Everything and Less

Everything and Less

The Novel in the Age of Amazon

Mark McGurl

VERSO
London • New York

First published by Verso 2021
© Mark McGurl 2021

1 3 5 7 9 10 8 6 4 2

Verso
UK: 6 Meard Street, London W1F 0EG
US: 20 Jay Street, Suite 1010, Brooklyn, NY 11201
versobooks.com

Verso is the imprint of New Left Books

ISBN-13: 978-1-83976-385-4
ISBN-13: 978-1-83976-387-8 (US EBK)
ISBN-13: 978-1-83976-386-1 (UK EBK)

British Library Cataloguing in Publication Data
A catalogue record for this book is available from the British Library

The Library of Congress Has Cataloged the Hardback Edition as Follows
A catalog record for this book is available from the Library of Congress

Typeset in Sabon by MJ & N Gavan, Truro, Cornwall
Printed and bound by CPI Group (UK) Ltd, Croydon, CRO 4YY

for Celeste, for everything

Contents

Acknowledgments

I am grateful to have had the opportunity to share my work in progress on this book with audiences at many institutions in the US and elsewhere. Their queries, suggestions, and criticisms have been a tremendous help. Gratitude is also due to Michaela Bronstein, Ulrika Carlsson, J. D. Connor, Celeste Crystal, Nathan Nebeker, and Sianne Ngai for reading things on short notice. Parts of chapters 1 and 4 have previously appeared in *Modern Language Quarterly*, *Public Books*, *American Literary History*, and a volume of essays edited by Amy Elias and Joel Burges. I am thankful to the editors of those publications for editorial assistance on those portions of the book. Thanks also to my colleagues and students in the Department of English at Stanford University, who have enabled the research and writing that went into the book in innumerable ways.

Preface

Bezos as Novelist

The first thing that needs to be noted about the collected works of MacKenzie Bezos, novelist, currently consisting of two titles, is how impressive they are. Will either survive the great winnowing that gives us our standard literary histories? Surely not. Precious few novels do. Neither even managed, in its initial moment of publication, to achieve the more transitory status of buzzy must-read. But this was not for want of an obvious success in achieving the aims of works of their kind—that kind being *literary* fiction, so called to distinguish it from more generic varieties. In Bezos's hands it is a fiction of close observation, deliberate pacing, credible plotting, believable characters and meticulous craft. *The Testing of Luther Albright* (2005) and *Traps* (2013) are perfectly good novels if one has a taste for it.[1]

The second thing that needs to be noted about them is that, after her divorce from Jeff Bezos, founder and controlling shareholder of Amazon, their author is the richest woman in the world, or close enough, worth in excess (as I write these words) $60 billion, mostly from her holdings of Amazon stock. She is no doubt the wealthiest published novelist of all time by a factor of … whatever, a high number. Compared to her, J. K. Rowling is still poor.

It's the garishness of the latter fact that makes the high quality of her fiction so hard to credit, so hard to know what to do with except ignore it in favor of the spectacle of titanic financial power and the gossipy blather it carries in train. How can the gifts she has given the world as an artist begin to compare with those she has been issuing as hard cash? Of late it has been reported that Bezos, now going by the name MacKenzie Scott, has been dispensing astonishingly large sums of money very fast, giving it to worthy causes, although not as fast as she has been making it as a holder of stock in her ex's company. Driven by the increasing centrality of online shopping to contemporary life, its price has been climbing. There are many fine writers of literary fiction, maybe too many—too many to pay close attention to, anyway—but only one world's richest lady.

For this book, however, the weird disjunction between the subtleties of literary fiction and the garishness of contemporary capitalism and popular culture is the point. The book argues that the rise of Amazon is the most significant novelty in recent literary history, representing an attempt to reforge contemporary literary life as an adjunct to online retail. In making that case and pursuing its consequences, the fact that the former wife of the founder of Amazon is a novelist is as good a place to begin as any. On the one hand, as we'll see, Amazon is nothing if not a "literary" company, a vast engine for the production and circulation of stories. It started as a bookstore and has remained committed ever since to facilitating our access to fiction in various ways. On the other hand, the epic inflection it gives to storytelling could hardly be more distinct from the subtle dignities and delights of literary fiction of the sort written by MacKenzie Bezos.

It was she who, according to legend, took the wheel as the couple drove across the country from New York to Seattle to start something new, leaving her husband free to tap away at spreadsheets on his laptop screen in the passenger seat. If this presents an image of Jeff as the author of Amazon in an almost literal sense, it surely mattered—mattered a lot—that his idea for an online bookstore was fleshed out while living with an actual author of books or aspiring one. "Writing is really all I've ever wanted to do," she said upon the occasion of the publication of the first novel in 2005.[2] By this time Amazon was already the great new force in book publishing, although it had yet to introduce the Kindle e-reader, the device that made a market for e-books. Neither had it hit upon perhaps its most dramatic intervention into literary history, Kindle Direct Publishing, the free-to-use platform by whose means untold numbers of aspiring authors have found their way into circulation, some of them finding real success. It had not yet purchased the book-centric social media site Goodreads, or Audible.com, or founded any of the sixteen more or less traditional publishing imprints it now runs out of Seattle.

That self-published writers have succeeded mostly by producing the aforementioned forthrightly generic varieties of fiction, and not literary fiction, is part of the story this book will tell. Romance, mystery, fantasy, horror, science fiction—these are the genres at the heart of Amazon's advance upon contemporary literary life. They come at readers promising not fresh observations of the intricacies of real human relationships—although they sometimes do that by the way—but compellingly improbable if in most ways highly familiar plots.

In one recent self-published success, a man awakens to find he has been downloaded into a video game. Rallying himself surprisingly quickly, he lives his version of *The Lord of the Rings*, but now with a tabulation of various game statistics appearing in his mind's eye. In another, a young woman is gifted with the power of prophesy, making her a target of the darkly authoritarian Guild. Run, girl, run! In still another, a woman has a job as a "secret shopper," testing the level of customer service at various retail stores, stumbling into a love affair with the impossibly handsome billionaire who owns them all. Then there are the zombies. There are as many moderately successful self-published zombie novels as there are zombies in any given zombie novel—hundreds of them. Whether dropping from the air into the Kindle or other device, or showing up on the doorstep in a flat brown box, these are the works that Amazon's customers demand in largest numbers and which it is happy to supply.

The Testing of Luther Albright is nothing like them, though no doubt it, too, has been delivered to doorsteps by Amazon on occasion. What I find fascinating is how the traces of genre fiction are visible in the novel all the same, if only under the mark of negation. Told in the first person, it recounts the strained but loving relationship of a repressed WASP father to his wife and son. He is a successful civil engineer in Sacramento, a designer of dams, and has built the family home with his own hands. Leaning perhaps too heavily into the analogy between the structural soundness of buildings and of family relationships, the novel has an ominously procedural, even forensic quality, reflecting the quality of mind of the man who narrates it. Luther is not a negligent father or husband, just a painfully self-conscious and overly careful one, so much so that he might be creating the cracks in the foundation of his life it was his whole purpose to avoid.

But no dam breaks and nothing ever crashes to the ground.

Indeed, it can seem that the novel is structured by a systematic refusal of potential melodrama, the kind of thing that would naturally have been at the center of a thriller. He buys his son a nice new car and watches nervously as he drives it a bit carelessly, but no horrific accident ever occurs. His strikingly pretty wife gets a job at a crisis helpline and begins to stay out late. She is acting a bit strange. Is she having an affair? Actually, no, she is just working hard talking people off the ledge. There has been an earthquake near Sacramento. Will the dam he designed break, drowning thousands? No, it holds, despite the best efforts of a local reporter to scare people into thinking it won't. Best of all: Luther has hidden the gun he inherited from his alcoholic father in a secret compartment in the basement. He worries about it being there. It throbs in his mind like a telltale heart. Chekhov's law tells us it is required eventually to go off, but it never does.

This is not just literary fiction, but militantly literary fiction, however politely so. It insists on the dramatic tension built into ordinary middle-class life. It is a declaration of autonomy from the ginned-up fakery of genre fiction even as it watches the latter out of the corner of its eye. The same is true of *Traps*. Told in the present tense, alternating the stories of four quite different women in Southern California and Nevada over the course of a few days, it contrives their convergence at a crucial juncture in each of their lives. It has something of the structure of the modern thriller à la Dan Brown but without the global conspiracies and evil monks and rigorously indifferent prose. Instead it features a subtle background motif of our relation to dogs, those creatures we care for but who can also occasionally be dangerous. It attends to details—"a bulletin board behind her fringed with notes and flyers and a few canceled checks, and on the counter next to the register sit a bowl of peppermint candies, a March of Dimes donation can, and a rack of *People* magazines, the one with mothers and children on the cover"—with no significance other than as an intensification of what Roland Barthes called the *reality effect* of realist fiction.[3]

Unless it be those copies of *People* magazine: one of the four protagonists of *Traps*, the easiest to connect to the situation of her author, is a skittish movie star and mother who sees her family life become fodder for paparazzi. Another, we learn, is part of the private security team that protects her as one surely protects MacKenzie herself in real life. Against the luridness of Hollywood gossip, the novel is on the side of the sanctity of private histories and intimacies. It finds interest and even some excitement in the difficult work of maternal care, which can turn the traps of life and love into opportunities for growth and renewal. Like *Luther Albright*, it is a testament to the decisive importance of family. "Family life" being some of the favored territory of literary fiction, much less prevalent as a theme in romance, mystery, fantasy, or science fiction. Appropriately, the novel is dedicated to the author's parents, and its acknowledgments speak touchingly of the personal importance of her four children and then husband, Jeff.

A man who, meanwhile, is known to have a taste for popular fiction, especially for works of epic science fiction, although he has a documented interest in literary fiction, too. Perhaps he was encouraged in that direction by MacKenzie, who studied creative writing with Toni Morrison at Princeton. He attended the same university but studied computer science. As the author (he would prefer the term "inventor") of Amazon, he has created something akin to a work of epic science fiction sprung to life. The sprawling logistical networks, state-of-the-art warehouses, superpowered information technologies and interfaces—all of it, to which we might add his personal investment in space travel through his privately held company Blue Origin, an investment said to be running at the rate of about a billion dollars a year. For one commentator, Amazon's "core competence" is really "*storytelling*," not the other stuff. "Through storytelling, out-lining a huge vision, Amazon has reshaped the relation between company and shareholder."[4] Has it done the same for the relation between writer and reader?

In the early years of Amazon, Jeff Bezos was very much a showman—a goofily ingratiating alternative to Steve Jobs with a notoriously honking laugh. Amazon was something that had to be sold hard to shareholders and customers alike. These days, with nothing left to prove to anyone, his public persona has cooled, his gaze sharpened, the laugh traded in for a quietly bemused smile. As could have been predicted by one of his ex's novels, with their suspicion of predatory media, he briefly found himself at the center of a "dick pic" blackmail scandal involving his new TV-anchor-cum-helicopter pilot girlfriend, but handled it with admirably preemptive efficiency before it could really get off the ground. Even so, the distance Jeff has traveled from domestic life with a camera-shy, preppie novelist wife could hardly have been made clearer. From now on, the founder of what once billed itself as Earth's Biggest Bookstore would himself be living large, larger than life.

In truth, it's not quite fair to associate all of this with popular genre fiction, only one sort of which runs toward the epic—the big, the bold, the world-forming. Neither is literary fiction always obsessed with the intimate and small, having its own avatars of epic in writers like Thomas Pynchon, David Foster Wallace, Karen Tei Yamashita, and the like. If works like MacKenzie Bezos's are sometimes held in contempt for their avoidance of politics in favor of domesticity, the epic versions of literary fiction are harder to criticize on those grounds. As this book will explain, the dynamic opposition of "more" to "less" and vice versa has been fundamental to the aesthetic development of contemporary fiction in all its forms, high and low. One might speak, for instance, of how the romance novel, that most generic of genres, is all about the forging of the small world of a marriage as a space apart from the alienations of modern life. This is as opposed to the epic sprawl of *Game of Thrones*, where marriages are wholly public, wholly political, and deadly; or for that matter a science fiction epic like Neal Stephenson's *Anathem* (2008), whose concerns are so cosmic as to leave that level of human relations behind altogether.

More and less. If the keynote of Amazon is certainly the first, the second is never far behind as a rejoinder to it in an aesthetic economy shadowing the real one. A real one where, in a sense, every meaningful decision is a matter of having or acquiring or selling or spending *more* or *less* of something, including of course money. Whether in the form of literary fiction or genre fiction—the first, in the Age of Amazon, being in essence a subset of the second, simply a genre in its own right—the novel will appear in these pages as what I would call an existential scaling device. It is a tool for adjusting our emotional states toward the desired end of happiness, whatever that might look like to a given reader, however complex or simple a state it might be. Fulfilling that task depends upon the rules of genre, upon the implied contract it draws up between author and reader for the reliable delivery of stories of a familiar kind. Genre being a version, within the literary field, of the phenomena of market segmentation and product differentiation. Before that, dating back to antiquity, it was a way of piecing through the different things that stories can do for us and instructing writers to construct them accordingly.

Gravitating as a matter of course toward literary fiction, to the genre that likes to think of itself as non-generic, scholars of contemporary literature have generally been neglectful of this all-important organizing feature of literary life, and no wonder. When it comes down to it, works of literary fiction are more reliable providers of discussable interpretive problems than works of genre fiction, whose interest often snaps into focus only at the level of the genre as a whole. Coming alive in the classroom, works of literary fiction advertise their interpretability in many ways, not least by refusing to fully subordinate the unit of the sentence, with its potentially artful intricacies, to the purposes of plot. Neither do they forgo thematic subtleties, things you could miss on a quick read. That, paradoxically, is their generic appeal.

To be sure, individual works of genre fiction have been known to generate volumes of learned commentary. Mary Shelley's *Frankenstein* (1818), Bram Stoker's *Dracula* (1897), and Kurt Vonnegut's *Slaughterhouse-Five* (1969) are works of apparently inexhaustible literary interest, however historically belated their recognition as masterpieces by scholars and other arbiters of aesthetic rank. Furthermore, if it were ever really the case, the days are long past when one could safely assume that any given new work of genre fiction must be artistically unsophisticated. Genre categories have by now found themselves internally differentiated into more or less "literary" instances appealing to relatively distinct if no doubt overlapping audiences. Ironically, this is true even of the category of literary fiction, whose more routinely sentimental examples are no more likely to find themselves the objects of scholarly attention than their more luridly generic brethren. They might even find themselves categorized as something else altogether, as "women's fiction" or "chick lit" or other offshoot of romance.

But artistic complexity of the kind congenial to the classroom is not necessarily what readers of genre fiction require. Just as important, frequently enough, is the work's reliability as a competent new execution of a certain generic narrative program. That is where it falls in line with the ways and means of Amazon as a paragon of reliable service, and why genre fiction is the heart of the matter of literature in the Age of Amazon. Only as it were accidentally, because it is something a number of readers still prefer, does the company serve up the dignified delights of literary fiction.

This determines the overall shape if not the finer details of the sketch this book draws of the situation of the novel today. Contrary to the usual procedures of literary scholarship, it welcomes literary fiction to the party as one genre among others, insisting that we not divorce it either from the larger system— from the corporate culture, writ large—that facilitates its coming into being or from that system's more characteristic products. The long-term implications of telling the story this way for the future of academic literary studies are not necessarily encouraging, corporate culture being no friend to the slow-paced reading and rumination on works of genius (or at least of very high quality) for which the discipline has historically been the occasion. Even so, what's happening on the ground of literary commerce in our time as the result of Amazon's efforts is undeniably fascinating, a work of genius in its own right.

Positioning literature lower on the hierarchy of human needs than we might like, putting books on the virtual shelf alongside other staples one might order from the Everything Store, the company is not so much anti- as omni-literary, making an epic narrative out of the speedy satisfaction of popular want. What literature loses in that transaction—too much, no doubt, for scholars to accept without a fight—it partly gets back as an endorsement of its everyday necessity. For whole cultures as well as for individuals, stories are of prime importance, and not just on special occasions. They are what guide our purposeful and pleasurable movement through time. Certainly, they have been necessary to Amazon, whose rise as a titan of contemporary commerce would have been unthinkable without the inspiration provided by works of fiction and the market opportunity presented by books.

Introduction

Retail Therapy

Once you've bought a novel in your pajamas, there's no turning back.

—Richard Powers, *The Overstory*

There are lots of interesting things to be seen on the internet, and equally many things to be said about them, but "the internet" itself and as a whole has become predictable, a cliché machine. To talk about it is like talking about the weather—which, in a way, is what it is: the weather of our emotional lives, the informational air we breathe, the media environment from which we extract the nutrients of our everyday existence as social, economic, and political beings. A quarter century or more after the internet's arrival on the world stage, the things we say about it are beset with a deflating sense of déjà vu, of a rightness that is no match for overfamiliarity. I blame the internet for this problem, naturally. With its multiplication and acceleration of the quintessentially modern phenomenon of public *commentary* on this, that, and everything, observations about the internet drawn forth from its humble individual users long ago ceased to gain meaningful interpretive leverage on it.

Which isn't to say that the internet is not, after all, important, possibly as vast in its implications as the arrival of the printing press was to the early modern world and carrying just as many unintended consequences in train.[1] Certainly it has been important to my object of study in this book, the contemporary novel, which now, even when it comes to us in the familiar form of the physical book, is as often as not advertised, ordered, reviewed, and discussed there.[2] It is only to say that any analysis of the novel in online times that seeks to move into fruitfully new conceptual territory needs a better protagonist, or perhaps antagonist, than "the internet" or even "the digital" can supply on its own. It needs a vehicle of meaningful focalization, something to lend analytical coherence to what might otherwise seem the impersonal unfolding of scattered techno-capitalist processes.

For this book, that protagonist/antagonist is the retailer Amazon, launched in 1995 as an online bookstore. Amazon has insinuated itself into every dimension of the collective experience of literature in the United States and increasingly of the wider world. It has done this as the purveyor of more than half of the print books sold in the US and the overwhelmingly dominant force in the e-book market, a market it essentially made; as the proprietor of the booming enterprise of Audible.com, which is encouraging a remarkable return of sorts to the original orality of long-form storytelling; as facilitator, through its Kindle Direct Publishing (KDP) program, of the self-publication of countless thousands of works of fiction, and progenitor of a path to a successful literary career independent of traditional presses; as the home of sixteen more or less traditional literary book imprints of its own and proprietor of the book-oriented social media site Goodreads. Increasingly, it is the new platform of contemporary literary life.

Could it be that the torch of cultural experimentation once confidently carried by modernism and the avant-garde is now carried by an online retailer? Does the spirit of innovation now reside in new ways and means of textual distribution rather than of either content or form? To claim so would be a stretch, surely, but would not be entirely outlandish. Has, for instance, anything as consequential as the Kindle happened *inside* a novel since 2007, when Amazon unveiled its e-reader and instantaneous wireless download system, Whispernet? Granted, the Kindle has not killed off the print book, not by a long shot, but it is something substantially new in the universe of reading, while whatever excitement may once have been associated with, say, postmodernism in fiction long ago subsided into more or less excellent permutations of familiar forms.[3] If it were ever true, the narrative of continual innovation running from realism to modernism to postmodernism no longer compels belief that the future of the form will depart significantly from the repertoire of techniques it inherits from the past.

By contrast, set free from the original Kindle device onto the Kindle app used on phones and tablets and laptop screens of all kinds, e-books have gone in that span from rarity to ubiquity as the preferred medium of many millions of readers; readers who are thereby connected as by an invisible umbilical cord to the mother ship of commodity provision in a whole new way. Whether they know it or not, these readers typically do not own the books they have downloaded—you will not find e-books in any used bookstore, and you can't easily lend one to a friend— having instead been licensed to use them on a limited number of personal devices. As detailed by Ted Striphas, this is interesting in its own right as an event in the colorful history of copyright and intellectual property. On the one hand, it assuages the sense of loss writers and publishers have often felt at the hands of a used book market from which they profit not at all. On the other, it enables the piracy of electronic editions of books available to any internet user with a modicum of navigational savvy.[4] For *Everything and Less*, the digital liquidity of the e-book has an even larger significance, one that reflects backward from its relative physical evanescence even to the print version: in either form, it is from Amazon's perspective not so much an object or even text as the bearer of a service.

Unlike the distributed communicational infrastructure we call the internet, with its trafficking in any and all kinds of information, Amazon's is a powerfully *interested* platform—interested in doing business of a certain kind, to be sure, but also interested in narrative. Take the Kindle. Partly modeled on the similar devices that preceded it to market by several years, inspiration for their dramatic improvement was found in Neal Stephenson's novel of a post-scarcity nanotechnological future, *The Diamond Age: Or, A Young Lady's Illustrated Primer* (1995). So much so that in the Kindle's development phase at Silicon Valley's Lab126, it was codenamed Project Fiona, after the engineer protagonist's daughter.[5] She is the inspiration for his design of a new kind of interactive connected book geared to the evolving educational and emotional needs of the individual who owns it. The actual achievements of the Kindle may not equal the book of this nanotechnological future, but (as we'll explore at greater length in chapter 4) the novel was crucial in inspiring them. And that's not the only work of literature to have influenced Amazon. As we'll see in chapter 1, although Bezos is better known as a reader of science fiction and would end up hiring Stephenson as the first employee of his space exploration company, Blue Origin, it would not be entirely crazy to say that we owe the existence of the company to his reading of Kazuo Ishiguro's literary novel *The Remains of the Day* (1989), which employees of the company have long been encouraged to read.

It is sometimes thought that Amazon started as an online bookstore purely as a matter of convenience, the book market having certain qualities made it the ideal means to Jeff Bezos's larger entrepreneurial ends. Most important was an extreme number and diversity of distinct titles, a tiny fraction of which could be displayed in even the largest brick-and-mortar store, matched with rigorous trackability by way of their International Standard Book Number (ISBN). In retrospect, we might add to this that book buying, while it is a mass phenomenon to be sure, skews upward in socioeconomic level toward persons with greater-than-average disposable income and who have that all-important prerequisite of convenient online shopping, a credit card. Reading for pleasure is predominantly a phenomenon of the educated middle class in broadest definition, and so is Amazon.[6]

Books and book buying do have some commercially advantageous qualities and may have always been a proof of concept for an intent to sell everything, but as we'll see, the relation of Amazon to fiction, to story, is more than one of convenience, going to the core of its corporate identity. So much so that we might think of the company not only as the protagonist of contemporary literary life but as its most emblematic "author," as deserving in its way of lending its name to the literary period in which it appears as Samuel Johnson was of the Age of Johnson (otherwise known as the second half of the eighteenth century) or Ezra Pound was of the Pound Era (the era of literary modernism). Which is to say, only debatably deserving of the honor, but not implausibly so, and helpful in bringing certain phenomena to our attention.

There is no denying the many other sources of external agency in the making of contemporary fiction, beginning with the massive conditioning of the originality of any contemporary writer by the weight of literary history, by the long and illustrious career of the novel as a repository of generic forms and techniques and expectations. It is a thing very much of the present, a platform in its own right. One could also point to the publishing industry more broadly conceived, including the small handful of multinational conglomerates standing bestride the global book market and the smaller independent presses working in their shadow.[7] To a certain extent, what fiction has been in recent years is only what they and other constituents of the contemporary trade publishing system, most importantly literary agents, have enabled it to be.[8] And then there is the institution of the school, with its inculcation in some of us of habits of literary leisure from a very young age, and the university creative writing program, my own object of study once upon a time, with its reorganization of the setting and shape of the literary career.

Finally, there is the simple specificity of the historical-existential surround, the way we live now, some of us as recreational readers, almost all of us constantly accessing information on the web. Back in the 1990s, Bezos had an inkling that the new communication medium quickly wrapping the world in its embrace might be made highly consequential to our lives as consumers, first of all as consumers of books, and he was right. It took him a bit longer to realize that it could be useful to marketers of various kinds, including those looking to market the novels they have written. Without denying the many other agents and institutions that coalesce to form the environment of literary life, many of whom will make appearances in its pages along the way, this book will make a case for Amazon, seeing how far that will get us in exploring the fate of the novel in online times.

I spend a certain amount of time each week breaking down cardboard boxes, lots of them from Amazon, getting them ready for the garbage pickup.

Not all but many of those boxes over the past few years have contained copies of the books consulted in the writing of this book on fiction in the Age of Amazon. You can take from this that, while it is at times highly critical of Amazon-enabled consumerism, *Everything and Less* will not presume its virtuous remove therefrom. Any honest account of fiction in the Age of Amazon must first reckon with the company's success in redesigning the world for the greater ease of shoppers, including those looking to buy books. Amazon has many detractors, but it has many more—a thousand-fold more—loyal customers, having become over the quarter century and more of its existence one of the few most admired institutions in the world. If we could bracket the million troubling implications of its rise, we could easily admit that it is one of the most impressive ventures of our time, equal in its way to the aqueduct systems, cathedrals, and moonshots of the past, those triumphs of logistics it distantly resembles. If nothing else, it stands as a monument to the continuing possibilities of large-scale endeavor, one that even its enemies should take to heart.

For many decades now, since the 1960s if not earlier, the leftist rejoinder to the rise of consumerism has been to argue that its satisfactions are illusory because they are predicated on a larger insatiability, a never-ending itch to further optimize. Capitalism in this view does not so much satisfy desires as deceitfully promise a mythical future state of complete satisfaction that by definition

—and at the risk of the collapse of the entire system—can never be allowed to arrive.[9] This is a powerful account of the harnessing of optimistic hedonism to a program of perpetual deferral of fundamental change, but it runs the risk of underselling the real pleasures of commodity consumption in the here and now. Which isn't to argue for more of the latter. On the contrary, borrowing the thought from Todd McGowan, I would rather say that consumption is *already* so enjoyable to those who can afford it in reasonable abundance, if only we could see it, that we needn't look to the capitalist future to finally supply us with what we need.[10] The pleasures we seek are already at hand.

In other words, the standards for satisfaction in traditional critiques of consumerism are too absolute or even theological in nature, missing how much of consumerism's power is derived not from the promise of a perfect future but from the simple delectation of its fruits. The pleasures of the present are if anything stoked by the kernel of incompletion at their core. As readers are particularly well positioned to know, what we call satisfaction has a processual or narrative character, not a binary one. It is a matter not simply of lack or possession but of more or less enjoyable intensities in the transformation of the first into the second. In the adventure of literary consumption, as of anything else, a complete satisfaction is one that is already beginning to fade away, requiring us to search for the next great read, which we happily do.[11] More and more, we do so by clicking our way to Amazon, which the evidence would suggest largely succeeds in delivering what its customers are looking for, or at least what they are willing to accept, again and again. That's how its founder looked up one day to find he had become the richest man in the world.

And yet this is not to deny the implication of contemporary fiction in a system of behavior and belief that surely needs to change. That *will* change if the warming planet has anything to say about it, requiring the invention of alternative forms of hedonism.[12]

The problem with Amazon arises in the first instance from the fact that human beings are not only consumers. They are many other things, too, including employees. This is the message of well-known critics of Amazon like legal scholars Lina Khan and Timothy Wu, for whom the rise of Amazon must be understood in light of the troubling collapse of resistance to monopoly power in US jurisprudence and regulatory enforcement since the 1980s.[13] Their central point is fairly simple: if the only valid criterion for the enforcement of laws against monopolistic restraint of trade is the ability to prove damage to consumers on the level of price, this leaves out most of the ways monopoly diminishes our collective economic life, especially over the long haul. Today's predatory pricing, a boon to consumers benefiting from a company's willingness to lose money until its competition gives up the ghost, is tomorrow's shrunken labor market, with fewer and fewer employers competing for workers' time.[14] It is also tomorrow's diminished innovation in products and services and finally, coming full circle, when the coast is clear, tomorrow's rising prices and poor service. It is a paradox that champions of the competitive "free market" have never been able to solve: what to do when the competition has been definitively won, the competitor become king.

Indeed, in recent years, there have been few free marke-teers consistent enough to see this as a fundamental problem (one of several) with the system they rally behind. Instead they have mostly become tribunes of concentrated economic power, warning us against "punishing success." Hence the rise of what I take to be the most sadly and surreally representative figure of our time, the self-pitying billionaire. He is everywhere in the news media and has taken pride of place in popular literature, too, in works like *Fifty Shades of Grey* and its many lesser-known imitators.

Surely, say his apologists, he should be able to keep his winnings and use them however he sees fit? Has not he, too, simply obeyed the dictates of the market conceived as the ongoing revelation of aggregate consumer preferences? Have we not, through that mechanism, revealed our preference for his domination of us? Then why all the player hating? The centering of the world on the putative authority of the consumer to the exclusion of our other roles reflects the long and baleful influence of neoclassical (or micro) economics—an economics of the chooser, the utility maximizer—on the everyday life of the mind and soul.[15] Amazon is in some ways its apogee. The consumer's other guise, all the more admired for its association with risk-taking and thrift, is the shareholder, the choosy figure whose interests, never mind the damage, are taken to be more pressing than those of any other stakeholder in the fortune and fate of the corporation. This despite the fact that the corporation itself, constructed by law as a fictional person, could not exist except with the consent of governments that decide to believe in that fiction and recognize it as a bearer of civil rights.[16]

The shareholder is the addressee of the one of the most important documents in the corporate history of Amazon, Bezos's fabled 1997 Letter to Shareholders, in which he announced his intention to forgo profit for the foreseeable future in favor of rapid growth. In retrospect, although uttered by a relative underdog among the movers and shakers of the corporate world of the time, it was a declaration of monopolistic intent. Supplemented by two decades of systematic state sales tax avoidance, the deal that shareholders licensed Bezos to offer his customers would prove to be irresistible. It was also depressing if not deadly for his brick-and-mortar-bound competitors, much of whose equity has been absorbed by Amazon since then. Now having safely established utter dominance in e-commerce, the company has begun to assert the profit motive as a primary one, with uncertain implications for the quality of its service.[17]

Paying adequate respect to the aspects of our social being not reducible to the role of consumer or shareholder might better equip us for the pursuit of happiness in the life we actually live, where, as often as not, our situation is not meaningfully a matter of choice. It might reduce our need for the consumerist salve we take in whatever dose we can afford. For now, the task here is to trace the circuits that link our lives as workers, citizens, and consumers insofar as they become visible in our lives as readers and writers. More, it is to take the measure of contemporary fiction through the analytical lens of what I would argue is the most remarkable and consequential novelty of recent literary history.

If that seems too strong a claim for Amazon, especially coming from somebody who argued the same thing about creative writing programs not so long ago, in a book called *The Program Era*, then let it stand as a thought experiment: What does the contemporary literary field look like when seen in light of this extraordinarily vivid entity?[18] What otherwise hidden aspects of contemporary literary life become clear when we acknowledge their conscious or unconscious intimacy with the ways and means of an online retailer?

The plausibility of proposing the writing program as the great novelty of postwar US literary history had much to do with the concreteness of the now hundreds of institutional spaces for which it has become the occasion since the founding of the Iowa Writers' Workshop in the 1930s, which fewer and fewer writers of high literary ambition have felt they can abstain from entering either as students or teachers; and with the explicit intent of these programs to define for their inmates what counts as good (and even more so, bad) writing. While it is no less novel than the creative writing program, the agency of Amazon in the making of literature is a more diffuse-seeming affair. Founded in the mid-1990s, the whole point of the company in its initial phase was to act without the constraints of physical spaces and face-to-face interactions, shedding the weight of brick-and-mortar storefronts in favor of connecting vast warehouses of books—at that point not owned by Amazon but the distributor Ingram—to individuals in their homes. Acting as a virtualized middleman, the company has never made strong claims to know what literary value is except as it is revealed by the preferences of its customers. The latter's judgments on the matter are reflected in the yearly Goodreads Choice Awards, billed as "the only major book awards decided by readers."

The rise of the writing program is one of the great success stories of higher educational marketing, maintaining its growth even in times of austerity, but the experience of attending or teaching in one is more immediately felt as a temporary buffering of the dictates of the literary market in their rawest form. By contrast, Amazon is the market personified. As a literary institution, it is the obverse of the writing program, facilitating commerce in the raw, but with the irony that aspiring writers interacting with it typically incur no debts in doing so. Its basic publishing services are free of charge until the event of a book's sale, whereupon Amazon takes a cut of the proceeds, usually 30 percent. (Advertising one's book on Amazon is another matter—it turns the author into a customer.) The "rules" it presents to would-be writers bear upon not the forms of narration, structure, characterization, or diction their works should exemplify as instances of the noble tradition of craft, things about which it has very little of substance to say. Rather, they bear upon the kinds of social relations—social relations *as* customer relations—the writer should accept as the basis of her aesthetic endeavor, pointing her to the network, the internet, as the ideal medium and indeed fetishized embodiment of those relations.

Swelling the ranks of writers with ready access to a market for their wares, the "influence" of Amazon on contemporary literature is more abstract but also more pervasive than that of the writing program, being in essence an efficient bundling and presentation of market forces and opportunities. Our pathway to understanding it is less through a tour of its historical locations and key personalities than in finding concepts that will help us get a handle on how novelists respond to those forces and opportunities. In giving over literature wholly to the market, collapsing as far as possible the distance between literature's residually sacral significance as a repository of higher values and its everyday function as commodity, Amazon in one sense intensifies a phenomenon occasioned by the consolidation of publishing in recent decades into immense multinational media conglomerates.[19] By all accounts, this consolidation has brought with it an increasingly merciless attention to yearly revenue growth and profit in the conduct of the business. And yet, unlike these behemoths that have absorbed virtually every historically prominent book publisher and imprint, from Knopf and Scribner to

Farrar, Straus and Giroux, Amazon for its own part brackets the question of the profitability of the products it makes available. Its clients are free to publish as many flops as they'd like, and there are a great many of those. Accumulating year after year by the tens if not hundreds of thousands, they make up a kind of *underlist*, a vast ocean of inert literary content stored on the server at marginal cost. This is one advantage of being a *platform* rather than a *publisher*. It's when the self-published writer wants to make a living from their labor that the market snaps into focus as something very close to the surface indeed, visible right there on the KDP dashboard telling them how many units they have managed to move.

Offering itself as the new platform of literary life, Amazon has redefined—for itself, if not yet for us, not entirely—some of that life's most basic components. It has done so not from scratch, of course, but by magnifying long-standing latencies of print capitalism, seizing upon them and making them all but perfectly and shamelessly explicit.[20] That said, as I explore throughout this book, the various components of the Amazon Way as applied to literary life make that life "liquid" in substantially new ways. This sparks the following series of key questions:

What is an author? For Amazon, authors should consider themselves a kind of *entrepreneur* and *service provider*. They are the opposite of the aloof or absent modernist god who, in James Joyce's telling, recedes from his work to pare his fingernails, letting the reader make of it what she will. If they come to seem godlike all the same, that will be because of their transcendent sales. The more ordinary case is one of modest sales won through exhausting effort in content generation, self-promotion, mailing-list cultivation and search engine optimized marketing. While it is tempting to describe this as "disintermediated" authorship, with writers and readers finally able to connect without the interposition of a publishing industry middleman, Timothy Laquintano is right to insist that it is instead a matter of refashioned and to some extent virtualized corporate intermediaries. These include the spookily judgmental ghost in the Amazon machine writers refer to as "the algorithm." It will recommend their book to readers—or not—based on closely studied if still somewhat mysterious criteria.[21]

And that's before we account for the obvious persistence of gatekeepers in the operation of the literary field at large, even in the offices of Amazon, with its many in-house imprints. The first two chapters of this book will examine the writer as service provider in the broader context of the transformation of the labor market from one centered on the production of goods to one centered on the provision of services, tracing the complex circuits connecting the individual imagination to the service platform. Exploring the transformation of authorship in an internet-enabled world, contemplating the corporation itself as a kind of super-author, these chapters are the two in the book most explicitly *about* Amazon in a sustained and concrete sense. They are followed by a series of chapters for which Amazon plays the role of the framing device by which we can see other things. For instance:

What is a reader? Amazon sees them as a *customer* with needs, above all a need for reliable sources of comfort, or *utility* in its original sense, where it had more to do with a feeling of well-being than with the no-nonsense infrastructural austerity the term evokes today. The reader-customer is looking for various things from a novel, no doubt, but all of them can from this perspective be assimilated to a program of self-care, of informal bibliotherapy or, leaning hard into the crisscrossing etymology of selling and telling, *retail* therapy.[22] Largely carried out alone in the private experience of absorption in a text, this program is made social to some degree when knitted into a book club or classroom discussion, or posted to one's followers as a Goodreads review. It takes place against the backdrop of what Philip Rieff in the mid-1960s could already call the "triumph of the therapeutic" in Western culture. By this he meant the conversion of traditional modes of "binding address" for the shaping of self-seeking desires toward a greater good into individualist "techniques" with "nothing at stake beyond a manipulable sense of well-being."[23]

Where once the "limitation of possibilities was the very design of salvation," Rieff declared, now the "answer to all questions of 'what for?' is 'more.'"

> Everything conceivable can be made universally available. Variety has become a term of control as well as remission. Confronted with the irrelevance of ascetic standards of conduct, the social reformer has retreated from nebulous doctrines attempting to state the desired quality of life to more substantial doctrines of quantity. The reformer asks only for more of everything—more goods, more housing, more leisure; in short, more life. This translation of quantity into quality states the algebra of our cultural revolution.[24]

"Everything conceivable can be made universally available": a motto for Amazon devised decades before the fact of the Everything Store. It is inaccurate, as we'll see, only to the extent that it misses the countervailing impulses to asceticism, or minimalism, with which the maximalism of the Age of Amazon is in fact tightly braided. It might also be fleshed out such that some of the diversity of those therapeutic "quantities" becomes visible, from those directed toward enduring self-improvement, at one end of the spectrum, to those designed to provide more fleeting blasts of well-being at the other. Then, too, it should be observed how a kind of binding address returns in alienated form in Amazon's world-historical success in customer *lock-in* through the Prime paid subscription program. The soul of the customer is delivered to the company on the wings of free delivery.

Therapy is the heart of the matter in chapters 3 and 4, which examine the history and present of a genre that is by any quantitative measure the central one in popular literary life today: the romance, the love story. Here is where something at stake throughout the book is examined most intensely: that our desires are fundamentally generic in nature, and that the literary forms we call with varying degrees of intended insult "genre fiction" are profoundly related to that fact. But so are those of what we call "literary fiction," the assertion here being that, according to Amazon, *all fiction is genre fiction* in that it caters to a generic desire. This includes—on occasion, depending on where you're coming from—a desire for complex literary artistry. Observing the many contemporary novelists of high artistic esteem who have been playing with popular genre forms, recent criticism has found one of its recurrent themes in the so-called genre turn in literary fiction. It is a real phenomenon, and we will return to it later in this book, but what we have here is something else: a colonization *of* literary fiction *by* the logic of genre that conserves literary fiction in its relative difference.[25]

To desire generically is to desire repetitiously, a feature of our life as readers that first shows up in early childhood in the demand to be read a favorite story again and again.[26] This essential feature of the reading life is modified as we grow older but never eliminated entirely, as the forceful appeal of genre consumption (one romance after another, one zombie novel after another) attests. It was implicit in formalist studies of an earlier era, such as Vladimir Propp's, that took folktales and other popular forms as data sets for the study of repetition and variation in cultural production.[27] But with few exceptions, their insight that repetition is crucial to the very being of narrative—and perhaps also to its appeal—has not been sustained.[28]

No wonder if critics have wanted to draw attention to works of singular achievement on the theory that the repetitive mediocrity and badness of commercial culture will take care of themselves. But the pursuit of finer things is a habit like any other, and one with mostly therapeutic benefits if we're honest. This is not necessarily an insult. The Aristotelian account of *catharsis*, to take an unassailably dignified historical example, is an argument for the therapeutic value of tragic drama. By the same token, the meaning of "self-care" is not exhausted by its conferral of expensively radiant skin upon the bourgeoisie, but is also crucial for the survival of persons whose well-being is otherwise a matter of complete indifference to the powers that be. Neither do the therapeutic benefits of literary consumption necessarily contradict other efficacies of the text—ideological ones, for instance, which are presumably enhanced by the repetition of the message. What's more, and most importantly, there is much to be learned from plumbing the sources of badness in the artistic automatism that yields *merely* generic forms.

In the meantime, great works of genre fiction are those that don't seem generic in this pejorative sense, their authors having mastered their conditions and conventions of possibility in such a way as to convince us that we are encountering something unique. (Think here of the mind-boggling cleverness and gender-political relevance of Gillian Flynn's thriller *Gone Girl* [2012], or the sublimity of world-building one finds in Steven Erikson's ten-volume work of dark epic fantasy, *Malazan Book of the Fallen* [1999–2011], as impressive in its way as any high-modernist masterwork.) A step down from these relative rarities are what we might think of as brilliantly successful performances of familiar generic forms, where, somewhat on the model of the musician playing a score, originality is displayed in the interpretation rather than in the invention of new forms. (The mystery genre is unusually replete with talent deployed in this way.)

Reading these works, we begin to see how what is in one sense the "formulaic" nature of genre fiction is in another sense a rigorous and potentially elegant *formalism*.[29] Granted, familiar generic forms are in the nature of things subject to novelty in the cultural references of their particular use, but the novelty of this novelty only goes so far. For instance, while Young Adult fantasy has in recent years been the scene of hyper-pluralistic inclusion of new voices and non-European cultural contexts, a development one can only applaud, the durable ubiquity of certain tropes—the identification of the protagonist as the Chosen One, the appearance of the love interest and rival, the ordeal of training, the literalization of neoliberal meritocracy as a death match—is easy to see. The inclusion of racial and cultural difference at the level of proper names and physical character descriptions apparently requires no rethinking of the form of the story at all. In this, something like Joseph Campbell's "monomyth"—the idea that heroic narratives from all cultures share basic components—licenses a return to these tropes as a recipe for success.

If the deepest truth revealed about human beings in genre fiction is the truth of our repetitiousness, beginning with our propensity to take one breath after another, to eat one meal after another, read one book after another, and on and on, this is not to deny the incomparable creativity and flexibility of humanity over the long haul, so far in excess of any other creature we know of.

It is however to insist, as confirmed by the oft-noted enthusiasm of the relatively aged for YA fiction, that *all literature is children's literature* at its core.[30] This is the revelation of Norman Holland's classic of the 1960s, *The Dynamics of Literary Response* (1968), which I return to in chapter 4.[31] Half a century after the fact, Holland's adherence to old-school Freudian developmental categories will not work for everyone, but if we peel them back, we see a critic pondering with unusual tenacity the actuality of the psychic relation between readers and literary works. What's going on in that relation? For Holland it is a matter not of knowledge acquisition but structured fantasy, the most elementary basis of which is the promise of a world made just for you, the reader, as it may have seemed when you were a babe in loving arms. That's why it matters that these worlds are *fictional*, even the hard-core realist ones: fictionality signifies the bending of narrative representation to our various imaginative needs. Every act of reading is in this sense a *return* to something primal, the gently bowed page of book figuring as a kind of breast. (So, too, the audiobook that facilitates the return of sorts of the bedtime story in the life of the adult commuter.)

Staging an encounter with our most basic motives for reading novels, the middle chapters are also where the book registers a truth about the contemporary literary field somewhat veiled from us by the overwhelming critical focus on prestigious literary fiction—and that is its profound gendering. Superficially minimized in the space of literary fiction, which generally prefers to be thought of as universal in its address, the gendering of literary life is otherwise fairly intense, with genres and authors marked as either boyish (Tom Clancy) or girlish (Nora Roberts) in a way that is all but taken for granted. This is true even as literary reading as a whole is still significantly statistically skewed toward women, as it has been for centuries. As we'll see, the gendering of literary life is echoed even in the toggling of Amazon's corporate identity between a sort of world-dominating epic heroism and a more modest self-presentation as a family-friendly conduit of domestic provision. More immediately, attention to the gendering of genre is useful in showing how stark inequalities along the axis of sex matter to contemporary literary history.

What is the internet? What in particular is it as a literary-historical phenomenon? As the technological precondition of the Age of Amazon, the internet appears throughout this book but is the preoccupation of its final two chapters in particular, where the coexistence of contemporary fiction with all the words and images of the World Wide Web is approached from several angles. To the domains of production and consumption that center the earlier parts of the book, these chapters add the matter of circulation or distribution, asking what the novel is when intermixed with the rough-and-tumble of real-time global communication and social media.

There are several ways of answering that question. Thematic reflections on and formal mirrorings of the internet in contemporary fiction are by now quite common, and there can be little doubt that the larger attention economy in which the novel now competes has entered its bones in more subtle ways. This will be the subject of chapter 5. The ultimate answer to the question appears in chapter 6, centered on the progressive *commoditization* of the novel. The commod*ification* of the novel by contrast is an old story, a given, as important as the fact remains: novels are offered for sale. What will catch and hold our interest in this chapter is instead that they are on average so cheap, so ubiquitous and ordinary as to seem like sacks of flour or boxes of nails. This is especially true in and around the Kindle store, where as Nick Levey notes, novels can often be had for as little as 99 cents, and where consumer price sensitivity applies a strong downward pressure on what a given writer can charge for their wares.[32] (The otherwise unbelievably good royalty rate of 70 percent of the cover price Amazon pays to self-publishing authors only holds for works priced between $2.99 and $9.99, outside of which range it falls to a still healthy 35 percent.) In the world of commoditized commodities, the value-adding aura of brand matters little as long as the product fulfills its function.

The novel will perhaps never be fully commoditized in this sense, inasmuch as the author's name is one of the original forms of the brand, a model for the differentiation of the product by reference to the identity of its producer. It is a fine example of what Lucien Karpik has called an economic singularity, a commodity whose deeper nature is, for its potential purchaser, always somewhat opaque inasmuch as you don't *really* know what you're buying when you buy a novel until after you have read it. This as opposed to a standard-issue carton of milk, for which the mediation of "judgment devices" such as promotional materials and product reviews are hardly necessary.[33] And yet the sheer ease with which authors now introduce themselves to a web-enabled world puts the singularity of any one of them under unprecedented pressure for recognition. It squeezes the time for their meaningful presence in the culture, when they achieve it, to a minimum, readying their work for interment in the remainder pile or server stack.[34] In more ways than one, as we shall see, the Age of Amazon is an age of *surplus fiction*.

And *what, finally, is fiction really*? I think Amazon would have no particular quarrel with the traditional answers to this question, whether it is as repository of cultural identity, exercise of our powers of empathy, proving ground of our interpretive abilities, source of cultural capital, or place of imaginary escape. But the one suggested by Philip Rieff above is I think a more comprehensive expression of the Amazon ethos than any of these. As is made clear throughout the book in a variety of ways, fiction in the Age of Amazon is the symbolic provision of *more*—above all, of more various and interesting "life experience" than can be had by any mortal being, let alone one constrained by the demands of work and family. It is a commodification of this experience, shaped to the reader's limitations and recurring therapeutic needs.

A physical book is in this sense a box of time, and an e-book the virtualization of the same. It is a *volume* in which time has seemed to stop.[35] Or, rather, it has been put on a kind of imaginary endless loop inasmuch as fictional time moving in sequence from a novel's beginning to its end stands still until the reader is ready to reactivate its flow. This is also to say that, in the novel, time itself is commodified, made *commodious*. It is imagined as something that waits on our convenience and conduces to our existential comfort, which in the real world, the working world, it fundamentally does not do. Like all forms of therapy or self-care, the fictional supplement is taken in repeated doses, each of them a tiny upward tick in our accumulation of human experience, each of them a temporary reset of our mood. And, too, like many nutritional supplements, their actual value to the health of the reader might well be viewed with some skepticism.[36] At the limit, they may be the vehicles of what Lauren Berlant has influentially called cruel optimism, pointing us toward shiny objects whose pursuit is slowly killing us.[37] But that is not the official story. The official story, so different from the panicked and admonitory one retailed in the eighteenth and nineteenth centuries, when novel reading seemed a scourge, is that reading fiction is *good for you*. It is part of a repertoire of habits of experiential optimization and self-care.

This ambiguity—fiction as virtue and vice—sheds light on a larger truth about all the components of Amazon's administration of literary life just enumerated: as state of the art as they may be, they are to some degree self-contradictory, or at least conflicted. For instance, if what fiction most essentially is for us is a volume of commodified time, one of the most notorious facts of contemporary literary life is that there is so little time for it. This is especially so inasmuch as reading a novel is a relatively long-term commitment compared with other forms of cultural consumption. It is an expense of leisure not everyone has or feels they have. In other words, the sped-up culture that delivers that novel to your doorstep overnight is the same culture that deprives you of the time to read it.

Similarly, if the writer in the Age of Amazon is a kind of

service provider, and the reader a valued customer, a customer who is as they say "always right," that reversal of traditional authority in the writer-reader relation taken to its extreme would defeat the purpose of reading fiction. This is a key difference between a literary work and a free-form fantasy. Our interest in fiction is in part an interest in encountering different degrees of (albeit, properly formatted) otherness, the better to assimilate it to ourselves in the spirit of personal augmentation. It is the otherness of fictional characters and their experiences, most obviously, but also the otherness of the author's gradually revealed intentions. To varying degrees, and notwithstanding the self-centeredness of literary self-care, our interest in the novel is an interest in encountering the author's autonomy, which is the real difference—and addition —they bring to our existence, in however mediated a fashion. Only in some instances does it make sense to think of this as an increase in one's portfolio of cultural capital. Reading in the Age of Amazon is a matter not of pride or power but need, the need for "more" in a basic, sometimes desperate sense.

The happier side of these contradictions is that they bespeak the gap between Amazon's aspirations to colonize the literary imagination and the reality of the present situation, where pockets of autonomous consciousness—and action—abound. Without denying the aggressive advance of consumer capitalism into places heretofore protected from it, to think that love and friendship and human creativity are "capitalist" in any fundamental sense gives that system too much credit, and why would we do that? Weighed down though they may be with rancid ideological encrustations, these blessings are the resources we will use to build something better, or not, and works of fiction reflect them even now.

Not only that, but novels are generally written in conditions— alone at a computer, unbothered by the boss, with responsibility for the whole thing from first to last—not of alienated industrial production but of craft. The tolerance (in the engineering sense) this installs in the fit between the work and the working world surely matters.[38] It matters even if the would-be self-supporting, self-published writer is signing up, whether they know it or not, for a life of considerable repetitive toil.[39] One of the joys of my sometimes painful commitment to reading more than my share of "bad" fiction over the past few years has been witnessing its unruly perversities, sometimes in the very act of doubling down on generic conventions. I have also encountered a few instances of what I don't hesitate to call brilliant if sometimes quite niche literary visions.

Accurately or not, novel writing retains its image as the quintessence of unalienated labor living on in the present, an antidote to the dominance in our world of labor of the other kind. That's no doubt why so many people hope to find time to do it, and so very many, a dizzying number, succeed. And some of the things they come up with—my god. Among the many who write fiction as though vaguely remembering a TV show are some who really surprise you with the vividness and individuality of their imagined worlds.[40] If, in their effort to scan the literary field from Amazon's point of view, the pages that follow try to see things as if this margin of autonomous creativity weren't so, and as though the whole world were already Amazon, they also watch for signs of the enduring limits of the corporation's power as the super-author of our time. There are many to detect. What, if anything, will spring forth from them, and what difference it will make, is a separate matter.

This is not a book about Amazon. It is a book about the novel in the Age of Amazon. The former can be found in the works of Brad Stone, from whom I borrow the locution "Age of Amazon," and several other excellent financial journalists.[41] As fascinating as the company is in its own right, this book observes it only in the interest of understanding the situation of the contemporary novel. By the same token, a systematic confrontation with the nitty-gritty realities of contemporary publishing is available in the works of John B. Thompson, which are replete with sophisticated conceptualizations of the business drawn from the testimony of some of its key players.[42] By contrast, this book wants to know what's going on inside the books that business brings to market. It wants to *read* them—some number of them anyway—as evidence of what the novel is now. The novel: that is the thing the book really cares about and assumes its reader does, too. Framed by the rise of Amazon, the story told here is the story of the arrival of the genre's illustrious history in the present.

And yet, I use the term "novel" advisedly, not wanting to suggest that it is the only form of narrative fiction Amazon asks us to be interested in. In fact, in the Age of Amazon the term "novel" is a notably slackened one, more the designation of a certain quantity of narrative product than the specific thing whose historical appearance has been theorized by the likes of Ian Watt, Georg Lukács or Mikhail Bakhtin.[43] For the last two especially, the novel could not be understood except in negative relation to civilizational epics like the *Aeneid*, whether as a point of pride or shame. For the early Lukács, the novel reflects a mournful falling off from epic wholeness, that semi-mythical state of cultural integration that modernity brings to a close. For Bakhtin, it represents an exhilarating release into that modernity in all its carnivalesque, democratic glory. For Watt, it is the cultural expression of a certain rising class in Europe, the modern bourgeoisie, the merchant class. With its hospitality to the many-ness of modern desires, Amazon seems more of a Bakhtinian venture than either a Lukácsian or Wattian one, but in fact the novel per se is not really its thing. What it seeks is a reinstitution of the epic on new grounds—grounds it owns.

It is an epic whose ultimate form would be the narration of the historical unfolding of the enterprise in all its dimensions far and wide, from its biggest and boldest bets to its intimate capillary infusion into the daily lives of millions. That is what it means when the company entreats its hundreds of thousands of employees, as it constantly does, to have fun and work hard while they "Make History." Unlike classical epics, which speak of worlds sealed in the amber of the past, distant in time even from their authors, this one would have to be written from the perspective of a hypothetical future in which all our needs and desires are fulfilled in the glory of the corporation. In the meantime, it sponsors the creation and/or distribution of a plenitude of smaller narrative satisfactions—contemporary literature as we know it—in which that future is intimated even as blockages to its arrival are scrutinized.

It is not a neutral fact that Amazon started as a bookstore, or that it continues to show such a large commitment to the facilitation of storytelling even as it has moved on to a hundred other more profitable things. They might be short stories, novellas, novels, novel series, "omnibus" anthologies or trilogies —especially trilogies, which I've come to think of as the most characteristic of contemporary literary forms—and they were almost certainly written with aims other than doing the bidding of their host. What matters from Amazon's perspective is their collocation as incidental expressions of the unfolding epic of the Everything Store.

That self-applied nickname is shockingly metaphysical when you stop to consider it, and nothing that Amazon has ever done suggests it doesn't mean it literally. Perhaps no other company of our time works so openly under the sign of totality, and with such total aggression toward entities with which it perceives itself to be in competition. It is in this sense the ultimate Hegelian corporation, a would-be Absolute Monopoly. It has long been clear that Karl Marx's close association of capitalism with the commercial bourgeoisie—a revolutionary class, remorseless destroyer of feudal relations, fated to be superseded by the proletariat—was the recognition of a contingent and not necessary relation between the two. The bourgeois era has passed but the capitalist one rolls on.

What this suggests is that, to the extent that the novel was indeed a bourgeois form, reflecting the newfound confidence of the middle class on the world stage of the eighteenth and nineteenth centuries, it may have been in some ways an anticapitalist one, strange as that sounds. It is at least an idea worth considering: wasn't the genre's notorious focus on the particularity of individual experience in some tension with one of capitalism's most essential features, its submission of all forms of value to a regime of abstract equivalence mediated by money?

Granted, the individual is a convenient unit of organization and administration for the purposes of the liberal capitalist state, and a bonanza for contemporary social media platforms, where self meets selfie meets the algorithm. Still, as against the deeper reality of relentless abstraction we feel in our bones, the bourgeois individual of novel fame could be taken as having been compensatory and nostalgic from the get-go.

If this is so, then the novel would naturally start to seem like a residual form, a genre not yet dead but in ongoing retreat from the center of the culture, where, as suggested by David Cunningham, not the bourgeoisie but *capital itself* stands forth as the subject of history—the one protagonist to rule them all.[44] But how can an impersonal force of value abstraction, everywhere and nowhere visible as such, possibly be a "subject" in this sense? Amazon has an idea, and the literary historian will follow along for a while to annotate the proceedings. The corporation itself, the Everything Store, will step forth to personify this otherwise invisible thing, arrogating to the corporate brand the role of hero for our time. Amazon is in this sense the very

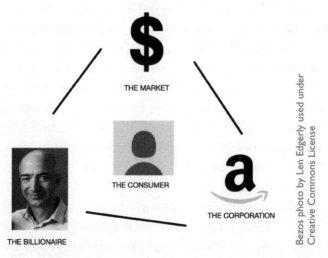

Personae of Contemporary Capital The symbolic trajectory from the human founder figure through the corporation to the pure abstraction of the market is one of increasing escape from responsibility for capitalism's harms, while the reverse trajectory moves toward the privatization of its benefits.

figure of capitalism's "real abstraction," as Marx called it, the abstraction that nonetheless has concrete effects in the material world. Real abstraction is indeed at the heart of its original business plan where, by contrast to slightly younger brethren like Google and Facebook, the idea has always been to traffic in real things, beginning with books delivered in boxes, while submitting these physical commodities, where possible, to state-of-the-art digital disembodiment and frictionless logistical flow.

And in cases where a human face is needed, the person of billionaire Jeff Bezos will do, completing the triumvirate of the billionaire founder, multinational corporation, and "the market" itself as personae of contemporary capital who putatively draw their authority from the revealed preferences of the consumer (see figure on p. 25).

The billionaire stands as the last redoubt of heroic individual agency in a world otherwise given over to abstract systems and bureaucracies. He is the guy—almost always a guy—who can self-finance space travel. And yet, he and his company are only manifestations of the even greater power of "the market" as the ultimate author and arbiter of our collective destiny. None of these personifications of capital fits comfortably into the role of a novelistic character. The novelistic protagonist is by tradition more of an antihero than hero in the epic mold, for reasons of his comic normality and necessary partiality as a representative figure. The epic poet Walt Whitman was perhaps the last writer who could safely assume that what he assumed you would assume, offering himself as the hero of his time, the conduit through which millionfold diversities of a nation are knitted together.

Whether in the form of Amazon or Bezos or any of the other avatars of transcendental Authority, the most comfortable literary vehicle of the personification of capital is the epic, the genre of civilizational totality but more precisely, as we shall see in chapter 2, of pseudo-imperial totalization. In practical terms, this suggests that to conceptualize contemporary fiction only with reference to the novel, let alone the art-novel, is to blind oneself to large swatches of the actuality of the literary field. At a minimum—and here we begin to see the surprising analytical

EPIC

ROMANCE

NOVEL

NOVELS

The Contempory Genre Triad While it is irresistible to attach specific recent titles to the triad of epic, romance, and novel, given how efficiently they help it come into focus, in fact it is better to think of them as forms of narrative value unequally distributed between different individual works. For instance, while it seems quite reasonable to call *Fifty Shades of Grey* a romance novel, what are we to make of the fact that it is part of a trilogy? From *The Divina Commedia* to *The Lord of the Rings*, the trilogy is the quintessential epic form. Partly, no doubt, it is a result of its derivation from Stephenie Meyer's *Twilight* trilogy—it having started life as a fan fiction extension of the latter—but that just begs the question of the relation of the paranormal romance to epic. Partly it responds to the demand for more product, conveniently turning one profitable transaction into three. By the same token, but for the slightly absurd idealization of its billionaire hero, and especially as compared with *Twilight*, the world depicted in *Fifty Shades of Grey* is more or less the same one we find in realist novels.

payoff in letting Amazon frame our analysis of that field—one needs to see the novel as one among a trio of dominant contemporary narrative forms made up of itself, epic, and romance; or, if one prefers, one might decide to open up the category of "novel" to internal differentiation along the same lines (see figure above).

While epic is the vehicle of capitalist totality, romance is the means by which we imagine the suturing of our individuality thereto, as when Ana Steele submits herself to the controlling impulses of Christian Grey but gets to live the billionaire lifestyle for her pains. If the corporate epic addresses the largest possible vision of the social in all its diversity, then the romance works to construct the smallest possible social world, a nation of two. The novel in its classic form—but especially in its *au courant* "lyric" or autofictional form—can then be seen as allowing individuals to find accommodation between these two scales of socialization, extensive and intensive, advancing into epic or romance territory as necessary for oneself to feel sufficiently aggrandized or comforted. In reading a novel, as the very result of doing so, the psychic economy of readers is adjusted and readjusted to the end of their happy coexistence with an overheated economy of information.

Notwithstanding their differences, all these genre forms and their respective social identifications are resistant to the formation of more militant collectivities, like unions, which contest the value of market efficiency as the only one that matters. That is why the effort to snuff them out is so relentless, nowhere more so than at Amazon.[45] Thus, if the problem with Amazon arises in the first instance from the fact that human beings are not only customers, it arises in the second instance from the fact that it presents, as a corporation, a degraded form of collectivity and collective action, a privatized and fundamentally socially irresponsible one. No amount of philanthropic goodwill arising in the breast of management could change the fact that it is and will always be disciplined by "market imperatives" and an amorally fiduciary responsibility to shareholders.

Bezos's 2020 Letter to Shareholders, the last in his tenure as CEO as he prepares to leave the daily operation of the business to others, is an interesting document to read in this context. It is the final installment in a series of such documents stretched out over the years since the company had its IPO in 1997. The final letter is interesting, first of all, for the very fact that it *is* interesting: for Bezos, the Letter to Shareholders has always been a medium of writing, a mode of corporate and individual self-expression of unusual intensity and flair. No doubt it was because he felt the weight of the occasion of his last entry in the genre that this one is a heady mix of victory lap (so many billions of dollars in value created), defiant public relations statement (despite what you've heard, Amazon is in fact "Earth's Best Employer" or will soon be), and fatherly lesson about the hard work required to succeed in this world. The key to the latter, he says, is to "create more than you consume," a slogan just vague enough to allow us to forget that, in the retail world, your creation is necessarily someone else's consumption.

The contradictions arising from an effort to view the self-interested exploitation of market opportunities as acts of generosity become obvious as the letter reaches its climax in a section called "Differentiation Is Survival and the Universe Wants You to Be Typical." If it isn't going to get Bezos hired by the Harvard Philosophy Department, it nonetheless makes for an unusually brainy CEO sayonara. Quoting biologist Richard Dawkins's observation that, considered in evolutionary terms, life is intrinsically hard, a matter of constant effort not to dissolve into deadly "equilibrium" with one's surroundings, Bezos finds in it a metaphor, a lesson of "utmost importance" for those who would be excellent:

> We all know that distinctiveness—originality—is valuable. We are all taught to "be yourself." What I'm really asking you to do is embrace and be realistic about how much energy it takes to maintain that distinctiveness. The world wants you to be typical —in a thousand ways, it pulls at you. Don't let it happen. You have to pay a price for your distinctiveness, and it's worth it. The fairy tale version of "be yourself" is that all the pain stops as soon as you allow your distinctiveness to shine. That version is misleading ... You'll have to put energy into it continuously ...
>
> The world will always try to make Amazon more typical— to bring us into equilibrium with our environment. It will take continuous effort, but we can and must be better than that.[46]

One imagines that the typical fulfillment center worker or delivery truck driver doesn't need to be told that a considerable expense of energy is required to continue to "be yourself" in the most basic sense intended by Dawkins—to survive. As a consequence of taking a biological truism as, instead, a model for success of a socially relative kind, the letter silently smuggles *competition* into the lesson, a thirst for glory.

But whose glory? There is a large irony in the CEO of a company with a famously conformist corporate culture (with management employees learning to spout Bezos's official fourteen "Leadership Principles" robotically before their first day at work) speaking this way. Working hard to "be yourself" is thus easily decodable as an invitation to submit one's identity to the corporation which, sure enough, arrives on cue in the passage above to let us know whose distinctiveness the outgoing CEO is really thinking about.

In any case, framing selfhood as distinctiveness, Bezos's valediction leaves out something equally fundamental to human life: interdependency. The "energy" you burn in maintaining yourself as a self is not only a matter of high personal character and drive. It is also a matter of ongoing metabolic interaction between you and your environment, including your social environment. That is why the border of any organism is not a wall but a porous membrane, a two-way street. The question in this case being what you owe, as an ethical organism, to the other organisms around you, and whether a profit-driven entity like Amazon can be trusted to settle its accounts on that score justly. Lying just beneath the letter's self-help-style exhortation to expend the energy required to be awesome is a pugnacious social Darwinist refusal to apologize for being the fittest company in the jungle.

Somewhat in the spirit of the postapocalyptic fiction with which contemporary literary history is, as we shall discuss, so richly supplied, we need to stare long enough at the wonders of Amazon that their all-too-real shadow referent flickers into view: a world beset by savage inequality and civic decay. And not only that. An even shorter allegorical route runs from postapocalyptic fiction to actual apocalypses, the ones already accomplished and the even bigger environmental ones to come. They will be found incommodious by everyone, even those with a ticket to leave Earth on a spaceship.

It's amazing that we manage to say "Amazon" so often without thinking about the river it is named after, one of many burning front lines in the current global climate crisis. Warding off this unflattering connection, the company's recent greenwashing of itself in various ways, although presented in characteristically epic terms, has as yet applied only the barest patina of eco-virtue to its massively carbon-intensive ambitions for itself and its customers.[47] The belief that we will be saved by miracles of technological invention functions in the present mostly as an alibi for putting no critical pressure at all on the structure of consumerist desire. Amazon can buy as many fleets of electric trucks as it wishes, and all breathers of air should be happy about that, but until it takes aim at its own revenue growth—until it asks its customers to consider whether they maybe *do not need* that thing they are about to order—it will be hard to take seriously as a force for environmental good.

This inspires one more line of judgment: the problem with Amazon arises in the third instance from hard limits we are hitting in the ability of the world ecology to sustain us in the way of life it encourages. As I watch the cardboard boxes accumulating out back—it has been raining, and the pile is achieving a slightly molten quality—I understand this as a point of self-incrimination, too.

To analyze the fictions produced in Amazon's shadow is hardly sufficient to the task of reconstructing our collective life on more sustainable grounds, but it is one place to start thinking about what it would mean to try.

1

Fiction as a Service

Amazon as Literary History

Should Amazon now be considered the driving force of American, perhaps even world, literary history? Is it occasioning a convergence of the state of the art of fiction writing with the state of the art of capitalism? If so, what does this say about the form and function of the novel—about its role in managing, resisting, or perhaps simply reflecting the dominant forces of our time? How has the novel's long history as a purveyor of fictional worlds prepared it, or not, to speak to those forces in ways that readers still find compelling? These are the broad questions with which this study begins and by which it hopes to begin to draw critical attention to what is surely one of the most historically novel if as yet largely unexplored features of contemporary culture.

Amazon is at once exemplary and odd. It is a paragon of the contemporary corporation operating under the conditions of what was once enthusiastically called the New Economy, in which dramatic advances in information and communications technology would in theory change the game to the benefit of one and all. Like the magic systems portrayed in epic fantasy, the new corporate IT would surely if somewhat obscurely magnify the possibilities of human agency, making wizards of us all. In the event, it has made some men very rich while reinforcing the precarious dependency of most men and women on a system of economic arrangements not of their making. A system in which, under the watchful eye of the stock market, what is rewarded is ruthlessness in the management of employee armies and casting of spells. And Amazon is nothing if not ruthless, having become notorious for the aggression with which it pursues its own interests under the banner not of king or country but *customer*.[1] With its brutally efficient management of the warehouses it calls fulfillment centers, with its predatory relation to the businesses with which it competes, Amazon exemplifies a corporate world that has returned in recent years to more savage conditions rather than advanced to a higher state.[2]

It is however strikingly distinct from its corporate brethren in several ways, not least in its uniquely intense and ongoing self-association with literature and the book. Not unrelatedly, and notwithstanding the controversy that so often follows in its wake, it has become a service so useful and convenient to readers as to thwart all but the most determined efforts to resist its charms.

Launched in 1995 as an online bookstore, Amazon's receipts from books had by 2014 shrunken dramatically as a percentage of the company's estimated $75 billion in yearly revenue, to something like 7 percent, as the company began to compete with Walmart for the prize of being the largest retailer in the world. That percentage is no doubt even smaller now, with 2020 revenue coming in at $386 billion, a nearly fivefold increase in only six years. And yet, if books are now only a fraction of the business of Amazon, that fraction is no small part of the book business, exceeding half of all US book purchases. The number is even higher for electronic books, a market Amazon did not invent but which it unquestionably made with the introduction of the Kindle e-reader in 2007.[3] Greater still is Amazon's dominance of the market in popular genre fiction. It has proved especially amenable to electronic consumption and is at the core of the $9.99 per month Amazon Unlimited e-book subscription service, now with several million subscribers. The latter points to an aspiration for serial plenitude over singular encounters in the reader's relation to literature; to literature as a service somewhat like internet service or some other "always on" utility.

Intensely more observant of the realities of reading than publishing has ever been before, Amazon Unlimited pays royalties to writers based on the number of pages of their works the Kindle user actually reads rather than on their download alone. This distinction was part of the inspiration behind Amazon's introduction in 2017 of Amazon Charts, an in-house weekly best-seller list divided into categories of "Most Sold" (familiar enough), but also "Most Read." The latter integrates the wealth of data Amazon gleans from Kindle devices reporting back to the mother ship along with information on audiobook consumption, presenting a picture of what people are reading as opposed to simply buying. This is in addition to the myriad best-seller categories, numbering in the thousands, one encounters in any ordinary book search on the website, where, for instance, at one point in 2019, Delia Owens's *Where the Crawdads Sing* (2018) held the No. 1 spot in Coming of Age Fiction, American Literature, and Women's Literature and Fiction, while John Grisham's *The Guardian* (2019) held the No. 2 spot in American Literature but was No. 1 in both Murder Thrillers and Small Town and Rural Fiction. Works like this claim the lion's share of attention in the publishing industry as it is currently organized, yet with so many lists covering so many niches—Women's Divorce Fiction, Australia and Oceania Literature, Teen and Young Adult Vampire eBooks, the list goes on—one feels there should be room near the top for almost everyone.

Book sales in the billions are no doubt motivation enough to keep the company focused on the readers who were its first customers, but in recent years Amazon has undertaken a series of initiatives that suggest a deeper existential commitment to the idea of literature, to getting inside literature, to *being literary*, than dollar figures can fully communicate.

It has, first of all, become a traditional publisher with sixteen separate imprints, each tied to a separate genre, including one for literary fiction called Little A. The latter speaks to the persistence of the category of literary fiction as something unto itself, something putatively "un-generic," but also to its demotion to the status of one genre among many, as we see in the figure on p.36.

Our Imprints

Amazon Publishing is made up of the following imprints that publish books
across genres and around the world.

 Lake Union Publishing
BOOK CLUB FICTION

 Thomas & Mercer
MYSTERY, THRILLER, AND TRUE CRIME

 Montlake
ROMANCE

 Little A
LITERARY FICTION AND NONFICTION

 Amazon Crossing
WORLD LITERATURE

 Amazon Crossing Kids
CHILDREN'S BOOKS FROM AROUND THE WORLD

 47North
SCIENCE FICTION AND FANTASY

 Skyscape
TEEN AND YOUNG ADULT

 Two Lions
CHILDREN'S BOOKS

 Amazon Original Stories
SHORT FICTION AND NONFICTION

 TOPPLE Books
CURATED BY JOEY SOLOWAY

 Amazon Publishing
GENERAL FICTION AND NONFICTION

 Jet City Comics
COMICS AND GRAPHIC NOVELS

Grand Harbor Press
INSPIRATIONAL

Waterfall Press
CHRISTIAN FICTION

 AmazonEncore
REDISCOVERED WORKS

Amazon Imprints A list of imprints that is also a snapshot, as from an over-
head drone, of Amazon's understanding of the contemporary genre system;
that is, of the parceling out of the universal human desire to be told a story into
separate modes of fulfillment keyed to different audiences and taste profiles.

Perhaps the most interesting and lively of these imprints is Amazon Crossing, which under the leadership of editorial director Gabriella Page-Fort has become the most prolific publisher of literary translations into English in the world. We will return to it in chapter 2, where the relation of Amazon's corporate multinationality to world literature is brought to the fore. All told, the Amazon imprints have published thousands of books and are still growing despite the unwillingness of most bookstores to carry them, not wanting to help a company gunning for their business. Notably, whereas in the publishing industry at large, total sales of adult nonfiction generally outdo those of adult fiction, the vast majority of Amazon Publishing's books are novels, suggesting an intriguingly excessive commitment on its part to fictionality.[4]

More innovative, and more consequential to this chapter and indeed this whole book, has been Kindle Direct Publishing (KDP), which, for 30 percent of the proceeds on any electronic text sold but at no further cost to the author, was designed to circumvent the traditional gatekeepers of American literary production, ushering in a new age of self-authorized popular creativity and low-cost literary entertainment.[5] Although it is difficult to find exact data, it would appear that millions of texts have been self-published via KDP, and that hundreds of them have sold hundreds of thousands of copies—albeit, at cover prices sometimes as low as 99 cents. KDP works in tandem with the hard-copy print-on-demand platform CreateSpace, acquired in 2005 and folded into KDP in 2018, and with Brilliance Audio and Audible.com, acquired in 2007 and 2008, respectively, thereby covering all the sensory modalities of the contemporary book. Kindle Singles, whose motto is "Compelling Ideas Expressed at Their Natural Length," is fascinating for how it leverages technology against the traditional constraints of the physical form of the book, which has to be of a certain size to be shipped and displayed through regular channels, allowing writers to sell a single short story, or a novella, etc., as an e-text. Amazon has also acquired the book-oriented social media site Goodreads, now with more than a hundred million eminently data-minable registered users. Through its Amazon Literary Partnership program, it has doled out millions of dollars in grants to various literary organizations since 2009.

Cumulatively, these ventures represent a highly interested practical theorization of the literary field, one which we are by

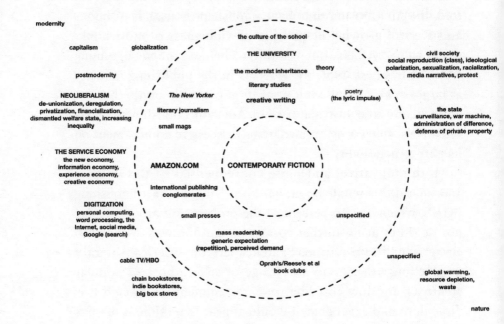

FICTION IN THE AGE OF _____

Contexts Distance from the center of the diagram is a measure of explanatory generality, which is a source at once of comprehensive power and of potential banality. To say, for instance, that contemporary fiction is a product of nature, or modernity, would be as absolutely true as it would be absolutely uninteresting unless those claims could be specified. To notice, in turn, that poetry lies on the periphery of the diagram is to see at once how all literary activity can be described as "poetic" in the loosest sense, but also how weak the specific influence of contemporary poetry on contemporary fiction is beyond its association with the "lyric impulse," that is, the human predisposition to artful self-expression in words. A more specific influence on fiction is exerted by the university, and in particular by the creative writing programs where so many professional poets now work alongside fiction writers. As discussed at length in my book *The Program Era*, creative writing programs didn't exist in anything like the form we know them until the postwar period, but they now figure as perhaps the most crucial institutional infrastructure underlying the production of literary fiction and poetry in the US, the sine qua non of innumerable careers.

no means obliged to accept, but which anyone hoping for an adequate sense of the realities of that field will be increasingly obliged to observe.

So where exactly is Amazon in this field? What does the institutional ground of contemporary literary production actually look like? This is the signal question asked by a new institutionalism in scholarly approaches to contemporary literature in recent years as it has sought to move beyond the abstractions —pre-eminently "postmodernism"—that have guided its interpretation for so long. Perhaps its looks something like the diagram in the "Contexts" figure on p.38, which, taking the relative coherence and reality of something called "contemporary fiction" as a given, represents a highly schematic plotting of the various institutions that can be said to influence its form.

At the top of the diagram one sees the university, whose importance to contemporary literature of a certain kind would be hard to overstate, especially to the lives of the great many authors who make a better living there as writing teachers than they could through book sales alone. Given that they stand alike as such striking literary-historical novelties, it seems fair to begin by asking: What is the relation between the "Age of Amazon" to

How-To The writing pedagogy facilitated by Amazon focuses more on marketing strategies than on the form and content of stories.

the creative writing program? Observing the situation in 2021, one would have to say that they are merely adjacent literary-historical phenomena, although there is nothing standing in the way of their partial convergence in, say, the publication as KDP e-books of otherwise dead MFA theses. Juxtaposing these two entities, we immediately notice something interesting and possibly surprising, which is the relative lack of any real pedagogical dimension in and of the KDP literary ecology, which acts more or less as though the writing of good books will take care of itself. Confirming this lack, what the company calls KDP University is mostly a series of chats with self-published authors reflecting on how they achieved their success. In the same vein are the raft of how-to books sprung up to help writers navigate KDP, which could be thought of in a pedagogical light (see figure on p. 39). Certainly, Amazon is already hard at work conquering the campus bookstore and textbook (and other sundry) markets, as Barnes & Noble and Borders once did.

What the worlds of KDP and MFA already share is a professed allegiance to the artistic will of the people, and creativity in general, although Amazon represents a significant intensification of this populism, relatively unburdened as it is by that other half of the writing program's mission: the conservation of more or less high modernist literary values and pursuit of traditionally exclusive literary prestige. One way of thinking about the Age of Amazon, then, is as a possible successor formation to the creative writing program, thereby foretelling the end of the Program Era. To the extent that the motive for getting an MFA is to become a "published novelist," KDP offers considerably more efficient means to that exalted end. But, of course, there are many reasons to pursue an MFA degree other than that, so a literary historian must entertain the thought of pure supersession with skeptical caution. Indeed if, as seems to be the case, the rise of Amazon has been associated with an overall lowering of the incomes of full-time writers, the impetus for supporting themselves by teaching writing has become all the stronger, assuming enough students can be found to shore up the enterprise with their tuition money.

Here, however, I want to concentrate on the sector on the left side of the diagram, where one finds various ways of characterizing the properly economic environment of contemporary fiction. Amazon has a different sort of relation to so-called neoliberalism —that is, to the ideology of de-unionization, deregulation, privatization, financialization, and the dismantling of the welfare state that has dominated policy debates since the 1970s—than it does to the university writing program. While its relation to the latter is one of as yet uncoupled adjacency, its relation to neoliberalism is one of specification and thus, inevitably, idiosyncrasy. In the back-and-forth between empirical analysis and concept generation in materialist literary historiography, this specificity can be a real advantage, pointing, for instance, to the sheer oddness of the novel as a "neoliberal" commodity—not least, as we'll see, in the way it structures time.

The same is true of Amazon's relation to the internet, or more broadly to digital technology, including the personal computer, word processer, data server, and now social media. On the one hand, in a way that is not quite true for its competitors in the publishing business, the multinational conglomerates— HarperCollins, Hachette, Macmillan, Penguin Random House, and Simon & Schuster (at this writing, the latter two have planned to merge, pending approval by regulators)—who between them produce the lion's share of books published in the United States, the advent of advanced digital technology and internet communication is the sine qua non of Amazon. Although it moves a great many physical objects through space, it is one of the original "dot-com" companies, as they were once called, a congeries of digitizations on the front and back end of its business.

To say that Amazon has arisen as a new and highly consequential agent in the unfolding of literary history is necessarily to say that the internet has, too. It was, after all, the latter that made Amazon possible, directly inspiring the company's founding as an answer to the question, much on the minds of would-be entrepreneurs of the late twentieth century like Jeff Bezos: what is to be done with this new medium of globally networked communication? Bezos's answer was to start a business billing itself as "Earth's Biggest Bookstore," and later the "Everything Store," on its way to becoming the internet-enabled octopus of contemporary retail, warehousing and fulfillment, media production, consumer electronics, and web services we know today.

Conceived in 1989 as a means for the sharing of scientific research and data, by 1991 the browsable layer of the internet known as the World Wide Web had already been opened to commercial activity. For Bill Gates, famously, the web would be the medium of a newly "friction-free capitalism," from the overcoming of barriers to trade, to the efficient management of the global supply chain, to the accelerated advertisement, sale, and eventually direct digital consumption of wares.[6] In the event, even as the web indeed transformed the communicational infrastructure of capitalism, the arrival of this friction-free future would be slowed by that irritatingly inescapable hindrance, embodied humanity, with its retrograde wants and needs. An online identity might not have a body in the usual sense, but it is irrevocably tied to one or more bodies in real life. The energy of which it is constituted in all its "immateriality" comes from some grossly physical power plant or other. Thus, *pace* Bill Gates, and nowhere more aggressively than at Microsoft, was the web quickly partitioned and privatized toward the end of the efficient exploitation of deliberately manufactured inefficiencies. It was conceived as a new kind of territory to be claimed, a territory made in the claiming, half-hallucinatory, measured by nodal traffic density, deal flow, and mindshare.

Amazon would secure plenty of the latter, becoming one of the few most admired and ubiquitous brands in the world, but its most profitable venture, revealed only in the second decade of the twenty-first century, would be in offering web services to other companies on the invisible back end of e-commerce. This was the brainchild of Andy Jassy, who recently took over from Bezos as company CEO. What the company does for would-be authors with the KDP platform, and for small businesses looking for a distribution channel with Amazon Marketplace,

Amazon Web Services does on even larger scale for other corporations, hosting and organizing their data in hyper-scale server farms. While one cannot by any means equate Amazon with the internet, the move into web services has by one account made the company the single most pervasive private infrastructural presence on the web, all but unavoidable in any internet user's daily rounds whether they know it or not.[7] Nick Srnicek and others have called it "platform capitalism": having captured the playing field upon which competing commercial interests do battle, the platform monopoly recedes from the scene of risk even as it profits from the risky transactions of others using its services, harvesting data and selling advertising space as it goes.[8]

Amazon provides service. That is the thing it sells, and if it is a paragon of the New Economy, that economy is also simply a technologically enhanced form of the *service economy*. The latter is neither an *ideology* (neoliberalism) nor a *technology* (the internet) but a form of *social relation*, the result of a large-scale transformation of industrial "relations of production" into postindustrial relations of service. As we see in the figure below, the situation described by the term "service economy" is

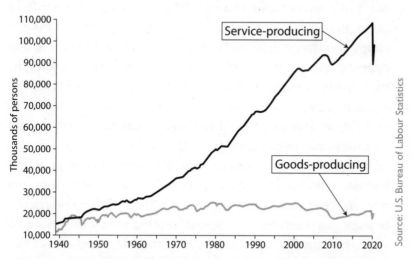

The Rise of the Service Economy Having been at near parity with the goods-producing sector during World War II, the service sector has since taken off in the US, now employing almost 80 percent of US workers. The numbers are similar for the UK and slightly less stark in Germany, France, and other highly developed Western economies, while they are still at near parity in China.

arguably the most dramatic socioeconomic transformation of the past century in the US and other advanced economies, but it is one that has received surprisingly little attention from cultural critics in these precise terms.[9]

The service economy comes freighted with a complex social psychology of servility and entitlement, servility and domination, and indeed, as we'll see, servile domination.[10] More simply, it gives us the first general concept or ideal under which fiction in the Age of Amazon might be experimentally subsumed: customer service. The author as servant, as server, and service provider; the reader as consumer, yes, but more precisely as *customer*, which has an importantly different, because implicitly social relational, meaning.[11]

Published in 2014 via KDP and CreateSpace, John Rossman's *The Amazon Way: 14 Leadership Principles behind the World's Most Disruptive Company* reads as a kind of corporate catechism and hagiography of the founder of Amazon, Jeff Bezos. It provides a useful condensation of the company's self-understanding, derived as it is from the list of fourteen principles that to this day circulate throughout the company as a constant point of reference and anchor of the corporate culture.[12] Even as he prepares to step down as CEO, Bezos remains its dominant executive and controlling shareholder, and that raises an important issue. When thinking about the corporate identity of Amazon, an entity now with more than 1 million employees, one cannot forget the charismatic individual at its center, although in this case, we might want immediately to open the lens wide enough to include MacKenzie Bezos (now MacKenzie Scott), his novelist ex-wife. As the company's fourth employee and original bookkeeper, she was on the scene of the company's rise since the very beginning. She is now, after her divorce settlement, no doubt the wealthiest novelist in history, and we'll see if her already impressive philanthropic endeavors reflect that fact over time. Although this hasn't to my knowledge been remarked, it would seem to matter, intuitively, that the domestic space occupied by Amazon's famously numbers-obsessed founder CEO was also a scene of serious literary ambition.[13]

So what is Amazon all about? According to Rossman, a former Amazon senior executive, principle number one is "Obsess Over the Customer":

> Jeff Bezos's customer obsession is really something beyond a mere obsession—it's a psychosis that has generated many of his most vitriolic tirades or, more often, sarcastic comments at Amazon associates who have fallen short of his own standard for customer service. It stems from Jeff's unique ability to put himself in the customer's position, deduce his or her unspoken needs and wants, and then develop a system that will meet those needs and wants better than anyone else has ever done.[14]

Notice the quasi-literary structure of identification this imagines, where Bezos adopts the point of view of the customer and in so doing makes himself the ultimate customer. In a sort of New Economy revision of the king's two bodies of medieval political theology, there is the real body of the CEO and abstract body of the customer from whom he draws his worldly power. So Hachette wants to charge more for e-books than $9.99? *Sorry, that wouldn't be good for the customer.*[15] You want to unionize that fulfillment center? *Sorry, that would hurt the customer.* This is what is meant by "servile domination." The ideal toward which it points is a world composed entirely of customers and no workers, even as the workforce actually assembled by Amazon continues to grow. Some might take this as a beautiful ideal, pointing toward a fully communist post-scarcity technotopia, but in the meantime it is exceedingly contradictory in its real-world implications of mass redundancy and poverty. As Rossman puts it, explaining Bezos's massive investments in customer self-service technologies, "He long recognized that the biggest threat to the customer experience was human beings getting involved and mucking things up."[16]

The plan for Amazon was conceived when Bezos, with a computer science degree from Princeton, was working at D. E. Shaw & Co., a Wall Street investment firm known for its invention of high-speed trading via advanced technology. To that extent,

Amazon can be said to have been born among numbers, but it was words that sealed the deal. Not only were books, in their relative physical uniformity, durability, and differentiated numerousness, the ideal commodity with which to venture into the new world of online commerce, but one book in particular was decisive in convincing Bezos to leave his job at Shaw. As Brad Stone reports,

> At the time Bezos was thinking about what to do next, he had recently finished the novel *Remains of the Day*, by Kazuo Ishiguro, about a butler who wistfully recalls his personal and professional choices during a career in service in wartime Great Britain. So looking back on life's important junctures was on Bezos's mind when he came up with what he calls "the regret minimization framework" to decide the next step to take at this juncture of his career.[17]

By this account we owe the existence of Amazon.com to *The Remains of the Day*, to a novel about a servant, and indeed about the transformation of the role of the servant in an increasingly Americanized world. At first one assumes this meant Bezos wanted to avoid being the servant of his legendary Wall Street boss Mr. Shaw, wanted himself to be the lord and not the butler, but a closer look at the novel suggests a more complex psychology at work. It is as much a matter of emulating Stevens the butler, who has his own "psychotic" obsession with service, as with *not* becoming him. In any case, the influence of literature on Amazon did not stop at its origin, but persists in certain of its more peculiar corporate customs, such as the requirement that internal meeting presenters forgo PowerPoint in favor of brief prose narratives read in silence before the meeting begins.[18] New product proposals are delivered in the form of futuristic fictional press releases reflecting on the product's success, and indeed the entire company appears animated, at times, by the spirit of the epic science fiction, a genre of which Bezos is known to be an ardent fan.

This is fascinating, and we'll return to *The Remains of the*

Day and to epic science fiction alike, but first we should simply note how Amazon's commitment to service transforms literary experience into customer experience. KDP is about as open a publishing platform as one could imagine, a veritable romp of unbound and unrestricted authorship, but even here, if one looks closely, one sees that the customer, and not the writer, is king, except insofar as the writer is also a potential customer, a purchaser of advertising or product placement. In the interstices of the KDP platform website one finds a "Guide to Kindle Content Quality," warning the would-be self-publisher, "Content published through Kindle Direct Publishing is held to the high standards customers have come to expect from Amazon. If readers tell us about a problem they've found in your book, we will make sure you know about it and point you in the right direction to get the problem fixed."[19] These problems include "typos," "formatting issues," "missing content," "wrong content," and even "disappointing content." There may be different and frankly lower standards at KDP than at Knopf, but there *are* standards, and they take their bearings from the implicit presence of the customer as reader.

When one clicks through on the category of Disappointing Content, the service becomes more rhetorically aggressive on behalf of the customer: "We do not allow content that disappoints our customers." And what kind of content might disappoint those customers? Content "whose primary purpose is to solicit or advertise" would be bad, as would content that is "too short" or "poorly translated." And yet rounding out the list of forbidden qualities is one almost metaphysical in extent and implication: "Content that does not provide an enjoyable reading experience." This could be taken to preclude an awful lot of things—including presumably any kind of literature that resists "reader enjoyment" as its ultimate end. Surveying the vast sea of KDP content, one highly doubts that this rule is rigorously applied, if it even could be. "Provide an enjoyable reading experience" *to whom*? That is the multibillion-dollar question.

The quality strictures would seem to go more to the articulation of a disciplining ideal, and justification for removing truly objectionable content at will, than to the company's routine operations. The question is the extent to which these operations have begun to shape a literary culture—or literary culture in general—in their image.

The Man of Letters as a Man of E-Commerce

"You are a start-up ... The next great business is you."[20] The merging of identity and enterprise asserted in Hugh Howey's 2013 pep talk to aspiring authors is notable for the precision with which it calls forth the rhetoric of contemporary American business culture, projecting its most cherished legends of high risk, long hours, and outsize reward into the domain of literary ambition. At the outset of their career, the writer makes investments and absorbs losses and may even take out some loans. They do so in hopes of future profits, yes, but also toward the realization of a state of autonomous capitalist being. If you *are* the business, you can probably also be considered its founder, controlling shareholder, main publicist, and CEO—the Jeff Bezos, as it were—of the independent content-provider that is you. Freed now, by the good graces of Amazon, even from the strictures of traditional publishing contracts, your one remaining fetter will be the reader as customer, a quasi-deity around whose needs—assuming you want to earn money from your writing—your creative labor must revolve.

Not two years before issuing this advice on the website where he interacts with his readers, Howey had been a South Carolina bookstore clerk, viewing the publishing world from one of its lowest rungs, working on his stories in between shifts. That all changed when, frustrated in his attempts to win the interest of major publishers, he uploaded a short story to the servers of Kindle Direct Publishing and watched it catch fire.[21] Soon thereafter, Howey would achieve renown not only as a best-selling writer of several volumes of fiction but also as the chief ideologue of a highly self-conscious group of self-described "indie" authors, some of whom, like him, have cultivated devoted readerships and achieved considerable commercial success. Possessed as never before with a set of real-time sales-tracking mechanisms, and with a set of tools for strategically marketing their work, indie writers tend to be exceptionally knowledgeable of the protocols organizing the markets they enter, whether via Amazon or one of its smaller rivals such as Smashwords or Lulu.com.[22] They assume duties that would otherwise fall to the editorial and marketing staff of traditional publishers, but also avail themselves of a thriving secondary market for cover design, copyediting, and even—at the margins of legitimacy— paid "reviewing" services. (Indeed, the line between a robustly informed literary professionalism and simple gaming of the system can sometimes blur. Amazon's move to pay authors for pages read rather than works downloaded would appear, in part, to have been an attempt to counter the efforts of a certain kind of KDP scam artist.)

Generally hostile to the publishers who scorned them—"the phrase '*vanity publishing*' was almost certainly invented by traditional publishers years ago in order to squash the competition from entrepreneurial authors," writes one—indie writers sometimes act as unofficial spokespeople of the company from whom they in effect rent virtual shelf space and automated marketing services. Over time, the relation between indie writers and Amazon has grown more fraught, as every new policy or program shift reminds writers that they are dealing with a corporation just as "faceless," and in some ways more so, as any of the conglomerates.[23] (A corporation that, for instance, asks authors to sign a strict exclusivity agreement for their work to be included in the Kindle Unlimited subscription service offerings is not likely to be perceived as wholly benign in its intentions.) Strategically conceding indie writers the avant-garde status they crave, we can then go on to ask how the "Age of Amazon" might define the situation of contemporary American fiction as such.

Entitled "Wool," the story Howey uploaded imagines a future world in which, to all appearances, the entire human population lives in one large silo extending 144 stories into the ground, while visions of the toxic wasteland at the surface are projected on screens within.[24] No one remembers how or why this highly regimented and hierarchical, if also patently socialistic, form of life came into being, all memory of the past having been lost. There are those who dream of something more, but even to speak of such things is punishable by exile into the waste, where crumpled bodies of past transgressors dot the lifeless brown landscape. Before they leave the silo, they are dressed in short-lived survival suits and given some wool with which to scrub the ever-clouding lenses of the cameras at the surface. Strangely, none of them has ever been known to fail to complete the task. The most recently exiled was the protagonist Holston's wife, who, having grown obsessed with some inexplicable code she recovered from the servers of the silo computer system, became convinced that the images of devastation on the screens inside the silo are a lie. The world might actually be beautiful and green. Now, two miserable years after her suicidal departure, her husband prepares to follow.

As with any outsize literary success, one can only speculate what it was about this story, among the millions, that lit a fuse, but explode it did. It couldn't have been the story's uplifting ending, where—spoiler alert—Holston steps out of the silo and first sees exactly the green world his wife promised. He scrubs the lens in eagerness for his silo brethren to witness the truth that will set them free, and only then begins to choke and die. He desperately pulls his helmet off, trying to breath, and sees the same old wasted world. So the false image is not the dreadful one projected inside the silo, but the inspiring one projected inside the visor of his helmet. The end.

But not the end. Responding, by his own account, to overwhelming reader demand for the story to continue, over the next few years Howey produced a series of novella-length installments that were finally gathered in three large "omnibus" volumes known collectively as the Silo Saga. But how could the original short story possibly have continued? Should it have? As a stand-alone work it is perfect, a resonant retelling of Plato's allegory of the cave that stands comfortably beside any of the canonical political parables of twentieth-century fiction, from

Darkness at Noon to "The Lottery." But what exactly is its message? And whatever that might be, does it remain the same at over 1,500 epic pages in length as it did at the original 58?[25]

I think not, and I further think that the reason why might be tied to the evolving circumstances of its publication. Put simply, what had figured as a bitter negation of utopian sentiment— but also an ironically utopian representation of non-capitalist existence as necessity, since there is no room in the silo for capitalist expansion—evolves by customer demand into something like the opposite, an epic of corporate populism, of open-ended "freedom." How could one possibly continue on from the chillingly perfect closure of the first story? Well, is this the only silo? No, it turns out that there are two of them; and then later fifty of them, all gathered outside a now-ruined Atlanta. Each one is isolated from the others, thinking it is the whole world, but all are governed from a malignant central command silo. The epic drama then becomes one of rebellious networking, as characters find ways for different silos to communicate freely, as though on a primitively reconstituted internet. Finally, they commandeer a drone and begin to explore the wasteland that surrounds them. With one more wonderful twist, it turns out that this wasteland has a sharp border several miles away. Beyond the immediate environs of the fifty silos, the depopulated world *really is* green and beautiful after all, ripe for renewed habitation, unrestricted reproduction, and economic growth.

Now, to say the least, not all of the countless thousands of fiction writers who have published via KDP have Howey's considerable storytelling talent and obvious concern for craftsmanship. But it would seem that they all, like him, and despite the putatively anti-generic implications of "indie" cultural production in music or film, write in popular generic forms. Indeed, noticing the recent migration of several otherwise "literary" writers into the space of genre, one might go as far as to say that fiction in the Age of Amazon *is* genre fiction, a highly gendered and age-differentiated genre system complexly structured by the poles of epic and romance and their characteristic modes of wish fulfillment.

On the side of epic one finds, as in Howey's Silo Saga, innumerable scenarios of apocalypse, postapocalyptic survival, and world rebuilding, along with other sorts of fantasy and science fiction epic sequences. On the side of romance, one finds a highly differentiated array of amatory and erotic genres. In this system, the "novel" per se—the genre described in critical discourse on the "rise of the novel," and brought to a high point of achievement in the realist tradition of Austen, Eliot, and James—is not particularly important except as a unit of discourse in the formation of a trilogy or longer series. Offering tested models of market success, genre is important to indie writers because it implies the existence of an audience ready to be pleased again and again within the terms of an implicit contract. Success, and even a highly qualified version of originality, in this system are the results of effective variation and permutation within established generic structures.

One lively recent subgenre has been the paranormal romance, anchored in its latest incarnation by the traditionally published *Twilight* books of Stephenie Meyer. The genius of one Amanda Hocking, then a twenty-six-year-old eldercare worker from Minnesota, was to see that popular thirst for high school–centric vampire romance had not yet been sated. And so she competently upped the available supply and became a millionaire.[26] Similarly, customer demand for billionaire romance extends far beyond the ability of the former fan fiction *Fifty Shades of Grey* and its E. L. James–authored sequels to satisfy it. Jasinda Wilder saw an opportunity here for her *Alpha* series.[27] In the first volume, a marginally employed young woman burdened with huge student loan debts and a terribly sick mother starts finding checks for $10,000 in her mailbox. On some level the fantasy could stop there. There's a real eloquence in the duress expressed in the opening chapters of this novel, and consequently a great sense of relief when the pressure is off. But, of course, a helicopter ride, jewels, a blindfold, and hot sex with what turns out to be an incredibly handsome if domineering billionaire makes things even better.

Loving the White Billionaire

There is indeed, at least in one of its regions, an undeniable convergence of the contemporary genre system with porn categories, and in the world of KDP there is no real restriction on their finer and finer subdivision in the interest of "target marketing."[28] For instance, I don't know how large the audience is for "sexy BWWM Billionaire Romance," in which an African American woman finds satisfaction with a handsome white billionaire, but Monica Brooks's *Loving the White Billionaire* trilogy leaves no doubt that it is here to service them (see figure above).[29]

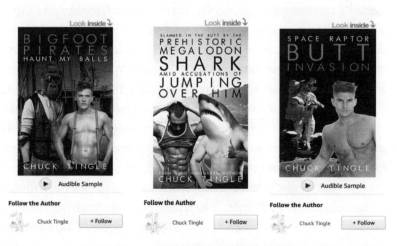

KDP as Queer Performance Art

Sometimes the theme of giving service to the billionaire is made perfectly explicit, as in M. S. Parker and Cassie Wild's billionaire romance *Serving Him* and its many sequels.[30] It would take some real dialectical ingenuity to redeem this fantasy structure, which reimagines the central beneficiary of a system of savage economic and racial inequality as the sexy Samaritan savior of the lower orders. Indeed, one is tempted to dust off the term "false consciousness" to describe it, and to wonder whether the KDP apparatus is somewhere being deployed, as it might conceivably be, to more progressive or even radical ends. Certainly, in the literary field at large, genre forms sometimes play this role, from the anti-racist crime novels of Walter Mosley to the complex genre stylings of Colson Whitehead and Viet Thanh Nguyen to the forthrightly pulpy leftist feminism of Aya de Leon's *Justice Hustlers* (2016–19) series.

"Radical" is one word we might use to describe the zany multiplicity of self-described "tinglers" published by one Dr. Chuck Tingle, author of *Space Raptor Butt Invasion* (2015), *Bigfoot Pirates Haunt My Balls* (2015), and *Unicorn Butt Cops: Beach Patrol* (2015), and hundreds of other works of self-published surreal satirical gay porn (see figure on p. 53). Brought to increased notoriety by his ironic nomination for a Hugo Award by a group of right-wing dissenters to what they perceived as the award's increasingly politically correct bent, Tingle is as much a performance artist as writer, and he projects something of the same sly innocence as Andy Warhol, although in a sweeter, more life-affirming vintage. Some of his works—for instance, *Slammed in the Butt by My Hugo Award Nomination* (2016) or *Slammed in the Butt by the Prehistoric Megalodon Shark amidst Accusations of Jumping over Him* (2017)—veer into a condition of pure self-reference we might more easily associate with the highest of high modernisms if it weren't for the comic crudity of it all.[31] One might also point to avant-garde poet Kevin Killian's uncannily earnest-and-yet-fake collection of Amazon reviews, *Selected Amazon Reviews* (2006), originally posted on the site over a long period, or to Nick Thurston's *Of the Subcontract: Or Principles of Poetic Right* (2016), which describes itself as a "collection of poems about computational capitalism, each of which was written by an underpaid worker subcontracted through Amazon.com's Mechanical Turk service."[32] Finally, as we will see shortly, one might look at some of the products of small presses that are essentially adjuncts to the Amazon apparatus in all but name.

In any case, in the purity of their lust for the highest-status person they can imagine, works like *Loving the White Billionaire* are arguably preferable to the more "sophisticated" love for billionaires shown in Howey's contribution to the billionaire romance genre. *The Shell Collector* pits an environmentally conscious investigative journalist against a handsome oil company magnate in a near-future world where most shellfish have died off owing to the acidity of the oceans. Midway through the novel, the mixed-race female protagonist has what has to be considered, in generic terms, a convenient realization:

> Getting to know Ness as a person has been a mistake, rather than a boon for my piece. The issues I want to write about are larger than one man, larger than any of us; they concern the entire globe; they concern our environment, our politics, our collective choices. Tearing him down felt good before. Now it feels hollow.[33]

So no more blaming the white billionaires, okay? The barely politically contestable, because socially diffuse, culprit of our woes is "all of us." Which isn't to say that a viable environmentalist political program can be mounted only on the critique of billionaires. Howey's journalist is right about that. But surely there should be limits to our solicitude for them as, in effect, personifications of the system that needs to change? Predictably enough, after their love has been consummated, it turns out that Ness has been nobly funding a secret program to genetically alter shellfish so that they can survive in the new conditions for enjoyment by future generations. Technological innovation and industrial development led by captains of industry may have caused our environmental problems, but in this novel they can still be called upon as saviors.

To say that we have only skimmed the surface of the deep ocean of KDP content here would be an understatement, and who knows what interesting literary fish might be found swimming there if we only had the means to see it more fully, perhaps by giving scholars access to the data so they can explore it using computational tools. For now, some are doing what they can by, for instance, scraping data from the millions of reviews posted to Goodreads and analyzing it for patterns in contemporary literary consumption.[34] If we could inspect every fish in the KDP sea, we would probably find more than a few texts that do not passionately worship billionaires, and some other surprises besides. At this point, however, we'll want to move in the opposite direction, asking: What about the world of the contemporary literary novel, the world of highly esteemed works like *The Remains of the Day*? What can the experiment of positing Amazon as the protagonist of contemporary literary history help us to observe in that world?

Contemporary Fiction as Virtual Quality Time

Among the handful of time concepts that can be said to be original to the postwar period, two are prominent enough to lay claim to decisive significance for understanding the Age of Amazon: "real time" and "quality time."[35] While the first is associated with the technical operations of data management, war fighting, media, and markets, and the second with the warmth of interpersonal relations, they converge in present usage as complementary signs of a general condition of *hurry* that also defines the logistical achievement of good customer service. As one early Amazon employee put it, "We're supposed to care deeply about customers, provided we can care deeply about them at an incredible rate of speed."[36] What's interesting about the terms "real time" and "quality time" is how, upon close inspection, they are found to be not in perfect, but rather in broken or partial, opposition, as though they are the mutually reflecting shards of some prior, and presumably deeper, dialectical collision in the late capitalist life-world. I would propose that it is in and among these shards that one finds the form and function of contemporary fictional narrative as therapy, or self-care. This is how one might begin to move from the organic expression of Bezosian billionaire consciousness in the world of KDP to a more expansive account of contemporary fiction.

The term "real time" dates from the early 1950s, when it emerged in the professional literature of computer science and weapons systems engineering.[37] To acquire information in real time is, most simply, to do so without the usual delay attendant to processes of mediation. Real-time data closes the gap between the occurrence of an event and its apprehension as information, crowding reality and representation together in the urgent space of a perpetually self-renewing *now*. As a relative notion, "real-time" processes in fact run a wide spectrum of tolerance for lag. In computer science we are often talking about delays measured in nanoseconds, or billionths of a second, while in the real-time computer trading pioneered at D. E. Shaw, it is less than a second. In transactions through Amazon, the interval covers a span between a few seconds or minutes, in the case of a digital download, and a few days or more for the delivery of a package facilitated, in turn, by a precisely timed and continually self-informed sprawl of distribution networks.

The theory of real-time retail was made explicit in 1997, in Regis McKenna's *Real Time: Preparing for the Age of the Never Satisfied Customer*, which predicts a world where increasingly "the gap between need or desire and fulfillment collapses to zero."[38] Amazon's announcement, in 2013, that it was developing a drone package delivery service to be called Amazon Prime Air is almost too perfect a reminder of the origin of "real time" in the development of military technology. The same could be said of the entire discipline of industrial logistics that, as Jasper Bernes has noted, was itself born of the massive organizational projects of war fighting.[39] Spreading into the world of commerce, real-time computing has gradually restructured the economy in a manner it is not far-fetched to call violent, converting "rigid" workforces—which is to say those that are unionized, stable, and secure—into "flexible" ones engaged in "just in time" production.

Inhabiting a world ruled by real-time transactions, a human being might well find themselves longing wistfully for some quality time with family or friends. Quality time is the time of intimacy, of analog, face-to-face, inter-subjective attention. As a term it originates in 1970s theorizations of child-rearing, founded on the idea that it is not enough to spend large quantities of time with one's child—say, cooking and cleaning while the child plays nearby.[40] To develop his maximum cognitive potential, the child must be taken as an object of attention in his own right and acknowledged as a fully functional human interlocutor. The unspoken implication was that childcare must take the form of compulsory sociality and even auto-infantilization on the part of mothers. (Fathers barely appear in this literature.) Role modeling, setting an example of efficacy in the world— these would not be enough. The ideal mother would have to meet her child halfway on the road to adult social intercourse. This is the origin of the concept of quality time.

And yet, even as quality time was being theorized, the structure of family life it took for granted was in the process of rapid transformation, if not disintegration. To the extent that it had ever been a norm, the 1950s image of the stay-at-home mother was becoming ever more rarified. This explains how what began as a call for compulsory sociality on the part of mothers evolved in short order into a relative convenience to parents—and even more so to their employers. A woman with a full-time job typically spends a much lower quantity of time with her children than her stay-at-home counterpart, but this was less troubling than it might have been if what really mattered was the *quality* of that time. It was in this context, too, that the idea of quality time began its promiscuous spread to other domains, including that of adult friendship, arriving finally at the subsidiary form of quality time known variously as "alone time" or "me time," which is quality time with oneself—or with a book.

"Oh, I'm not in a hurry at all," says the butler Stevens as he begins the journey that frames the events of *The Remains of the Day*. "For the first time in many a year, I'm able to take my time and I must say, it's rather an enjoyable experience. I'm just motoring for the pleasure of it, you see."[41] Granted to him by his new American employer, Stevens uses his free time not only to travel, but also to write, in the form of diary entries, the series of reflections on his life of service we in effect hold in our hands. In Amazon's early years, employees were constantly reminded that their goal was to "Make History," and so, too, in this novel do we find a subtle meditation on the relation of the employee-servant to "matters of global significance" in the context of World War II. Now, in the novel's present, Stevens is experiencing a transformation in the ideal of service. He has been used to standing silently in the presence of his superiors, but now feels increasingly called upon to engage them socially as part of the job: "In America, it is all part of what is considered good professional service that an employee provide entertaining banter."

And so he dutifully practices bantering, the problem being the hurry required in the offering of witticisms. As a diarist, by contrast, he is able to be ruminative, enjoying the titular remains of his day, his life, in the form of leisurely retrospection. And I think we might generalize this point: what makes fiction so interesting as a "neoliberal" commodity is its partial temporal disjunction from the real-time regime.[42] In the Age of Amazon, we might say, fiction is nothing if not the virtualization of quality time. Consumed during alone time, it finds its thematic substance in dilation upon human intimacy and intrigue, while its most typical grammatical form—the past tense—indicates its imaginary removal from the real time of the reader's present.

If *The Remains of the Day* is the novel that gave us Amazon, the novel of which that whole sprawling enterprise is, in a sense, a reading, then it is formally and thematically connected to that enterprise more deeply than we might have imagined. As, in a sense, is every work of fiction insofar as it is an act of time shifting, compression and dilation, an act not so much of filling up otherwise boring "empty time" as of carving out spaces for sentiment as against the relentless demands of work. But to nail the point down, we'll want to attend briefly to another author who makes this connection quite explicit. Nicholson Baker is a highly respected writer as attuned to the temporality of the Age of Amazon as Ishiguro, and one who, furthermore, as against Ishiguro's relative delicacy, connects the time of reading with time for erotic wish fulfillment in a way that recalls KDP. Like *Remains of the Day*, Baker's *Vox* (1993) and *The Fermata* (1995) were published by Vintage, an imprint of Random House, in turn controlled by Bertelsmann.[43] Conceived not within, but alongside Amazon.com in the early 1990s, they explore the lifeworld neither of the billionaire nor of his personal servant but of the office worker and temp, and will allow us to see the Age of Amazon from the point of view of labor even more directly; or, rather, from the point of view of the laborer temporarily freed from the real-time demands of work into the realm of fiction. In each case the experience of fiction is reflexively thematized as an experience of virtual quality time.

The first takes the form of one single prolonged phone sex conversation between Jim and Abby, who are paying two dollars a minute to retain their privacy as they share fantasies and finally reach the simultaneous orgasm that is also the novel's climax. The first sequence involves Jim ordering lingerie via phone from a catalog. "I had a vision of myself jerking off while I ordered that pair of tights," he says, not yet in a historical position to be able to order them online. Still, the commingling of Eros and customer service that would come to define KDP romance is already quite clear, as the catalog sequence evolves into a series of classic porn scenarios where forms of service, including from house painters, become intensely erotic. As Jim says, "Really I think two dollars a minute is cheap for this. I need this. I'd spend twenty dollars a minute for this. We're actually talking!"[44] *The Fermata* is, if possible, even more on point. It is about an office temp and would-be writer with the ability to stop the flow of time while he himself remains free to act. Mostly he uses it to fondle women—the creepiness of which the novel has trouble ever dispelling—until it occurs to him that the "chronomaly" can be used for a purpose even more fulfilling. Stopping the flow of time, he can now write his long-planned autobiography, which he will self-publish:

I could ... have, say, a hundred copies made up. I'll typeset them myself. I'll get Copy Cop to bind them. I'll design a jacket that uses the logo of some flush, big-name publisher like Random House ... I'll use a color copier to make the cover. It will look like a real book! And then ... I'll go to Waterstone's ... and put this book in people's hands just as they think their fingers are closing on some other, real, book. They will read me. Word will spread.[45]

It would be hard to imagine a more perfect premonition of KDP, and of the achievement of mass self-expression it envisions. And yet Baker's version helpfully points toward the phantasmatic dimension of the KDP ideal, not least in the way it puts the *time of writing itself* into a black box, as though the typical fulfillment center worker wouldn't experience extreme difficulties in writing something *self*-fulfilling, let alone something good, in their spare time. (Say what you will about creative writing programs, they understand that good writing takes time. Indeed, by all accounts, the hiatus they provide from ordinary responsibilities is one of their most unambiguous benefits.) To a certain extent, the same is true of the *time of reading*. The mystification enters at the level of pricing. Except, perhaps, in maintaining a pleasant sensation of consumer choice when turning on the device, after a certain point there is little value to the reader qua reader in accumulating ninety-nine-cent e-books if they do not have enough time to read them.

The problem with quality time, in other words, is that it happens in real time—which is to say, first of all, that it happens within what Jonathan Crary describes as the "24/7 world," a world of "generalized inscription of human life into duration without breaks, defined by the principle of continuous functioning."[46] Real time is the technical expression of systematic impatience and, as such, has proved notoriously difficult to contest, politically, culturally, or otherwise, since arguments against it take time. If fiction promises to "resist" the real-time regime, we will have to admit up front that it is for the most part a virtual resistance, more compensatory than revolutionary, although not necessarily unimportant on that score.

For instance, if *The Remains of the Day* is an exercise in leisurely retrospection, the diary form in which that retrospection unfolds ("Tonight, I find myself here in a guest house in the city of Salisbury")[47] continually refers to the real-time present of the motor trip. Like traditional epistolary fiction, it is written "to the moment." Similarly, while *Vox* portrays the flagrantly erotic expenditure of quality time, its unusual narrative form—one extended dialogue—is the most direct possible narrative instantiation of real time, abjuring the temporal compressions and dilations that are the pride of narrative fiction.

But in some ways the point, the problem, the perplexity, is even more basic than that. To spend quality time with a child or with family or friends or lovers implies bodily co-presence, the live-action sharing of experience without significant delay—it implies, that is, communication in real time. In the Age of Amazon, real time is not only the external context for the therapeutic experience of virtual quality time; it ticks at its core. Indeed, could it be that the original "real time" medium is sensory perception, the relation of subject to object, experience itself? If so, and if Amazon can fully monetize *that*, it will have truly become our Everything Store.

The Great Conscription

One of the sourest and most brilliant endings of an American novel is the one found in Chester Himes's *If He Hollers Let Him Go* (1945) when, about to be jailed for illegal possession of a firearm, African American shipyard worker Bob Jones is given the option of instead enlisting in the US army to fight the Japanese. Having already been absorbed into the wartime workforce as a supervisor and found himself fairly nicely paid on that account, his all-too-predictable prying loose from a small pocket of privilege by the lever of white supremacy has been bitter enough. Now, suddenly, he is given a choice that can only make him laugh—go to prison or be absorbed even deeper into the war machine. "Two hours later I was in the army."[48]

Himes's novel is important for putting up resistance, in advance, to the latter-day idealization of US participation in that war and of the unity of the segregated nation that fought it. It is also, as Frantz Fanon emphasized when he discussed the novel in *Black Skin, White Masks* (1952), an important document in the fictional exploration of colonized male subjectivity.[49] Another way to look at it is as a landmark in the stream of African American literary history, a place where the foundational theme of enslavement and liberation is complicated by being converted, in part, to one of wage slavery and, in many senses of the term, conscription. For the first, as embodied most powerfully in the slave narrative, to write is to write oneself into the condition of a full, free human being. It is an act of political self-representation in the most literal sense. Here, however, the act of self-representation embodied in Bob Jones's first-person narrative has found itself ironized: holler as one might, to speak can only be to pledge allegiance to the social structure that has captured you by your apparent consent.

Projected forward into the context of the contemporary service economy, Bob's dilemma echoes a broader phenomenon analyzed by Deborah Brandt in her important study *The Rise of Writing* (2015), which describes the gradual conversion of writing from a medium of self-expression into a technology of conscription to wage labor—indeed, as the very thing, written messages, the typical service industry employee now produces as part of their core job tasks.[50]

Brandt reminds us that it had been *reading* that had been most important to the production of an "informed citizenry" as conceived by the US Constitution, and *writing* somewhat of an afterthought, something that could be left implicit in the broader concept of freedom of speech. What we call "literacy" had always harbored this asymmetry, indicating first and foremost an ability to read—preeminently, in a predominantly Protestant culture, to read the Bible—and only secondarily an ability to write. In pedagogical practice, of course, the two almost always go together, but the understanding has always been that readers would be relatively many and writers relatively few. To the extent that, as the title of a widely used composition textbook has it, *Everyone's an Author* (2013), that quantitative asymmetry can no longer be taken for granted in the same way. Hence the very meaning of writing as an exercise in the privilege of self-expression has been altered, too. For Brandt, the societal norm must now be considered to be one of conscripted or dependent authorship across the economic landscape, and self-expression a compensatory afterthought:

> According to the Supreme Court, people do not really write at work as citizens or free beings but rather as willingly enlisted corporate voices. At least in their official capacities, workaday writers don't write as themselves at work … Consequently, they don't really mean what they say. Their speech rights are corrupted and, hence, inoperable. From this perspective, writing starts to look a lot less romantic, and a lot more feudal.[51]

Noting how surprisingly common the task of ghostwriting—for example, producing the memo that will go out under the boss's name—turned out to be in the middle-class population she studied, Brandt's implication is that "ghostwriting" can be taken as a broader figure for what writing now predominantly is. Legally, at least, and perhaps in a more pervasive sense, too, the firm must now be considered the "author-in-chief."[52]

That this shift in emphasis would appear most powerfully in African American literature is not surprising, and not only because of the long-standing association of self-representation and political empowerment in that tradition. One might also point to the vibrancy of what Kinohi Nishikawa has called the Black literary underground as it emerged in the 1960s. It did so around autobiographical "urban" novelists like Iceberg Slim and Donald Goines, for whom the pimp or gangster embodied a version of the heroic entrepreneur of US mythology relevant to life on the street.[53] A more recent figure working in this tradition is Vickie M. Stringer, author of the Goines-inspired autobiographical fiction *Let That Be the Reason* (2001), detailing her turn to drug dealing in pursuit of financial independence that would facilitate her freedom from predatory men: "Whew! This champagne is good, I thought. And the strawberries were super deluxe fabulous ... It had been so long since I did anything for myself, and this was a nice evening. I was on a honeymoon with myself. I needed to start loving myself."[54]

Beginning to write the novel just before she was released from a seven-year stint in jail, Stringer published it in what we might now think of as the old regime of pre-digital, pre-Kindle self-publication, selling self-financed physical copies out of the trunk of her car. From these inauspicious beginnings, the entity she called Triple Crown Press would go on to become a successful publisher of thirty-some authors of what she marketed under the label Hip-Hop Fiction. To read Stringer's remarkably earnest primer, *How to Succeed in the Publishing Game* (2005), is to see how drug dealing and book publishing might be conceived as twin versions of a bid for independence—but more realistically, survival—in a world whose rules you did not make.[55] It is also to tune into a moment just before KDP would utterly change that game, pressuring, if not altogether disintegrating, the sensation of communal aesthetic endeavor emanating from homegrown entities like Triple Crown.

These earliest moments of the reshaping of the business of authorship by the internet are seen from a different, higher-status perspective in Colson Whitehead's *John Henry Days* (2001), published by an imprint of Random House on the way to what has become perhaps the most celebrated career in contemporary American fiction.[56] Recounting a search on the part of a freelance journalist for the truth behind the legend of the railroad worker and former slave who died competing with the steam drill, this novel has been read as an instance of what Linda Hutcheon calls "historiographic metafiction"[57]—that is, as instancing the widespread preoccupation in the postmodern novel with the unreliability of historical knowledge—and that makes sense.[58] And yet, the meta-historiographic dimension of *John Henry Days* may have impeded recognition of its meditation on the transformation of slavery into wage earning and, in turn, of the wage relation into what has come to be called the gig economy.

In this case, the freelancer is the original version of the gig worker whose "freedom" is a benefit especially to employers divested of the regulatory and other costs of long-term commitment to its employees. The novel's alternation between the imagined life of legendary John Henry, he of the Black body in spectacular competition with the machine, and that of J. Sutter, the wise-cracking African American journalist traveling from one press junket to another, reinforces that fact. It asks us to consider both the continuities (racism) and discontinuities (labor relations that split the working-class African American from his educated, middle-class descendants) in the progression from the nineteenth to the twentieth and twenty-first centuries.

While John Henry competes against the machine, J. Sutter's job is to feed the maw of the internet, a technological mediation that ironically, or so it appeared in 2001, calls forth an army of human content-producers, including the article on the John Henry festival Sutter is writing for a new travel website:

> J. hasn't worked for the web before but knew it was only a matter of time: new media is welfare for the middle class. A year ago the web didn't exist, and now J. has several hitherto unemployable acquaintances who were now picking up steady paychecks because of it ... It was only a matter of time before those errant corporate dollars blew his way ... All J. can think is *content*. It sounds so honest. Not stories, not articles, but content. Like it is a mineral. It is so honest of them.[59]

While John Henry pounds spikes for the railroad, J. Sutter mines content for the internet, a job at once much easier than heroic industrial labor but also given to existential dread because of its meaningless nature, being that it is, in effect, mercenary corporate ghostwriting.

The question is, what connection should we draw between J. Sutter and his author, Colson Whitehead, a writer of a presumably starkly different kind, or is he? Is the novelist just a kind of freelancer? Have the novels he writes been reduced to "content"? Is he, too, for all of his elevated status, a kind of ghostwriter for the corporation, and thus for capital as such, fated to accomplish nothing but further its ends? Against this possibility, the growing intensity of Sutter's identification with his subject as a man deeply aware of the vengeful immovability of racial mountains suggests a more serious agenda, even if a relatively hopeless one. It is not enough merely to incorporate the legend of John Henry into the workflow of the writer-junketeer. And yet the general conscription of writing to the needs of the corporation in the Age of Amazon leaves ample room for doubt that a space apart from racial capitalism will be found.[60]

As it arguably does for all the novel writing taking place now. We know that the genres pertaining organically to social media—the post, the tweet, the take—by which the contemporary subject is invited to express herself are on another level the unpaid creation of content for the corporation as author-in-chief, who by means of letting the people have their say achieves the network effects that are the precondition of its monetization as an advertising platform. Are self-published novels any different—or different enough?

That's one question provoked by a work like Jarret Kobek's novel *I Hate the Internet* (2016), which was published by a microscopic LA-based entity the author founded for that purpose called We Heard You Like Books.[61] Approaching life in the age of social media analytically and satirically, the book differs strikingly from the generic zombie novels, alpha billionaire romances, and vampire erotica that dominate sales among Amazon's KDP offerings. And yet the boundary between "direct" publishing, as Amazon euphemistically calls it, and being published by others has always been blurry in the literary avant-garde, whose market is often not large enough to sustain the kind of impersonal relations we think of as underlying the feat of "getting published." Avant-gardes are, among other things, groups of acquaintances, friends, and lovers who publish each other and themselves. The age of Kindle Direct Publishing has simply confused things further, making it difficult to separate the various meanings of "independence": from having the right to total delusion about your actual literary talents, to being free to misconstrue your dependent relationship to the giant corporation, Amazon, which saves you from exploitation (or more likely rejection) by traditional publishers, to staking out a space of genuine opposition to the reigning taste, as in Triple Crown or in the various projects examined in Nicholas Thoburn's study of radical publishing, *Anti-Book* (2016).[62]

Kobek's novel, whose full title is *I Hate the Internet: A Useful Novel against Men, Money, and the Filth of Instagram*, enters this interesting point in literary history safely in the last camp, trailing a blurb from Jonathan Lethem. Kobek's previous works include *Atta*, brought out by the distinguished publisher of experimental writing Semiotext(e) in 2011, and a strange 2012 chapbook called *If You Won't Read, Then Why Should I Write?* The former inhabits the mind of the 9/11 terrorist ringleader up to the very moment of his collision with the North Tower, refusing to moralize about his murderous delusions, while the latter is a hard-to-describe collection of fragmentary transcripts of moments from the ordinary lives of celebrities accompanied by cardboard inserts detailing the trouble they have had with the law. Both of these works, especially the first, have their virtues, but *I Hate the Internet* is a minor landmark in the field of contemporary literature, if only for the rare energy of its attempt to speak against the very thing that made its existence possible: the same corporate capitalist world that gave us the internet it hates.

I Hate the Internet is often very funny, wending its way forward with the punchy rhythm of a stand-up routine, following a group of friends living in the supremely annoying San Francisco of 2013. In its humor and casually quick pacing, it reads somewhat like Kurt Vonnegut, Kobek's acknowledged model, although without the dangerously cute dorkiness that leavened his predecessor's pitch-black assessment of our place in the universe. *I Hate the Internet* has no Billy Pilgrim figure, no holy innocent who throws the cruel absurdity of the world into relief, unless it is this novel's Ellen Flitcraft, a minor character whose life is arbitrarily destroyed when lewd pictures of her are posted online. What it does have is inexhaustible comic rage at the sea of "intolerable bullshit" in which its urbanely ironic characters are forced to swim.

To hate the internet is, first, to hate the hateful men who congregate there to express their hatred for women like the narrator's best friend Adeline; second, it is to hate racism, even as public discussion of race is understood as a screen for the more basic exploitations of capitalism, which is a third thing the novel hates, especially the self-adoring kind associated with the beautiful but eminently hateable Bay Area. Finally, there is humanity, which is revealed as essentially a "bunch of dumb assholes," as is daily displayed (coming now full circle) on the internet. As it reads on the book's first page: "The Internet was a wonderful invention. It was a computer network which people used to remind other people that they were awful pieces of shit."[63]

This last component is one of the techniques the novel uses frequently, and to interesting effect: the deflating definition. Kobek gets it from Vonnegut, who got it from Ambrose Bierce's *Devil's Dictionary*, which got it from Dr. Johnson. It works really well in the context of the tech industry, where the tolerance for intolerable bullshit has always been very high indeed. Sometimes the deflating definition works by simple sarcasm, other times by using the technical jargon of scientific truth. Most consequential for our experience of *I Hate the Internet* is the narrator's early redefinition of race as a misreading of a merely technical fact about human skin, which is that its color "is a visual byproduct of eumelanin's presence in the stratum basale layer of the epidermis."[64] Thereafter in the novel, some seventy or eighty times, each character or group of persons is described not as belonging to one race or another but as having more or less "eumelanin in the stratum basale layer of the epidermis." It is Kobek's equivalent of Vonnegut's "So it goes," which follows each death in *Slaughterhouse-Five*; but whereas Vonnegut's version rides on its disturbingly fatalistic brevity, Kobek's point is to inject an unwieldy mouthful of scientific truth into every instance of racial identification. Although this becomes tedious and unfunny by about halfway through the novel, that is arguably the point.

For all its oppositional energy, *I Hate the Internet* is finally a text of conscription, of unavoidable complicity. Indeed, it is disarmingly open about its self-implication in what it critiques, pointing out how, for starters, it was created on a machine "built by slaves in China." As we read early on:

> This bad novel, which is a morality lesson about the Internet, was written on a computer. You are suffering the moral outrage of a hypocritical writer who has profited from the spoils of slavery.[65]

Bruce Robbins has memorably analyzed the potentially disabling perception of one's implication in a vast system of exploitative capitalism as the experience of the "sweatshop sublime," and part of what makes *I Hate the Internet* a good novel and not the bad one it purports to be is how intelligently it manifests the consequences of that implication.[66] Here it is the writing machine itself, the Apple laptop, that suggests his fundamental conscription in a system he opposes, but Amazon would have served just as well.

If there remains a blind spot in its lucid deflation of our bullshit balloons, it would appear to be an emotional one. Whatever else we mean by the "internet" now, we mean, by way of the rise of social media, a certain shared climate of feeling, an animated and sped-up hubbub of the discourse of human interest. By turns soothing and bruising, it is the very medium of what Lauren Berlant, correcting a long-standing tendency to think of emotions as internal and private, has described instead as *public feelings*. They are the affective substance of political life, the very thing, even more than political ideas, to which online citizenship has become attuned and by which it is increasingly deranged. (We will return to this important contextual feature of contemporary literary culture in chapters 5 and 6.) While the tenor of our online exchanges runs the gamut from deepest sympathy to savage snark, one of the internet's signature speech genres is surely the *rant*, the hyped-up rhetorical expression of mockingly contemptuous dismay. The novel as rant: in this way, too, *I Hate the Internet* is the internet it hates.

The Last Delivery

On a 2015 earnings call explaining his company's smashing results for the previous quarter, Jeff Bezos explained, "We manage by two seemingly contradictory traits: impatience to deliver faster and a willingness to think long term."[67] He referred in particular to the recent growth of Amazon Web Services, an entirely new business within the business, years in development, having nothing much to do with online retail except in providing state-of-the-art computing infrastructure to itself and hundreds of thousands of corporate clients. "Today a bookseller is setting the tone of the computing industry," was how one analyst summed up the situation, although of course it had been quite a while since Amazon could accurately be described as a bookseller.[68] Now even the term "Everything Store" would seem insufficient unless it were redefined to include more than the totality of downloadable or deliverable commodities. "Many of the startups are running on Amazon," noted the analyst to reporter Louis Bedigian. "No other company in the past or in the future will have that strategic asset that these guys have." In the beginning, when Amazon dubbed itself "Earth's Biggest Bookstore," there had been an element of imposture in the claim, since all it meant was that the company had someone else's books (the book distributor Ingram's) listed in its database; and there would continue to be those, over the years, who would point to the company's consistent unprofitability, the result mostly of its manic investment in its own growth, as betraying something unreal about the whole enterprise. And yet the "Get Big Fast" approach appears after a quarter century to be pushing profits to the bottom line at will. It can now be said that Amazon is really very large, and largely real.

But note that the "contradictory traits" to which Bezos refers go less to the company's size than to its relation to time, whose horizon is by his account both very short *and* very long term. What about that contradiction? What might it add to our sense of Amazon as an event in literary history? Getting big fast had always been about gaining quick leverage in and on markets, but it was also about survival on a truly epic temporal scale. "Too big to fail": after the 2008 economic crash we associate the phrase with the socialization of privately assumed risk in the banking system, but one feels that for Bezos its logic goes much deeper than that, holding the promise of resistance to the corrosions of time itself. The idea seems to be that, for Amazon to fail, the entire world in which it does business would have to fail along with it. Indeed, echoing a familiar quip to the effect that it is easier to imagine the end of the world than the end of capitalism, we could say that ideally, for Bezos, it would be easier to imagine the end of capitalism itself than the end of Amazon. Amazon, true to its name, is thereby understood as nature writ large in its satisfaction of human wants. The mistake would be to confuse its long-term orientation with futurism, with acting on speculations of what is likely someday to be the case. Any observer of the history of science fiction would know that robustly predicting the future is a sucker's game, with too many unknown variables to control.

The task here is instead is to stay *in the moment—forever*. As McKenna had explained in his 1997 management treatise *Real Time* (which I would bet all of his billions Bezos found time to read): "Instead of fruitlessly trying to predict the future course of a competitive or market trend, customer behavior or demand, managers should be trying to find and deploy all the tools that will enable them, in some sense, to be ever-present, ever-vigilant, and ever-ready."[69] Challenged to justify his violent disruption of the publishing industry, Bezos notoriously quipped that "Amazon is not happening to book selling; the future is happening to book selling."[70] The key point, in this context, is not Amazon's ideological abdication of responsibility in the face of metaphysical necessity, although Bezos is expressing that, but the way the company conceives of the future as always already happening *now*. In this cosmically expanded present, real time and long term are not at odds, but two intertwined dimensions of the will to corporate immortality.

That perhaps explains Bezos's interest in a project like the Clock of the Long Now, dreamed up by Brian Eno, Stewart

Brand, Daniel Hillis, Esther Dyson, and other Bay Area luminaries of the Long Now Foundation, which, against what they
see as the shrinking of the future in contemporary life, attempts
to foster long-term thinking. The enormous precision instrument they have devised and begun to build ticks once a year and
bongs once a century, while a cuckoo will emerge once every
millennium. If all goes according to plan, this will continue to
occur for 10,000 years.[71] A fascinating endeavor, and one meant
to cultivate our sense of responsibility to future generations, it is,
however, notably absent of any specific demands at all, least of
all for the restraint of capital or checking of economic growth; as
though the reframing of lives in a longer time frame will *in itself*
lead to right action of some sort, no doubt market-friendly. And
where is the Clock being built? Recalling the set of some James
Bond movie, it is being built inside a mountain on donated land
on the vast West Texas ranch of one Jeff Bezos.

A science fiction set brought to life, it comports well with
Bezos's other, much larger long-term investment in private space
exploration through his company Blue Origin. This venture is
animated by the idea that, someday, in order for the species to
survive, humanity is going to have to be prepared to leave planet
Earth for more survivable climes. One of its first employees
was the science fiction novelist Neal Stephenson, Bezos's fellow
Seattle resident, who seems to be remembering his billionaire
friend in the character Sean Probst in his novel *Seveneves*, which
imagines precisely the sort of scenario (exploding moon, rain of
fiery rocks) that might require such a departure.[72] It is Probst
who, defying the government space bureaucracy and sacrificing
his own life, saves the human race by using his private spaceship
to mine an enormous shard of ice from a passing comet, dragging it back to the vehicle carrying the last remnant of humanity.
Talk about Prime delivery service! Only thus, now that they are
possessed of a means of steam propulsion to a safer part of
space, does it even make sense for the novel to leap 5,000 years
into the future in its final section, where it can indulge in pure
speculation about what the space-bound geneticists will have
wrought in all that time upon the human clay.

In the book business, longevity is encountered on the back-list, in the long tail of literary value persisting through time, and for all its investments in instantaneity, Amazon has done more than any other entity in recent years to realize that value, giving it a market presence. Speaking of the digital revolution in general, John B. Thompson has observed how books "that had been left to die many years before" have been "suddenly brought back to life. It is one of the ironies of the digital revolution that, so far from ushering in the death of the book, one of its most important consequences has been to give the printed book a new lease of life, allowing it to live well beyond the age at which it would have died in the pre-digital world and, indeed, rendering it potentially immortal."[73] This is an ironic realization indeed of the immortality traditionally associated with literary greatness. In this version, even if people forget all about a literary work, even if it is judged perfectly worthless for present needs, it stands perpetually ready for reactivation as a commodity and—who knows?—work of art.

Amazon is often, and no doubt rightly, held in suspicion of having ominous implications for traditional literary culture writ large, but its critics miss something important when they think of the company simply as anti-literary, a mere numbers game. If anything, the problem is that it wants to be a great literary work in its own right. Weren't the original "contradictory traits" of Amazon already somewhat "literary" in their contradictoriness? Real time and long term. That is exactly the formula for something to have enduring literary value. If the literary text, transcending its mortal printed body, can now in theory live on forever, for as long at least as humanity does, or its servers, that life will only be meaningful insofar as the work remains available as an object of experience, an occasion for the real-time enjoyment of virtual quality time, that is, for reading.

2

What Is Multinational Literature?

Amazon All Over the World

Leveling Up

What if immersion in a role-playing video game were narrated as real experience? This is the premise of a thriving new literary genre called LitRPG. Its most successful example is Ernest Cline's *Ready Player One* (2011), now with more than 800,000 ratings on Goodreads and a 2018 Steven Spielberg movie version to boot.[1] Far more interesting than that movie, which dissolves the original's charming first-person narration into the usual CGI cinematic spectacle, Cline's novel is a small marvel of the management of narrative levels, the stakes of the fictional game-play remaining high enough to hold our interest in a world where our hero is "really" just an immobilized wearer of a VR headset—albeit one hiding out from an evil corporation trying to kill him. Far from deflating the drama, Cline's partial splitting of narrative levels heightens it, making young Wade Watts doubly vulnerable as his avatar Parzival races to win the online treasure hunt set in motion upon the death of a legendary game developer, Halliday. The prize: inheritance of the multibillion-dollar corporation Halliday has left behind.

The novel's ideological intervention in the real world can also be described as a kind of splitting. In this case it is the splitting of the bad corporation trying to win control of OASIS—more than a game, it is a fully immersive, near-future replacement for the internet—from the good narrator, the teenage underdog who will beat them to the punch. Getting to know Halliday through the biographical clues he has left toward the solution of his, come to think of it, stunningly narcissistic treasure hunt, we're meant to understand the vast fortune he has accumulated as the natural result of artistic suffering and genius, not of business savvy and monopolistic greed. Seeing Wade share his prize with the plucky band of gamers who have helped him win it, we're meant to feel good about total control of the online world falling into the hands of five people. Such is the success of the novel that we do all of the above until critical reflection arrives, assuming it does, to break the spell. Neither is it surprising that other writers would soon extract from Cline's novel a highly replicable idea, sensing further potential in the form beyond the usual quest motifs and fantasy tropes it also contains.

Unlike the traditionally published *Ready Player One*, most of the English language examples of LitRPG have been produced through Amazon's Kindle Direct Publishing (KDP) platform, which, if it has not dictated the shape of the genre, has no doubt greatly accelerated its growth into hundreds if not thousands of examples in just a few years, some of them with legions of readers in their own right. Whether the gatekeepers of traditional publishing were aware of it or not, it was a genre waiting to happen in multiples, and KDP enabled it to be so (see figure on p. 77).

Like *Ready Player One*, these works are almost without exception centered on the experiences of a young man whose underdog status in the real world is counteracted in the reality—not merely the fantasy—of the game. That last is a crucial nuance, testament to the genre's vestigial realism. After all, as Jesper Juul has noted, from the perspective of the player the *rules* of a game are real in a way that any storyline for which they might be the vehicle is not.[2] They demand real skill and

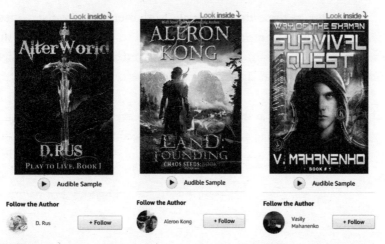

LitRPG Literary role-playing game narratives published via Kindle Direct Publishing

real decision-making even if not real swordplay. In LitRPG these decisions and that swordplay converge in a fictional narrative that leaves the reader free to sit back and watch the protagonist-avatar level up.

It's all fairly philosophically complex, a hall of mirrors of realities and fantasies, but the literary-historical novelty of LitRPG is fairly easy to state. It is in the way it *keeps score*, seeding narrative with quantitative performance statistics. Interrupting the flow of the story with periodic stats readouts detailing the relative power of various weapons and other objects the player-protagonist finds, as well as the new abilities and skill levels he has attained, these readouts are what distinguishes LitRPG from not just VR novels like William Gibson's *Neuromancer* (1984) and Neal Stephenson's *Snow Crash* (1992), but the entire tradition of what Thomas Pavel calls "dual structure" narratives, where characters traverse distinct levels of reality.[3] An important contemporary example of the latter is *isekai*, the popular Japanese storytelling form featuring the transport of an otherwise ordinary hero to a fantasy world, frequently enough one that exists in his original world as a fiction.[4] And yet *isekai* has no stats. Annoying as they might be to some readers, the stats are the heart of the matter for the literary historian looking at LitRPG, the thing we haven't seen before.

As when, at the outset of Vasily Mahanenko's *Survival Quest* (2015), about a computer hacker forced to do hard labor in the rat-infested mines of a corporate-owned virtual world called Barliona, a message appears in the air before his eyes:

> I quickly glanced at the message ... and waved it away, gathering the ore into the bag and starting on the second vein.
>
> *Experience gained: +1 Experience, points remaining until next level: 99*
> *Skill increase:*
> *+50% to Mining. Total: 50%*
> *+10% to Strength. Total 10%*
> *+5% to Stamina. Total 5%*[5]

And so on. Instances of the genre vary in how often these readouts appear, but for LitRPG's swelling legions of devotees they are crucial for how they maintain the form's idealized relation to something they also tend to do in their spare time: play video games. Nowhere is this relation between the two media, or the fact that it is an idealization, more obvious than in Dmitry Rus's *AlterWorld* (2013), the first of several volumes in his *Play to Live* series, about a cancer patient who escapes death when his consciousness is permanently downloaded into a massively multiplayer online role-playing game (MMORPG).[6] In Rus's novels, the first ever to be marketed by their author under the label LitRPG, the stats readouts are relentless, threaded into everything, and so is the upward trajectory of these stats, the game-player-cum-warlock narrator-protagonist ascending from triumph to triumph to a position of great power. At its most extreme it is novelistic narration as bragging.[7]

As the first to actually use the term, Rus has some claim to the title of "Father of LitRPG," but the writer who has been most aggressive in applying that term to himself has been Aleron Kong, an Afro-Asian American writer living outside Atlanta. He is the author of the *Chaos Seeds* series beginning with *The Land: Founding* (2016), which have become central to a swelling fan subculture surrounding the genre. Although not without controversy, it was Kong who attempted to trademark the term LitRPG, and it is he who is the genre's most ardent promoter. With his exuberant storytelling talent, his highly polished website and Facebook page, and impressive prolificness as a generator of new product, he is a fine example of the state-of-the-art writer-entrepreneur of the Age of Amazon. In Kong's rendition of LitRPG, an MMORPG called "The Land" is only apparently a game. It is actually a neomedieval "pocket universe" constructed by an ambitious court vizier to lure unsuspecting humans, or Chaos Seeds, into it for purposes we needn't worry about. Into this universe is thrown a twenty-four-year-old man, a skilled gamer, Richter, who immediately begins accepting quests and leveling up. By the end of the first volume, he is a highly respected master of his own village and has begun to build it up into a prosperous town, entering into various business negotiations to make it so.

Distinct from Rus's very Russian *AlterWorld*, Kong's novels are animated by the spirit of American liberal multiculturalism, the plot revolving around Richter's liberation of a diverse set of nonhumans—dwarves, elves, gnomes—from a kingdom in which they are treated as despised immigrants. As a kind of Moses figure, however, Richter is no less a paragon of gaming prowess than Cline's Wade Watts or Rus's Max, leveling up to master status in the virtual world at breakneck speed and taking political power there as his natural due. To the genre's innovatively quantitative score-keeping form, then, we might add another distinguishing feature, less original but equally hard to miss: its thematic emphasis on successfully leveling up, which transforms the ample frustrations of ordinary MMORPG gameplay into something more efficiently satisfying, if purely vicarious. In this it is in some ways the narrative equivalent of what has in recent years become a popular form of online entertainment on Amazon's own Twitch video-streaming service and YouTube, where hundreds of thousands of viewers have proven happy to watch multi-hour play-throughs of popular games conducted by players who have fully mastered them.

Thinking through the two most distinct features of LitRPG, the stats readouts and masculine triumphalism, it's tempting to venture a global interpretation of the genre, one that ties it to the corporate publishing platform that has been its most important support. Most simply, of course, it is the expression of the interests of millions of devoted gamers around the world (a group more numerous now than devoted readers) who in LitRPG have found a literary genre of their own. Scholars of video games like Nick Yee and Jane McGonigal help us to say more about this group, which is reported to be 85 percent male, with the highest concentration of users in their twenties and thirties.[8] In *Reality Is Broken: Why Games Make Us Better and How They Can Change the World* (2011), McGonigal touts the MMORPG *World of Warcraft*, which at its peak in 2010 had some 12 million subscribers logging on to play the game as many as twenty hours a week, as something that offers the sensation of "blissful productivity" and goal-oriented "work flow" as the player levels up, a kind of idealized mirroring of the much less satisfying jobs they tend to have in real life.[9]

We can speculate that LitRPG is similarly the expression of a world suffused not simply by technology but *tech jobs* in the broadest possible sense, from the work of actual IT engineers to really anyone whose livelihood requires them to manipulate information, or will do once they have graduated from school. *LitRPG as the dreamlife of corporate IT*: that tag is no doubt too confidently specific to be entirely convincing, but it gets at the way the form idealizes the medial and other conditions of contemporary employment in the tech and services sector. Launched from the existential situation of *early career*, with its particular vulnerabilities, LitRPG turns those conditions into a scene of narrative pleasure and imaginary self-aggrandizement, of "leveling up" in a comprehensive sense. In this it is a developmental successor to smash YA hits keyed to the particular martyrdoms of teenage life like *The Hunger Games* (2008).

With this interpretive key in hand, those stat readouts begin to make sense in a new way: they are the utopian negation of the performance metrics recorded in the employee's HR file. Why else import these hierarchical measures of status and self-worth into the free space of fantasy? LitRPG doubles down on quantification, concocting a space that, while obsessively hierarchical, is rigorously *fair*, with rules so deeply seeded in the programming of the game space that to play the game at all can only be to follow them. LitRPG is in other words a fantasy of meritocracy, of the successful investment in oneself as human capital. This is most obvious in scenes where the hero must decide how to apportion the points he has accumulated among various categories of skill enhancement and tools, predicting how, say, increased powers of spellcasting might combine with an invisibility cloak to lead to him to success in the battles ahead. It is also there in a telling scene in *AlterWorld* where Max pauses to do some online shopping, looking for useful equipment: "Was it better to invest in mid-range items like that King loot?" he asks himself. "It sure would last me another thirty levels. Or should I aim for some choice top items like those gauntlets that would serve me indefinitely?" The latter. "I pressed *Buy*."[10]

All of this stands in contrast to the reality of life in a global corporate culture where too many of the rules of success are hidden; where some people start the game with loads of the real equivalent of in-game cash; where someone turns out to be buddies with the game admin or an idiotic nephew of the Wizard. Where everything is *political*. Where women are often nowhere to be found, and when they are—watch out. The game world is by contrast a just world, for all its gory violence, with no manager lying in wait to take credit for your successes or secretly setting you up to fail. Here they are *openly* setting you up to fail, but with the honor of an avowed enemy combatant, a Level 12 Mage or whatever. And then, too, the damsels. Unlike the ones in real life, they are *game*. In the game you can be the spiritual equivalent of the chieftain-CEO, a possibility made perfectly literal in a minor offshoot of LitRPG called 4X Lit. An example is Andrew Karevik's *CivCEO* (2019) and its sequels, which are based not on RPGs but on games of grand strategy like the board game *Risk* or the video game *Sid Meier's Civilization*. Placing the protagonist above it all—"I was no longer in the cozy little library but was instead thousands of feet in the air, floating above the village"—rather than amid the action, these books have as yet had only minor success, but they are helpful in drawing out the nature of the fantasy in their more successful generic brethren.[11] Both 4X lit and LitRPG are structured as a fantasy circuit leading from the proletarianized corporate drone through the game space to the CEO and back.

If LitRPG can be said to be an adjunct to the psychic life of corporate IT, what does this efflorescence on the margins of the contemporary KDP genre system show us about literature in the Age of Amazon more broadly? For one thing, it makes clear the circulation of contemporary fiction in and among competing media, some of whose affordances are available for emulation in fiction, although rarely as literally as in LitRPG. Just as importantly, or so I will argue, it shows us how contemporary fiction is everywhere oriented toward what I would call, putting renewed emphasis on the term, the "corporate world."[12]

The second part of that term, "world," has received a lot of attention in recent cultural theory and criticism, mostly as a rejoinder to the "globe" of "globalization," which names the recruitment of all of Earth's far-flung peoples into one economic system. What in the 1990s and aughts seemed to many commentators an all but unalloyed good has since been called into question for its disintegration of traditional worlds—worlds that, far from simply being the quicksand of benighted inefficiency their capitalist detractors take them to be, are by this very term "world" credited with a kind of completeness as holistic settings for meaningful life. The theories of world literature built upon this concept take their bearings from Martin Heidegger's concept of "worlding" and essentially negate the more common historical understanding of world literature as cosmopolitan literature. To be "rich in world" in the Heideggerian sense is to experience oneself as part of a deeply meaningful collective narrative distinct from the remorselessly alienating equivalencies and inauthenticity of the culture of global capital.[13] Grounding the meaning of life, it is the world as ethnos, as primordial nation, as home. Its force is centripetal.

But corporate culture also has its meaningful world, or thinks it does. That is what we learn from LitRPG. It is a game world, a field of comprehensively quantifiable action and key performance indicators, and glory. As an *epic* world, and archaic to that extent, it is an object of desire as much as a real thing, but it is a game with real social consequences in the differential valuation of lives. Some "play the game" better than others and are rewarded for it; some aspire to own the game outright. It is no accident that Jeff Bezos, perhaps the most "heroic" figure today in multinational corporate capitalism (challenged for this crown perhaps only by Elon Musk) is also a fan of epic science fiction. The mistake here would be to think that either he or Amazon is committed to any one story as definitive of the company's ambitions. The aim instead is to imagine—and claim as property —the platform upon which all of our stories can take place.

The corporate world so construed is intimately related to the *world-building* at the center of science fiction and fantasy novels, the built-ness of which LitRPG never lets us forget. This stands in contrast to the traditional world, whose origin, frequently enough, is understood to reside in a mythical past. World-building is in turn associated in contemporary culture with the ever-unfolding franchise or brand—as in the Marvel Universe. While the built world is the occasion for stories, as Mark J. P. Wolf has noted, world-building is conceptually distinct from storytelling, a commitment above all to the realization of a durable fictional space.[14] As any one of the now innumerable how-to guides of literary world-building will tell you, world-building is a matter of "1) Creating a stable setting ... 2) where stories take place ... 3) that is consistent ... 4) and works by its own rules." This is from Steven Savage's self-published *Way with Worlds: Crafting Great Fictional Settings* (2016), the first of a sixteen-book series on the theme. But it is also a convincing description of the global Amazon *platform*—the rule-bound mechanism of selling and telling of many kinds.

Savage takes for granted that world-building is a matter of practical and theoretical concern only in and around science fiction and fantasy, not other genres like mystery, romance,

and realist literary fiction.[15] That's because, although his subtitle seems to deny it, the worlds of SF and fantasy are bigger
than mere "settings," taking leave of as many as possible of the
givens of the real or "primary" world that silently anchor the
reality-effects of fiction and are the common intellectual property of us all. They explore the primordial nature of things, not
merely local conditions, and imagine an equally primordial
form of ownership. Whereas the Heideggerian world concept is
an organic construction, indigenous to the land it occupies and
subject to ruin by modern technology, the corporate world is a
patently artificial but for that reason *totally winnable* one. It is
the world of Amazon, and expansion is its law.

Let Them Eat Story

Amazon is famous for the intensity of its corporate culture,
which succeeds in motivating impressive feats of labor from
its many hundreds of thousands of employees, or, as they call
themselves, Amazonians. Embodied in a signature set of best
practices and processes, guided by a series of slogans, symbols,
and carefully enumerated leadership principles, it meets resistance on the margins, especially at its fulfillment centers, but for
the most part barrels into a future of its own design. To read
the company's official blog is to be met with inspiring anec-
dotes, personalities, celebrations, and smiles, and behind them
all an unironic sense of mission. As though taking a cue from its
first-ever product category, books, not only the intensity but the
sheer *expressivity* of Amazon's corporate culture is what catches
the eye. In a way that does not seem to be true of, for instance,
Walmart, the company sees itself in terms of an unfolding epic
narrative of astounding achievement it can't find enough ways
to narrate.

So much so that one wonders whether its recent move into
film and television production wasn't destined to occur all
along, as early as the 1990s, when company founder Jeff Bezos
was still a honking nerd and not the chiseled starship captain

he appears to be today. Not that he aspired to start Amazon Studios when he started out on his journey from Wall Street to the garage in Seattle where Amazon was born, but the drive to manifest corporate identity in and as a series of *stories* meant that he was bound to discover this ambition and to act upon it, conditions being right. In theory, these expensive ventures into content production are meant to seduce consumers into remaining within the Amazon Prime retail ecosystem, enjoying its many fruits, conjoining their streaming consumption of filmed entertainment to the fulfillment of other—of all— domestic needs. But isn't there something obviously excessive in this membership-growth strategy? Does it not also bespeak a drive for corporate self-expression gone slightly off the rails, as though the usual channels of corporate communications simply do not offer enough bandwidth for the job?

To take the measure of the influence of Amazon on the contemporary literary field requires one to attend in this way to the confusingly dialectical reversals of the company's outward and inward orientation, where, to take another example, something like Leadership Principle #1, "Customer Obsession," a call to selflessness, is transformed into a mechanism of corporate self-regard and then back again. Intriguingly, one of Amazon's first ventures into film production was an adaptation of *The Lost City of Z: A Tale of Deadly Obsession in the Amazon* (2009), David Grann's best-selling account of the harrowing exploits of the early twentieth-century British explorer Percy Fawcett.[16] Let's just say that this project is not too difficult to align with the company's self-image as a pioneer of uncharted commercial territories, and one for whom "obsession" is obviously not a dirty word. The hero figure in that allegorical structure is Bezos, no doubt, but it is also anyone willing to route their ego through his, mortal man and immortal brand revolving in sync across the landscape like a vortex, sucking more and more of our world into its maw as it goes. Among the first and most important commandments by which Amazonians are asked to labor is to "Make History," the story of Fawcett serving as an object lesson in the manly capacity for self-punishment that making history might require, and in the forces of native opposition one might encounter along the way.

Can the same be said, then, of the other narratives of which Amazon's servers have been the host? How about the many hundreds of thousands of narratives published via its Kindle Direct Publishing service? Granted, in most cases it would be hard to establish any conscious intent on the part of self-published "indie" authors like Aleron Kong to enlist their imaginations in the task of representing the interests of the corporate sponsor who takes 30 percent of the proceeds on KDP book sales in return for its various services to them, but is the compulsion to do so deeper than mere conscious intent? How about the hundreds of books per year published under one of Amazon's sixteen more or less traditional book imprints, staffed by editors in Seattle and elsewhere who are as steeped as anyone in the company's culture? In what way, if any, do they reflect or promote the values of the mother ship?

But why stop there? Can the contemporary novel itself and as a whole be said in some sense to express the corporate identity of an online retailer? Is it in this sense an instance of multi-national literature?

That would be a stretch, surely, but it is worth asking the question in its biggest and baldest form, if only to begin to piece through the complex ways that literary works of the present necessarily reflect and embody the forms of economic life in whose shadow they come into being. Emanating outward from this core business model as platform, Amazon's corporate culture is to a greater or lesser degree of specificity one that we, too, participate in, even as non-Amazonians, as we go about our days. This has become especially true since Amazon's move into web services, where it has become the invisible back-end facilitator of, for instance, viewing shows on Netflix or experiencing any one of thousands of other popular destinations on the web. It would be difficult to overstate the growing omnipresence of the company in daily life both on- and offline. As a recent CNN Business report stated, "It's Amazon's world. We just live in it."[17] And yet Amazon is itself a product and mediator of forces larger than itself, lending the task of tracing the influence of economic forms on contemporary literature deliciously difficult in its complexity and overdetermination.

One could, for instance, as Leigh Claire La Berge and other critics have recently done, explicate contemporary literature as a reflection of the context of post-1980s financialization, with its large-scale shift of economic activity from investments in real goods and services to market speculation.[18] Where the production and pursuit of abstract "fictitious capital" is the order of the day, these accounts allow us to see how the realism of the novel is challenged in new ways. As we discussed in the previous chapter, Bezos himself got his start in the world of high finance and computer-assisted trading, whose lessons we can assume he brought to bear on the formation of a start-up otherwise conspicuously devoted to purveying real goods to its customers.

In line with the new institutionalism in contemporary literary studies, one might instead follow the lead of Dan Sinykin and others who have drawn attention to the rise of the multinational media and publishing conglomerates with whom Amazon has come to compete as the key determining factor in what literature looks like today. This is to see contemporary literary history as framed by what many would claim is the key feature of the twentieth- and now twenty-first-century advanced economies, a feature more basic even than financialization: their domination by Big Business. That term refers to corporations of gargantuan scale made up of separate business units knitted together in multitiered managerial hierarchies. In the case of publishing, it would be the many separate imprints, some of them quite illustrious in their own right, brought into the fold of conglomerates like Hachette and Penguin Random House.[19] Here the traditional practices of publishers—"reluctant capitalists," as Laura Miller calls them—extending back into the nineteenth century have been transformed by the requirement to show quarterly growth, retooled to search for and promote the next Big Book and devil take the midlist.[20] Amazon's own imprints no doubt feel some of this pressure to perform at modern multinational corporate standards for success. This is also the scene of the rise of the literary agent as a figure of decisive importance in the contemporary literary field, helping to manage an undifferentiated flow of potential product toward publishers that might otherwise be overwhelming.[21]

Closer to what we are interested in here, and crucial to accounting for the complex texture of contemporary literary life as a whole, is the ongoing event of economic deindustrialization, with its massive expansion of the service sector and of a service mentality in culture generally. If, as Jasper Bernes claims, in a capitalist economy "the work of art" must be understood as continuous with "work in general," then a shift "from work based on making things or objects to work oriented around the performance of administrative or technical processes" can be expected to alter the historical sense of what literature is.[22] For several hundred years, the book has been an industrial product, a thing made in multiples by machine, but in the Age of Amazon it is also conceived as the bearer of a service provided to readers looking to be told a story. Product becomes process in what is essentially the liquefaction of the literary object. This phenomenon is especially evident in something like Amazon's highly successful Kindle Unlimited e-book subscription service, where the individuality of any one of the more than 1 million works of literature available for download to its members is subordinated to the ideal of a continuous flow of product.

So, too, is the would-be professional fiction writer in the Age of Amazon encouraged to supply their readership not with the one book they will ever need, but with something more like a regularly updated *feed*, a series, or indeed series of series. This is the explicit intent of the recently announced Kindle Vella platform, which enables authors to dole out stories in serial format a few thousand words at a time. By all accounts, in order to take full advantage of KDP's promotional algorithms, the ideal pace at which an author should publish a whole new novel is about once every three months. No wonder, then, that for many writers authorship has become a small-scale corporate endeavor, whether via the mechanism of co-authorship or in the systematic parceling out of the tasks of editing, proofreading, and cover design to others, all of these services now readily available on the web. Failing that, there are works like Rachel Aaron's popular advice book, *2K to 10K: Writing Faster, Writing Better, and Writing More of What You Love* (2012), ready to help authors pick up the pace to 10,000 words per day, through which they could feasibly draft a decent-sized novel in a week or two. (I can't speak to the quality of most of Aaron's own fast-accumulating oeuvre of genre fiction, but *Minimum Wage Magic* [2018], her urban fantasia of the gig economy, is not half bad.)

Given the multiplicity of agents engaged in the making of literature now, the nomination of Amazon as first among them all can only be a kind of critical fiction, a way of framing the story of contemporary fiction in such a way as to throw a particular set of heretofore under-examined realities into relief.[23] It is a dangerous fiction, in some ways, in that it entails the analytical subordination of those other agents and the effort to see things—at least initially, as a preface to immanent critique— from the corporation's point of view. However fancifully, it is to insist that the literary history of the present has a *subject*, which is to say, a collective protagonist, a key form of identity in which individual identities converge and through which they exert a historically transformative force. For many, of course, this protagonist will look like an antagonist, if not simply a villain.

Once upon a time, it was the nineteenth-century proletariat who was supposed to be superseding the bourgeoisie as the subject of history, breaking the grip of the profit motive on human life and carrying us into the communist future. In our time it should have been the multitude of workers in service industries—upward of 80 percent of the labor force fitting this description in the United States—leading the way, but no. In any honest accounting of the twenty-first-century job market, it is the corporation that has seized the initiative, demanding that workers conform to its needs and meeting precious little organized resistance along the way. So, too, in recent *literary* history, it is Amazon that has been the force for innovation, with writers trailing behind, doing what they can to seize the opportunities presented by the new regime. The literary culture of the present can therefore plausibly be read as an adjunct to corporate culture in the broadest sense, with Amazon as the leading indicator of what distinguishes literature's present from its past.

Where did the idea—or rather the rhetoric—of "corporate culture" come from in the first place? Although it would be hard to establish a causal relation between the two events, the timing of the emergence and rapid diffusion of the idea in the United States suggests that it was born from the ashes of union culture, the culture of labor, and of working-class culture more broadly. While the one is rightly thought of as emanating from below, from workers themselves, and the other from above, from management, they can be taken to reflect successive historical states of the rapidly deindustrializing postwar workforce. If only for analytical convenience, we might locate the hinge between them in 1982, twelve years before the founding of Amazon, when, facing the stark realities of the economic downturn of the 1970s, McKinsey & Company management consultants Thomas Peters and Robert Waterman published *In Search of Excellence: Lessons from America's Best-Run Companies*. It would immediately become one of the best-selling business books of all time, a publishing sensation overshadowing the appearance in the same year of *Corporate Cultures: The Rites and Rituals of Corporate Life*, written by McKinsey consultants Terrence Deal and Allan Kennedy.[24] Between them, and despite their minor differences in emphasis, these twin products of the uppermost echelons of management advice giving in their time announced that, where once reigned strategic and structural rationality, "culture" would henceforth be king.

Why did they place this emphasis on culture? By their own account, it was because a strong commitment to culture is also the path to corporate "excellence"—which is to say, to a company's relative success against its competitors. The controlling fiction of a book like *In Search of Excellence*, logically incoherent on its face, is that all firms might achieve it. Looking a bit more closely, it becomes clear that the sudden appearance of the rhetoric of corporate culture circa 1982 in fact can be attributed to the need to control labor costs in an environment of systematically shrinking rates of profit. Robert Brenner has influentially described this period as the beginning of what is now known as the Long Downturn, documenting how, since the 1970s, in the aggregate, the increasingly postindustrial economies of the US and other countries have seen the profit rates characteristic of the industrial revolution precipitously decline.[25] This is the harsh background reality of what Peters and Waterman call the "corporate malaise that has us all in its vicelike grip," and to which the vigorous achievement of "excellence" would be the fantasy remedy.

And of what did excellence consist? "Whether bending tin, frying hamburgers, or providing rooms for rent, virtually all of the excellent companies [we investigated] had, it seemed, defined themselves as de facto service companies."[26] This points to a larger economic reality than they seem to realize, one that fundamentally conditions the prospects for any given corporation from the outset. Some companies might provide better service than others, gaining relative competitive advantage over their peers, and some, a precious few, may become money machines like Google or Facebook, who have carved out virtual monopolies in what is essentially a new branch of the advertising industry. But the sparkle of these examples cannot alter the less glamorous reality of the economic environment they inhabit, where the profits available in the aggregate of an economy tending toward provision of services are lower than they once were.

Enter Amazon, circa 1995, to literalize the insight that all companies must now be service companies, performing the virtual magic trick of not being required to show any profits to investors for more than two decades as a publicly traded company, even as it became notorious for the relative stinginess of its compensation packages. This is where its strong corporate culture and "long-term thinking" intervenes. To be employed by Amazon as part of its managerial workforce may mean working long hours for relatively uncompetitive pay, but in theory it is also to take meaningful part in something larger than oneself and eventually, typically after four years, to be richly rewarded with grants of stock in the company. As Peters and Waterman put it, "We desperately need meaning in our lives and will sacrifice a great deal to institutions that will provide meaning for us." The datum of our paycheck may be less impressive than we would like, but "we are more influenced by stories ... than by data."

> As we worked on research of our excellent companies, we were struck by the dominant use of story, slogan, and legend as people tried to explain the characteristics of their own great institutions. All the companies we interviewed ... were quite simply rich tapestries of anecdote, myth, and fairy tale.[27]

Here, then, is another meaning of "fictitious capital." Amazon's success was, among other things, in gathering these corporate fictional forms into a larger master narrative—an epic of business history—powerful enough to establish its platform as a world. Beginning with the hawking of books, history has been made at Amazon in the erection of an infrastructure of sales and fulfillment that can more efficiently get people what they want and need. If this seems impressive—and honestly, to not be impressed with what Amazon has accomplished, as distinct from approving of it, could only betray a willful ignorance of the facts on the ground—it still might seem categorically different from the way Napoleon or Gandhi or Susan B. Anthony made history.

But that overreach is entirely typical of the heady 1990s and in a way is the point, since it helps give cover to the depressing realities of the wage relation. As Deal and Kennedy put it, echoing Peters and Waterman, "A strong culture enables people to feel better about what they do, so they are more likely to work harder."[28] Needless to say, per unit of product, a *harder* worker is a *cheaper* worker, wages remaining equal, since there can be fewer of them. And sure enough, that is the macro story of the US and most other advanced economies since the turn of the millennium: a decreasing share of the national income for labor, an increasing share of that income for capital.[29]

This is something that labor unions had always feared and tried to combat in various ways. Where Peters and Waterman speak of "product champions" and Deal and Kennedy of "heroes" as crucial figureheads of the healthy corporate culture, the equivalent figure in union culture was the "knight of labor" or, more humbly but equally sentimentally, the "workingman." To read an account like Robert Weir's *Beyond Labor's Veil: The Culture of the Knights of Labor* (1996) is to be struck by the comprehensiveness and multidimensionality of this now all but extinguished "culture," which at its peak in the late nineteenth-century US encompassed both the anthropological and the more restricted meanings of the term.[30] The culture of labor surrounding the sprawling enterprise of the Knights of Labor was a way of life, a pattern of ordinary behavior, but also of arcane rituals of belonging, educational initiatives, sentimental poetry, fiction, and theater. Its goal was the production of class consciousness—a sense of commonality and solidarity in the working class as a whole.

In this case, remarkably if inconsistently, that whole was often understood to include women and non-white men. The subsequent rise to dominance of trade unions dedicated to the interests of specific subsets of laborers represented a falling off from the peak of semi-universalized and institutionalized class consciousness of the Knights of Labor era, but its aftereffects were felt well into the twentieth century, even to the 1970s, at which point the strength of trade unions precipitously waned.[31] They did so in part because the militancy of labor consciousness had by then been successfully diffused into what we now call mass culture—that is, the products of the culture industry. The latter is a "corporate culture" of outward rather than inward orientation, a culture not of the workplace but the newsstand, bookstore, internet, and airwaves. It is an ambient feature and reflection of an increasingly nebulous "middle-class" postwar domestic life.[32]

The cultural distance traveled from a sentimental melodrama like T. Fulton Gantt's Knights of Labor novel, *Breaking the Chains: A Story of the Present Industrial Struggle*, serialized in an Oregon workers' newspaper in 1887, to the bitter, neo-existentialist, temp-worker cool of a work like Halle Butler's *The New Me*, a work of literary fiction published by Penguin, is vast indeed but also on an evolving continuum governed by the transformation of a largely industrial economy into a largely postindustrial one.[33] The great irony of the transcendently large sales of *The Pursuit of Excellence* is that no one was really able to take its advice, much as they may have wanted to. I mean, who doesn't want to live a *meaningful* working life rather than doing some bullshit job? And what kind of sadist boss wouldn't want that for all his workers, assuming the numbers add up?

Alas, as Deal and Kennedy already lament in their 1999 follow-up book, *The New Corporate Cultures*, rather than success through culture and the provision of meaning, the period after 1982 would see its demotion in favor of remorseless layoffs, mergers and acquisitions, global outsourcing of labor, and pursuit of short-term inflation of stock prices benefiting share-holders and upper management and no one else.[34] It has seen the rise most recently of the so-called gig economy, where the corporation takes no responsibility for the well-being of its workers at all, redefining them as independent contractors. Such "culture" as what remains amid this wreckage of the Long Downturn is the profoundly cynical one reflected in the contemporary office satire, but it is also reflected in another way—and on a larger and more consequential level—in the rise of angry ethno-nationalism and scapegoating on talk radio, cable TV news and the internet, which is a "corporate culture" of another, disavowed kind.

In this context Amazon, along with a few other successful internet companies like itself, has been as much an anomaly as an exemplar of the new normal, leveraging the virtual "non-profit" status gifted to it by faithful investors to achieve global cultural domination by the corporate form. Wrapping the planet in its embrace, following upon the myriad capillary network connections of the World Wide Web itself, this form of domination emanates in the first instance from the ever-multiplying corporate offices, fulfillment centers, and other facilities around the world where Amazonians are busy making history, hoping thus to make meaning in their own lives, and also some money.

Consuming the World

I suppose it's possible to "Make History" in a small way, but not for Amazon, whose goal above all others, since the beginning —including up until its recent revenue spikes, the goal of profitability—has been to grow larger, as we see in the figure below.

For Amazon, markets exist to be dominated if not literally monopolized, and the market as such has no borders. Measured by the yardstick of increasing revenue and cash flow, but as a matter of course manifesting in many other ways as well, increased size has meant increased leverage, yes, along with some efficiencies of scale, but it has also meant visibility, aggrandized identity, self-esteem, *brand*. The "corporate person" is a legal fiction dating from the nineteenth century, a way of limiting the liability of the humans who own a company while

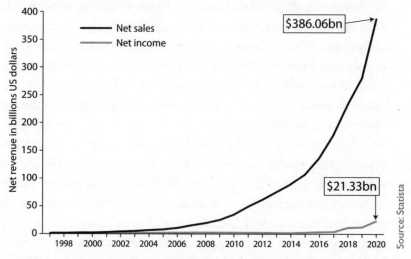

An Epic of Yearly Revenue Growth By 2020, Amazon's yearly revenue had grown to some $386 billion and is set to rise higher from there.

scandalously lending it their civil rights, but the metaphysical complexities, not to mention political implications, of this fiction are considerable.

On the one hand, the corporate form enables a transcendence of limitations of mere mortals, of which even Jeff Bezos is presumably one. While the individual human being can only grow so large or live so long, the corporate body is not bound by these petty physical laws. Neither can a corporation suffer or go to jail. To this extent the corporate person is the historical obverse of the African American person. For the former, visibility is a matter of choice and branding strategy, with moral invisibility—meaning responsibility to no one but shareholders—always an option. For the latter, visibility and invisibility alike are crosses to bear, the first an invitation for the state's abuse of the Black body, the second an index of unrecognized human worth.

On the other hand, in a competitive market, the corporate body might well be absorbed by other corporations or be torn apart and sold off by jackal bankers, or simply wither and die. For its part, Amazon has had at least one near-death experience in its quarter century of existence, when the bursting of the first tech bubble in the year 2000 reduced its market capitalization by 90 percent. One might also see its brief flirtation with Barnes & Noble, which sought to acquire its then-tiny upstart rival in 1996, in these terms.[35] It's worth remembering that in Amazon's early years, it was Barnes & Noble and the now-defunct Borders Books that bore the brunt of criticism as a controversial new force in bookselling, one that seemed to be laying waste to traditional ways of doing business and reducing the fortunes of independent booksellers. Now, Barnes & Noble is gasping for air while Amazon continues to thrive. But for how long? If, to take another relevant example, an iconic retail giant like Sears, Roebuck and Co., the Everything Store of its time, with a legacy dating to the late nineteenth century, can suddenly collapse as it did in 2018 when it filed for bankruptcy, why not also the company perhaps most responsible for that collapse? You never know. It seems unthinkable until—poof—it happens. This is why, as Intel's Andrew Grove famously put it, *Only the Paranoid*

Survive.[36] The identity of a corporation like Amazon is an interesting mix of superpower arrogance and perpetual existential dread, the latter only briefly quelled by reassuring reports of quarterly growth.

Making itself the occasion for millions of low-margin transactions, the goal for Amazon has been to become infinitely big in and across what it conceives of as a kind of universal marketspace, reformatting and rebranding reality in the image of the corporate world. It will settle in the meantime for global domination of e-commerce on the front and back end, doing so from a position beyond the control of any one national government. We rightly think of Amazon's retail and media operations as funneling stuff into private homes, carrying the spore of its corporate culture as it goes. But on the other side of that funnel is the surface of planet Earth in its entirety, crisscrossed by globally extended communications infrastructure and supply chains. Born long after the mid-twentieth-century heyday of US corporate nationalism, Amazon is headquartered in Seattle but has always been "multinational" and "globalist" at heart, setting its sights on a larger geography than could be contained within any city, state, or national border.

Not just history, then, but *world* history would be the thing Amazon makes, the inward-facing intensity of its corporate culture coinciding once again with an urge for infinite outward sprawl. In a program embedded from the outset in its naming after a South American river coursing through a vast expanse of jungle, the ongoing story of its rise would be an epic adventure, a heroic assault on everything, or it would be nothing. With major logistics and fulfillment operations in thirteen countries, it distributes goods to hundreds of millions of customers in 150 or more. Amazon Web Services reaches even farther, now serving 1 million different clients in 190 countries—all but a small handful of countries in the world. Spreading far and wide, carrying the banner of "customer obsession," the company pursues its interests in these places with unapologetic aggression even as it has found, in the Chinese e-commerce giant Alibaba, a more formidable indigenous competitor in the East than was ever encountered by colonizing imperial forebears like the British East India Company.

Amazon is obviously remarkable in its commitment to global growth, but also in a way unoriginal, or merely exemplary. As was already clear to the authors of *The Communist Manifesto* of 1848, the essential dynamics of capitalist development are such as to demand expansion of the enterprise beyond national borders, whether in the acquisition of raw materials or the opening of new markets, lending what they call a "cosmopolitan character" to all the world's economies. The merely national components of these economies "have been destroyed or are daily being destroyed." They have been

> dislodged by new industries, whose introduction becomes a life and death question for all civilized nations, by industries that no longer work up indigenous raw materials, but raw material drawn from the remotest zones; industries whose products are consumed, not only at home, but in every quarter of the globe. In place of the old wants, satisfied by the productions of one country, we find new wants, requiring for their satisfaction the products of distant lands and climes. In place of the old local and national seclusion and self-sufficiency, we have intercourse in every direction, universal inter-dependence of nations.[37]

Say what you will about this document's powers of prophesy, the acuity of its analytical distillations remains startling. Events were supposed to render its descriptions "historical," a way station on the road to communist revolution, but instead have made them seem permanently insightful and relevant, like great art.[38]

The *Manifesto* put its finger on something 1990s market pundits and politicians flattered themselves into thinking was original to their own moment—globalization. The world defined by what we now call "consumerism," with its perpetual discovery of "new wants," is already recorded there, too, a good half century before its advent would become obvious to everyone inasmuch as they were now the addressees of suddenly omnipresent advertisements. In classical eighteenth-century political economy, it was the draw of exotic luxuries that inspired world trade, and that dynamic presumably remains Marx and Engels's emphasis here. By now it has evolved into the fulfillment of what are widely considered basic needs by things mass-produced in China and other (from the US perspective) "distant lands and climes," launched upon the oceans in massive stacks of standardized shipping containers.

All this is furthermore accompanied and facilitated, according to the *Manifesto*, by the capacity for "intercourse in every direction," as though the fondest dreams for the newborn World Wide Web had already been realized 150 years before the fact. By the same token, if communication and "inter-dependence" were by themselves supposed to eliminate antagonisms, the more hopeful implications of those dreams have been substantially refuted, as we have become more and more aware of the internet's fertile affordance of paranoid fantasy, hate speech, and conflict mongering. Whether or not it makes sense to discuss this antagonism in term of "class conflict" as Marx and Engels understood it, their assumption that global interconnectivity would not of itself eliminate conflict has proven sound. In retrospect, it could fairly be said that an idealization of "communication" as the antidote to social antagonism was one the most persistent errors of twentieth-century thought.

And yet, for anyone looking to understand fiction in the Age of Amazon, the most uncannily relevant observation in the *Communist Manifesto* is surely its recognition of a specifically *literary* dimension of the always-already "globalizing" industrial capitalist economy:

And as material, so also in intellectual production. The intellectual productions of individual nations become common property. National one-sidedness and narrow-mindedness become more and more impossible, and from the numerous local and national literatures, there arises a world literature.[39]

The *Manifesto*'s brief gesture toward literary history has received considerable attention from scholars in a recent recrudescence of interest in the concept of world literature, part of a notional disinvestment, beginning in the 1990s, in the significance of the nation as a geographical frame for the telling of literary history.[40]

Born alongside the popular journalistic theme of globalization of the same period, post-national literary criticism has generally been committed to a new cosmopolitan ethos even as it has been troubled by the thought that it might simply be the unwitting cheerleader of the movements of multinational capital in the form of literary art. Is "world literature" a good or bad thing, finally? In working through this quandary, contemporary critics echo the tonal perplexities of the *Manifesto* itself, with its apparent enthusiasm for the capaciousness of world literature —the "one-sidedness and narrow-mindedness" it abolishes sound like obviously bad things, right?—struggling to reckon with its admitted origin in a global system of horrific economic exploitation. Goethe's original invocation of the cosmopolitan dream of *Weltliteratur*, in 1827, had not been freighted with this strange ambivalence, which in fact mirrors Marx's notorious ambivalence about capitalism as a whole: better than feudalism, to be sure, a step toward the fulfillment of human potential, but otherwise a massive historical crime, the theft of workers' time, which is to say, their lives.

That this structure of exploitation has, in the actions of Amazon, gone global is abundantly clear in Heike Geissler's *Seasonal Associate* (2014; trans. 2018), a novelization of the author's brief stint as a fulfillment center employee at Amazon's warehouse facility in Leipzig, Germany. Published by the left-wing avant-garde press Semiotext(e)—one of the main conduits for the introduction of French theory to the US intelligentsia of the 1970s and '80s, and oriented all along by what an anthology of its greatest hits calls a *Hatred of Capitalism*—Geissler's novel would appear to be hostile to Amazon down to its bones. Although labor conditions in its warehouse facilities have by now received a measure of resistance in the US, it might be significant that this theme emerged earliest and most prominently in Germany, with its far more robust and to this day powerful union culture. Not that it has succeeded in organizing the Amazon facilities there. Artfully constructed as a second person "you," the novel's writer protagonist is made subject to the whims of a thoroughly Americanized corporate culture, down to the reproduction in the lobby of that resonant symbol of the company's humble origins, Bezos's original door desk, made by the man himself from materials acquired at Home Depot: "Robert [the manager] has explained that the door, the door table, is a reminder that the customer is king ... Does the customer want us sitting here on comfy sofas? ... Exactly. The customer wants his order."[41]

Seeing things instead from the perspective of the worker—or rather, from the perspective of the whole human being—you as protagonist would "like to contradict him ... and say: I, who am also a customer of this company, would be glad to sit more comfortably here." Not only are the working conditions bad, but in Geissler's account, Amazon steals the worker's time in various ways, beginning with an unpaid worker orientation day and extending to the long commute to and from work. Subject to this loss, the German avant-garde writer as ordinary German worker will "start to see strata in society ... You'll see the strata before your eyes as clearly as the geologists see the structure of the ground where they've dug a deep pit." Intriguingly and appropriately, the birth of class consciousness is figured in terms of the "generic" nature of the protagonist's suffering of the low-level brutality of the fulfillment center workday: "Yes, you are generic; I intend to regard you as generic and introduce you to your most generic traits." As such, she is but a cog, as they say, in a global machine of which the circulation of books is only one small dimension:

> Many of the products you receive have travelled further than you have in the past five years. You're now processing mugs designed in Santa Monica, USA; made, printed, and packaged in China; then offered for sale in France; and now shipped from Amazon France to Amazon Germany as seasonal specials.[42]

In this framing, Geissler's novel recalls the *Communist Manifesto*, with its resolutely internationalist frame of reference, but they differ widely in their expectations about how soon a fundamental change of this system is coming, the wild-eyed confidence of the original having given way here to world-weary and even depressive plea for action of some sort.

The question is whether this novel, available for sale on Amazon, isn't in the interim doing the corporation a kind of service. Most concretely, it could be doing so by offering a potentially useful and wholly incorporable critique of practices that might someday get it into trouble. More abstractly, by providing a kind of confirmation of its corporate identity from without, from below.

This is the context in which we might read Amazon's recent movement into the world literature game, which turns the leftist cultural valences of a translation like *Seasonal Associate* 180 degrees around. Most of the novels ever sold by Amazon have been English-language ones, but that was never going to be enough, not symbolically. Enter Amazon Crossing, one of the aforementioned sixteen book imprints it hosts, and by the look of things the most active of them all (see figure on p. 103).

Characteristically, even as it represents a vanishingly small percentage of its overall business, Amazon's movement into the business of literary translation has not been modest in scope, as though what is at stake in the endeavor is not money alone but corporate identity and ethos. Based at the company's headquarters in Seattle, but with offices in Europe, Amazon Crossing is now the most prolific publisher of literary translations into English in the world, having outstripped prestigious New Directions for this honor a few years ago.[43] Facilitating the production of a multinational corporate culture, it has launched an online translation proposal portal navigable in fourteen languages and begun to sponsor translations into languages other than English, beginning with German.

While it has published more than a few works that might have appeared comfortably as New Directions or even Semiotext(e) releases, among them the gloriously unreadable works of Puerto

Amazon Crossing
Amazon Crossing introduces readers to authors from around the world with translations of international books, making award-winning and best-selling books accessible to new readers.

READ THE WORLD
Bringing readers from around the globe together through literature in translation

INT'L AWARD WINNERS

NEW & NOTEWORTHY IN TRANSLATION

Books from GERMANY

Books from CHINA

Books from around the WORLD

"Read the World" German and Chinese are two source languages of particular interest to Amazon Crossing, which has also begun to translate works from English into German.

Rican avant-garde poet and novelist Giannina Braschi, Amazon Crossing's bread and butter has been translations of genre fiction of various kinds. These range from the million-selling *Hangman's Daughter* series of medieval-period detective novels, originating in German, to Spanish zombie novels, Chinese historical romances, Russian fantasy, and Scandinavian noir. This in itself is extraordinary, a new wrinkle in recent literary history, where works of neither recognized high artistic merit nor necessarily even of transcendent best-seller status in their language of origin have found an avenue to international circulation. Why not, if translation costs can be kept low enough to at least break even on them?

If scholars have had trouble coming to a consensus on the phenomenon of world literature, torn as they are between enthusiasm and suspicion, the actions of Amazon represent something like the worst-case scenario of what it might actually mean: simply, works that manage to circulate in a global market dominated by a few languages; less an agent for the appreciative maintenance of cultural difference than an easily consumable agent of global cultural standardization—"World Lite," as one pithy headline put it.[44] The term for this is not "world literature" but "multinational literature." In this context, even a work like Braschi's *United States of Banana* (2011), utterly uncompromising in its rejection of the pieties of US nationalism and of easy consumability alike, starts to seem less like an act of genuine resistance than a loss-leader advertisement for the authenticity of the brand.

Bearing the motto "Read the World," Amazon Crossing launched in 2010 with the translation from the French of Tierno Monénembo's *The King of Kahel*, a novelization of the life of the late nineteenth-century adventurer and would-be self-appointed white king of the Fouta Djallon region of Africa, Olivier de Sanderval.[45] Here, then, is the original model for Amazon's cinematic adaptation of *The Lost City of Z* several years later. As though obedient to the requirement that the translated work function as an allegory of its conditions of translation, it is not difficult to draw a line leading from this colonial adventurer to the madness of the individual entrepreneur of the present day. A kind of belated Quixote, Monénembo's French nobleman explorer is credited with numerous appealing eccentricities as an obsessive dreamer of heroic dreams of individual exploit and economic development. He shows an almost comic willingness to suffer illness and abuse in order to realize them.

Near the beginning of his adventures, as though dreaming of the advent of the World Wide Web, Sanderval is faced with the sheer difficulty of travel in the jungle with a large retinue and delicate constitution. He finds himself "sorry to think he would be dust in the wind by that faraway time when inexorable progress made it possible to travel to Africa in a fraction of a second."[46] Mostly, though, his dreams of conquest are already anachronistic in the age of organized imperial expansion and the rise of the railroad trusts. And even if they weren't, Monénembo suggests, they would have proven impractical in face of the sheer political complexity of the African tribal world he enters. Bold as they were, the failure of Sanderval's dreams of commercial conquest was no doubt crucial, ironically, to their latter-day idealization by a French writer of Ghanaian descent, freeing him to patronizingly praise Sanderval's folly as an imaginary antidote to modern bureaucratized life.

Other offerings on the Amazon Crossing list go for a more straightforwardly positive retelling of the history of global capitalism. Works like Rebecca Gable's novelization of a popular board game, *The Settlers of Catan* (trans. 2011), and Petra Durst-Benning's *Glassblower* trilogy (trans. 2014–15), both translated from German, tell the story of the conversion of primitive European trading practices, first into individual entrepreneurial initiative, then into full-blown multinational corporate capitalism, the former serving to this day as the spiritual-ideological kernel of the latter.[47] Whether originally intended by their authors or not, the allegorical corporate self-representation (and self-congratulation) enacted in the publication of these works is hard to miss.

A more recent offering is Laura Gallegos's *Omnia*, translated from Spanish and released in 2016, in which an online retailer by that name succeeds in establishing commercial relations with other planets, exploiting as yet undiscovered anomalies in the laws of nature as we know them to offer even its alien customers free one-day shipping through a system of hyperdimensional Tubes.[48] Calling to mind Bezos's dreams of space travel, this is something Monénembo's hero could have used. Inhabiting the future, which is also a vision of the delocalizing present of the World Wide Web, Omnia's motto is "Everything You Could Ever Dream Of," *Todo lo que puedas soñar*. That's what it tells its customers, but its colonization of the consumer mind extends to the identities of its multispecies warehouse workforce, too: "'Bottom line, no matter where we come from, we all belong to Omnia,' says the human returns specialist Marlene. 'We all share the same nationality: we're all Omnians,'" agrees an alien employee named Belay, touting the efforts of Omnia's CrossWorld Department to maintain good relations with other planets full of potential new customers. "'Our road map,' announces the reclusive billionaire founder, 'includes the promotion of cross-world relations so everyone can benefit from the wonderful technological advancements we have made here [at Omnia].'"[49] These include an efficiency-obsessed artificial intelligence called not Alexa but Nia, who as the novel begins is gradually replacing the warehouse workforce with robots. In *Omnia*, Bezos's brainchild sees its epic aspirations radicalized and realized as cosmic retail.

A work like this—children's literature, really, although not labeled as such—is perhaps all too legible as corporate allegory, instancing a fundamental dorkiness that separates the book starkly from the works of more prestigious avatars of "world literature" like J. M. Coetzee, Roberto Bolaño, W. G. Sebald, or Elena Ferrante. So much so that one wonders if it doesn't in a sense cross over into the profoundest sort of critique of Amazon —critique by sheer ludicrousness. Once one has picked up on this possibility, there are hints in the novel that this may be true; that, indeed, if we could follow the Tubes all the way back to reality we would essentially find ourselves in the world of *Seasonal Associate*. Either way, it draws to the surface the globalization of the market in literature implicit in the circulation of those more prestigious works. The difference Amazon makes in the relatively rarified space of world literature is simply to step in and say "more, please"—more books, more *kinds* of books, more Goodreads lists, more countries, more authors, more languages, more transactions, and, if possible, all of them under the aegis of Amazon. And if a few works critical of Amazon are included in that mass? So be it.

Ultimately, with its command of the great global copy machine that is the internet, Amazon's efforts on behalf of world cultural circulation tend toward the production of a global surplus of fiction. Manifesting in this way the fundamental logic of capitalism, it establishes the network platform as the dominant context of contemporary literary production, the progenitor of glorious "network effects" where more is always better. This is so even as the sheer largeness of the epic surround becomes the occasion for dialectical correction in the opposite direction, as when Geissler focalizes the Amazon phenomenon through the eyes of one weary fulfillment center worker, or when autofiction as we find it in Ben Lerner, Tao Lin, Sheila Heti, or Rachel Cusk sets about rescaling the world to the needs of the authorial self. This scalar dynamic will be discussed at greater length in chapter 5. This centrifugal and centripetal, minimalist and maximalist dialectic is not new, only newly obvious to literary historians tasked with understanding the operation of the contemporary literary field.

It's always worth remembering that, as noted by Benedict Anderson long ago, books were among the first machine-made commodities, and have never been less than revelatory of the nature of the phase of capitalism in which their circulation occurs. The same is true today, when, as profit margins have steadily declined, the keynote of mainstream economics in the last half century has been a call for a return to more efficiently exploitative global labor relations and forms of trade. On the scene of contemporary literary production, the opinions of the gatekeepers—agents and editors—of the publishing conglomerates are what count as "regulation" in this sense, for good or ill depending on your position in the literary field. For its part, Amazon would convert that field into a kind of proprietary jungle, or terrarium perhaps, which anyone can enter but where only the algorithmically fittest survive.

This latter is the territory stalked by the so-called "authorpreneur," a locution almost too hideous to type out, but here we are.[50] Armed with book series development formulae, e-book pricing schemes, and impressive skills at search engine optimization, they are at once the state of the art of authorship in the Age of Amazon and a kind of throwback to the literary tradesmen of the eighteenth century for whom the tasks of printing and marketing a book were sometimes continuous with writing it in the first place. The difference of course is the presence of the internet-enabled platform monopoly underlying and enclosing all this literary laissez-faire.

Coda: The Great Firewall of China

The sheer force and effectiveness with which Amazon has begun to realize its epic ambitions is enough to send one searching for evidence of limits to its power, which are there to be found. One might point, for instance, to the spectacular failure of its attempt to become a player in the manufacture of mobile phones, which cost the company some $500 million. More relevant to our interests here, one might remark on its eventual capitulation to the publishing conglomerates, led by Hachette and fronted by some its most prominent authors, who before the dispute was resolved in 2014 demanded the right to charge whatever amount they wished for the e-books they sell on Amazon, not the $9.99 that Jeff Bezos on a whim arrived at as the right price for such a thing.

That conflict was sometimes presented as a match between the rights and interests of individual authors and the corporation —specifically, their right not to participate in Amazon's "non-profit" strategies for market domination—and that formulation is not entirely untrue. An equally salient takeaway, however, given the relative generosity of Amazon's payments to authors using its system directly, would be the realization that the publishing business is dominated by big business through and through, the combined market might of the publishing conglomerates remaining quite considerable. In this one instance, with the stakes much higher for one combatant than another, Amazon backed off. One imagines it was not exactly crushed to be forced to take a greater profit on books than originally planned, since the higher cover price increases its yield, too.

A more interesting and consequential limit to Amazon's power is the one it has encountered in China, with its 1.4 billion (and counting) potential customers. In 2019, Amazon announced that it was getting out of the business of selling Chinese goods to Chinese customers, that market having been locked down by the combined force of native online retailers JD.com and Alibaba. The latter is often thought of as the "Amazon of

China," with its tremendous market power, dazzlingly efficient distribution system, and similar array of business units. Content now to sell non-Chinese-made products within China and, even more important to the balance sheet, to import Chinese products directly to US and other non-Chinese customers through its Marketplace platform, Amazon has been forced to leave an agonizingly large and growing amount of business on the table. This provides an object lesson, if we needed one, in the difference between this historical moment and the nineteenth century, that original crucible of "globalization" and Western domination of the East revealed in the Opium Wars.

Two centuries ago, Western domination was total: now, not so much. And nowhere is the autonomy of China clearer than in the unapologetic control its government exerts over the internet within its borders, securing it against the free flow of information from without. That the Great Firewall of China, as it has been nicknamed, offends the sensibilities of the global neoliberal capitalist order is clear, predicated as the latter presumes itself to be on the free flow of information. But its implications for literary history, and indeed for world literature, are more complex than that, inasmuch as China now presents perhaps the best example of the maintenance of an autonomous and integral "world"—that ultimate desideratum of critics of world literature—in the face of forces of globalization. This is made clear, ironically, in a reading of the many translations of Chinese literature published by Amazon Crossing, a far greater number than from any other publisher in recent years. The commitment on Amazon's part to the works of this nation is exceeded only by its many translations of German fiction.

Perhaps the most illuminating text from this perspective is Jia Pingwa's *Happy Dreams* (2007; trans. 2017), a novel about a man and his best friend who leave the countryside of their birth for jobs as garbage pickers in the newly bursting metropolis of Xi'an. What sticks out about this novel is, simply, how little it reads like a novel on the "bourgeois" model of the West, a form often held to have taken hold in China only in the 1920s.[51] Instead it is a relentlessly *episodic* creation, a long series of more or less humorous picaresque encounters of its exceedingly upbeat protagonist with the world around him as he looks for trash to claim and sell. "The days went by, and Wufu managed to stay out of trouble. The two of us began to earn a good reputation on our Prosper Street patch. When there was no trash to pick, or I wanted a few minutes break, I would get out my flute and play." Thus opens a typical chapter of the book, making no promises that its peripatetic plot will accumulate into a larger whole. In the events the narrator recounts, there is no sign of his transformation, even as the reader is conducted into a social world invisible even to most middle-class Chinese readers. As the Author's Note at the end explains:

> Trash picking? I realized I had never given that job a moment's thought ... I had lived in Xi'an for more than thirty years, and I had seen trash pickers pulling their carts or riding their three-wheelers every day ... City folk, including me and my family, pride ourselves on our stylish, luxurious bathrooms, regarding them as a sign of progress and civilization, but the city is like its people: what goes in must come out; excrete as much as we ingest. Then why do we simply not see, or care about, the people who do the job of cleaning up our waste?[52]

Jia makes clear that trash pickers are but one highly resonant example of perhaps the key social phenomenon of China's recent past and present, which is the migration of workers from the countryside to cities, where they often remain relative strangers. And yet, such is the coherence of Chinese culture that even a trash picker like Happy Liu is well versed in Chinese storytelling traditions, referring throughout the novel to comedic analogies between his situation and those found in the so-called "Four Classics" of Chinese fiction, *Romance of the Three Kingdoms* (written in the fourteenth century), *The Water Margin* (fourteenth), *Journey to the West* (sixteenth), and *Dream of the Red Chamber* (eighteenth). In this *Happy Dreams* is like Chinese popular culture in general, for which these works remain pervasive points of reference.

AmazonCrossing translations from Chinese

If you, like me, were to venture fitfully into reading translations of these works (quite a task, as they are each several thousands of pages long) in hopes of better understanding Chinese fiction at the limit of the Age of Amazon, you would find that the episodic structure of *Happy Dreams*—its form—is something it shares with these classics. Like it, they are often described as "novels" but are so only in the most general sense, in that they are indeed long works of prose fiction. The irony is that the bourgeois novel in the West—Lu Yao's *Life* (1982; trans. 2019), proclaimed by Alibaba's Jack Ma as the book that "changed my life," is perhaps the closest among Amazon Crossing translations to fitting this bill—is itself being put under tremendous pressure by the course of cultural developments in the US and elsewhere in the West. Among them, as we have seen, are the renewed drive toward the seriality encouraged by Amazon's promotion algorithms, which reward KDP authors for releasing new-but-familiar works at regular intervals.

Webnovel With 165 million views and counting, the 2,000-plus-chapter Library of Heaven's Path stretches the definition of the term "novel."

Still, this is nothing like what one sees when one logs onto the massively successful Chinese venture called Webnovel, a subunit of the company Qidian, where "the novel" is subject to even more massive pressures by a medium built upon the expectation of steadily paced serial additions to works mainly of extravagant fantasy, many of them what in Japan would be called *isekai*. Demonstrating an enthusiastic embrace of literary reading on the screen on the part of Asian readers, these works don't exist except as a kind of digital drip feed. And yet, even though they seem "classically Chinese," Webnovel publishes these works in English to stake a claim for them as world or at least multinational literature (see figure above). Amazon will try to compete on this ground with its recently announced Kindle Vella platform, which essentially replicates the serial delivery mechanism pioneered by Qidian.

What's interesting about Pingwa's picaresque novel, in this context, is the resonance it constructs between Happy Liu's job and the nature of Chinese culture, which is above all a culture of symbolic *recycling*, which is to say, of collective cultural self-reference or worlding. Of great symbolic significance, then—and practical significance, too, as US municipalities scramble to adjust—was China's announcement in 2018 that it would quite literally no longer be accepting low-quality recyclables from the US and other Western countries as it had done for many years, preferring now to concentrate on domestic recycling efforts. To be sure, China is not likely to close itself to the world market upon which it depends, but it can be expected to operate there more and more on its own terms. Ironically, then, the structure of Chinese cultural self-reference we see in *Happy Dreams*, purveyed in translation to a curious American reader by Amazon, provides a potential model for the construction and maintenance of other autonomous worlds, worlds not reducible to the corporate world as defined by Amazon.

That said, very few nations have the kind of scale—the staggering enormity—that would appear to be the precondition of this cultural independence, and China has its own large corporations, including Qidian and Alibaba and the rest. The Chinese government sometimes makes a point of showing these entities who's boss, but for how long? Only the further unfolding of the Chinese Century, still in its early years, will tell. Perhaps it would be more accurate, then, to see China simply as the latest and greatest vehicle of the epic advance of multinational capital as such.

3

Generic Love, or, The Realism of Romance

The Consumer as Hero

To speak of fiction in the Age of Amazon is perforce to speak of it in relation to the consumer economy, a thing of long duration, a thing of historical stages in its making and only lately arrived at the popular embrace of online commerce. With its origins in the circulation of exotic luxuries in the seventeenth and eighteenth centuries, increasing spread in the industrializing nineteenth century, and ad-driven explosion in the twentieth, the consumer economy has changed the texture of daily life in countries in which has been able to take root, and continues to do so today, globally. Subsuming, virtualizing, and massively expanding the reach of two remarkable inventions of the mid to late nineteenth century, the department store and mail-order catalog, the company once billing itself "Earth's Biggest Bookstore" and then the "Everything Store" has helped set the scene for literary life in our time, when any given cardboard box might contain dog treats or sweatpants or tampons or a book; or when the novel as we know it might not even appear in its traditional physical form, downloaded instead from the company's servers to one or another tributary reading device.

But setting the scene is one thing: has the consumerist ethos embodied in Amazon's commercial practices been internalized in the novel's form? The previous two chapters of this book asked a similar question mainly from the side of literary production, tracing the penetration of an entrepreneurial ideal—the author as self-publishing "start-up," or corporate CEO—in the popular literature of an economy increasingly defined by the conscripted provision of services rather than the industrial production of durable goods. In this and in the following chapter of this book, that perspective will be flipped, allegories of supply giving way to those of demand as we focus on the novel as something, one kind of thing, a person might *want to buy*, simply, but as it happens not so simply.

"You sound like the ultimate consumer," says Anastasia Steele upon first meeting the hero of E. L. James's *Fifty Shades of Grey* (2011), which with over 125 million copies sold in its first five years in print is a strong candidate for the ultimate best seller.[1] She is interviewing him for the college newspaper, challenging him to explain his desire to possess so many things. Christian's response to Ana's charge is simple and remarkably un-defensive: "I am." That a man who is also introduced as a "mega-industrialist tycoon" who says he "like[s] to build things" and wants to "[feed] the world's poor" would so easily assent to thinking of himself in this way is interesting, if not exactly shocking.[2] We expect people who make lots of money building things to spend some of that money on other things, on the best things, amazing things. And yet, in a way that will reward further consideration, the consumer-tycoon runs counter to the most prominent image of the capitalist in the history of economic theory, the Protestant "acetic" described by Max Weber in the early twentieth century.

The latter was a figure characterized as much by the restraint of his worldly desires as by his vigorous actions. According to Weber, it was he who, seeing virtue in hard work and seeking profit for profit's sake, vaulted the Western world into full-blown capitalist modernity, quickly filling the world with new things. The Protestant ethic is expressed most directly, for Weber, in the writings of Ben Franklin, whose maxim "time is money" meant simply to draw the young tradesman's attention to the hidden costs of his leisure in hours not devoted to productive labor, but can sound like an even stronger metaphysical claim about the fabric of the universe. For Franklin, simply to *spend* money rather than to *invest* it toward future returns is akin to the profligate spilling of seed, disrupting the reproductive miracle of profit in which, in time, "money can beget money, and its offspring can beget more, and so on" toward ever greater wealth.[3]

Whether or not his conception of the virtuous capitalist had ever adequately explained the rapid transformation of the material environment of human life by modern industry, by the time of Weber's writing, the Protestant ethic was plainly falling out of sync with Western economies increasingly ideologically centered on mass consumption over and above production for the satisfaction of basic needs—economies in which, indeed, with the advent of modern advertising, forces had recently set about expanding what might count as a basic need. In this world the quasi-spiritual pursuit of profit without end finds itself inverted in the mirror—the maw—of consumer demand, which likewise escalates without apparent end or arrival at enough.[4] Driven by what Émile Zola and others would tendentiously describe as a distinctly feminine instinct for shopping, the economy so constituted would escalate in a virtuous upward spiral of wage-earning and inspired expenditure, with the latter taking the lead.

This much we know from any number of accounts of the rise of the modern so-called consumer economy whose latest phase is our own Age of Amazon, where upward of 70 percent of the gross domestic product of a country like the United States is driven by consumer spending, and one of the most closely watched economic indicators is the Index of Consumer Sentiment. What remains is to complicate our understanding of Weber's capitalist along the same lines—not erasing that figure, exactly, but forcing him to stand next to one of a substantially different nature. That other capitalist is what political journalists and cartoonists of the early twentieth century began to call a "fat cat," a figure whose very rotundity seems a rebuke to Weber's version, and to the tagging of the consumer as a woman (see figure on p. 118).

Pattinson photo by Eva Rinaldi licensed under Creative Commons

From Austerity to Excess and Back Frans Masereel, *Businessman* (1920), in the Weberian mode; the "fat cat" as seen in Clarence Budington Kelland, *Scattergood Baines* (1921); Robert Pattinson, star of *Twilight* (dir. Hardwicke, 2008)

While it has remained convenient to him to be thought of as doing God's work as a self-sacrificing "job creator," the capitalist in the mode of fat cat is distinct from ordinary shoppers only in the excessive purchasing power he brings to the checkout counter of life. Having exhausted the possibilities of direct commodity enjoyment, the fat cat indulges in the pleasures of investment itself. When he plays the markets, his work has all the thrill of gambling, but its more productive manifestations are satisfying, too, consuming human and other resources toward the end of amassing personal wealth and worldly power. He is a figure not of self-abnegating asceticism but self-gratifying Eros, not of stern rectitude but selfish excess. At the limit, he is the consumer as *predator*. Here they stand side by side, but only in their weird superimposition would we begin to see the character of Christian Grey come into focus. Add one more layer, the image of the brooding young movie star/vampire E. L. James had in mind as she was writing the original draft of the novel, and there he is. He is a man who has seen fit to buy himself a private jet, yacht, helicopter, hang glider, fleet of automobiles, scads of luxury real estate, and a string of submissive lovers, but who manages to project an aura of austerity all the same.

This is visible not least in his lean, pale physical form, but also in the minimalist architectural environments he likes to inhabit ("all curved glass and steel, an architect's utilitarian fantasy"), in the clean lines of the Apple electronics he and Ana use there, and even in his name. He is, after all, a great champion of *discipline*, which he assures Ana is the other side of the coin of softer pleasures. We could say he is a bundle of contradictions, but Christian's way of describing himself is even better. He is, he says, "fifty shades of fucked up," for reasons it takes Ana some time to learn.[5] Taking his cue, she nicknames him Fifty, and begins to explore his curiously hard-edged plenitude, accompanied in this endeavor by her own psychic multiplicity, an internalized audience of competing "inner goddess" and "subconscious" that corresponds, roughly, to the psychoanalytic id and superego. What follows in the novel and its two successors in the *Fifty Shades* trilogy are a series of narrative numerical reductions and integrations: from fifty symptoms to the one childhood trauma that explains Christian Grey; from many potential lovers to One True Love; finally, and most importantly for the genre of which *Fifty Shades* is the best-known member, from indecision in the face of a multiplicity of objects of desire to the assertion of unitary executive will in the solidification of the social form of the couple.

This genre is the contemporary romance novel, specifically a subgenre thereof called "alpha billionaire romance." Its instances are legion, with titles like *Beautiful Bastard*, *Hardwired*, *Dirty Billionaire*, *Loving the White Billionaire*, and *Bared to You*, many of them self-published on Amazon's Kindle Direct Publishing system, others appearing as mass-market paperbacks and e-books under well-known imprints, including Amazon's own Montlake Romance. All but wholly marginal to the contemporary literary field as seen from the perspective of academic literary studies and adjacent organs of literary journalism, the romance novel is absolutely central to popular literary life in the Age of Amazon, where readers are understood as customers, and the customer is queen.

What do we see when we center our view of the literary field on romance rather than on literary fiction? We see the inescapable identity of the novel as a *generic commodity*, to be sure, but also some of the surprising complexity of its engagement with the realities of consumer culture. While the characters and events of romance are not always "realistic" on the level of representational verisimilitude, they, by their nature, continually reflect upon the economic and otherwise crudely material bases of modern love and life in general, the world not as it might be built anew in some science fiction novel but as it already impinges on everything. In relation to these bases, romance instances what we might call a "functional" or "therapeutic" realism. As we shall see, it is enacted not only in the reader's encounter with the individual work, but also in the knitting of that encounter into a sequencing of reading experiences, one after the other. The individual work—a trilogy, in this case—is designed to manage a potentially problematic plenitude, sifting a haystack of potential lovers to discover the One, while the genre as a whole, offering readers an endless series of nominally distinct heroes as objects of desire, reinstalls that plenitude as a manageable reading habit whose function is to assuage some of the fundamental existential limitations of embodied life. And yet this complex is already encoded into the singular figure of Christian Grey, the One who is in theory everything a desirable man could be, a would-be epic hero corralled for domestic romantic duty.

Christian's unusual purchasing power is hardly needed the second time he and Ana meet, when he enters the hardware store where she works to buy some, as it turns out, not-so-innocent masking tape and cable ties. It is very much needed in the next act of purchase he makes in the novel, on his way to acquiring the services of Ana herself as a submissive lover. "*Odd*. I haven't ordered anything from Amazon recently," she thinks when her roommate tells her she has a package. It is not from Amazon but it does contain a book—a fine first edition of Thomas Hardy's *Tess of the d'Urbervilles*, one of the "British classics" Ana has told him that she, a graduating English major, likes to read. The gift is of course multiply self-reflexive. The inscription Christian has borrowed from the novel itself is meant as a playful warning to her about his intentions in giving it, which put her in the position of the novel's heroine: "*Why didn't you tell me there was danger? Why didn't you warn me? ... Ladies know what to guard against because they read novels that tell them of these tricks.*"[6] Of course, the circumstances of Tess's ruination are substantially different for Ana, whose virginity at the beginning of this novel is understood even by herself as an anomaly, the genre having modernized itself in various ways even as it has faithfully carried the flame of the marriage plot.

For the reader of the novel, meanwhile, the gift points to the book she (that is in all likelihood the reader's gender) holds in hand, which, if it is the best-known example of the alpha billionaire romance, is also in lineage with the English novel stretching back through Hardy and Henry James to Jane Austen and Samuel Richardson. Richardson's 1740 best seller, *Pamela: Or, Virtue Rewarded*, was the first major work to serve what would prove an endless demand in the modern book market for the story of a young woman's triumph in bringing an abusive male to heel as a husband. At the same time, and relatedly, it announced that female readers would be crucial to the market for novels in general, much more so than men.[7]

Grey's gift is at once the expression and negation of the Amazon economy explicitly referenced in this moment—pointing, in its high cost, to the nature of the book as a purchasable commodity even as that high cost is precisely what Amazon would diminish in its facilitation of popular literary commerce, where, as infamously asserted by Jeff Bezos, new books should be downloadable for $9.99 at most.[8] The stealthy e-book format reputedly so important to the novel's success as "mommy porn" is something like the opposite of the fine first edition. It converts the novel's obtrusive materiality into evanescent bits drifting profitably from device to device. This truth is brought home when, in the second volume of the *Fifty Shades* trilogy, *Fifty Shades Darker*, Ana is given an Apple iPad tablet supplied with a fictional British Library App, providing her electronic access to all the classic novels she could possibly find time to read. "I exit quickly, knowing I could be lost in this app for an eternity," she says, hitting upon one of the key features of literary life in the Age of Amazon, where a hyper-abundance of inexpensive product collides with a general scarcity of time for its consumption.[9]

It is, however, in the last layer of the trilogy's self-reflexivity that we see the deepest and most interesting fusion of the romance with the realities of consumer culture. It is reflexivity to the second degree, reflecting as it does a long history of reflexivity itself in the genre, whose heroines are frequently enough represented as readers. Think here of Jane Austen's Elizabeth Bennett, who "is a great reader and has no pleasure in anything else," or of the many female heirs—Emma Bovary, preeminently —to the original reader of romances in the history of the novel, Don Quixote.[10] If we have been taught to think of these reflexive incorporations of the reader as demystifying romance on behalf of hard-nosed novelistic realism, the persistence of the same phenomenon in works to all appearances wholly committed to the romantic fantasy suggests it is of somewhat larger significance, with reinforcing as well as critical tendencies.

Most fundamentally, it is a symptom of the modern "codification of intimacy," as Niklas Luhmann calls it. For Luhmann, this term gets at how, beginning in the seventeenth century, what had generally been thought the essential madness of romantic love was made functional in the routine task of social reproduction. In his account, faced with an increasingly differentiated and contingent modern social reality, chivalric forms heretofore centered on aristocratic extramarital relations (think Lancelot and Guinevere) were updated for use in the imaginative construction of reassuringly small and mutually self-confirming bourgeois worlds. Consuming the romance, that is, readers were systematically instructed in the pursuit of the intensive pseudo-totality of the marriage bond newly conceived as a source of deep emotional satisfaction to individuals rather than as an alliance between families. Structured as a quest for the One True Love as marriage partner, it was and remains an ironically generic pursuit, driven by an *"emotion preformed, and indeed prescribed, in literature,* and no longer directed by social institutions such as the family and religion." For Luhmann, modern love "seems to come from nowhere, arises with the aid of copied patterns, copied emotions, copied existences and may perhaps create a conscious awareness of this secondhand character in its failure."[11] It makes sense that the engine of these secondhand emotions, reading, would on occasion see its own reflection, as it were, in print.[12]

It only needs to be added that both these conceptions can be reinscribed in and as a function of the history of consumer capitalism. What Luhmann describes as the literary autono-mization of love in early modernity could be viewed instead as the gradual transfer of authority over amatory relations to a market, what is known as the "marriage market"—a locu-tion that took off in the late nineteenth century—in which bride and groom would each be reciprocally conceived as buyer and seller, consumer and consumed. The irony of this transfer for Luhmann's cocoon-like "pseudo-totality" is that it places unprecedented stress on the marriage bond, leading ultimately to high instances of divorce, including "no-fault divorce," the relationship equivalent of the free return.[13] While it would not often call for the purchase of first editions of classic literature, the ritual of courtship that ended in marriage, once conducted in the private parlor, would henceforth take the form of "dating," which was indeed an occasion for significant financial outlay in highly codified, mimetically inspired channels. As Daniel Harris explains, "Before the twentieth century, there were no dates, no lavish nights on the town in which men shelled out an entire month's wages for corsages, highballs at Delmonico's, five-course meals at the 21 Club, tickets for Broadway plays ..." There was no "love industry" and attendant genre of advertis-ing, whose repetitive forms assume that "love is such a universal experience that it reduces us all to the same generic person, the same beach-walker, the same sunset-admirer, who relies on the same commercially manufactured images of intimacy."[14]

This is true as far as it goes, establishing an important context for the modern romance novel, but arguably betrays too much confidence that modern lovers have ever been other than generic in their loving, let alone their lovemaking. Already in the seven-teenth century, long before anyone thought of going on a date to Delmonico's, François de La Rochefoucauld could deliver a maxim, "People would never fall in love if they hadn't heard love talked about," predicated on the reflexive unoriginality of that emotion; and it may be the case, then as now and at every moment in between, that the cognitive mechanism of *idealization* so crucial to love makes it an inevitably *generic* phenomenon.

People speak unembarrassedly of being attracted to one or another romantic "type," and can be observed behaviorally to define their objects of desire in terms assimilable to the acronymic code made famous in personal ads of the newsprint era, beginning with the still-regnant binary *M* or *F*—a code whose main use, now that the function of personals has largely been absorbed into more complexly algorithmic internet dating sites, is to label different types either of pornography or romance novel. An example would be the thriving genre of "BBW Romance," which features big, beautiful women and the typically burly men who love them. What's remarkable about the romance is how deep its knowledge of the essentially generic nature of desire goes even as it keeps faith, superficially, with the fantasy of One True Love.

Neither, relatedly, is Harris's formulation responsive to the paradoxical *generic singularity* of the alpha billionaire as a remarkable man. His godlike excellence would seem at least partly to refute the idea that we are "all the same," no? In the real world this figure is so often a repulsive grotesque; here in Amazonia he is a sleek server of emotional needs. He is the desiring man, the *subject* of desire, conceived and constructed as an *object* of desire, and suffused in that reverberating fantasy circuit with unpredictably utopian as well as reactionary ideological spirits. The romance novel is in this sense a set of imaginary negotiations with the realities of patriarchal capitalism, part of the long tradition in the novel drawn to our attention by Nancy Armstrong in *Desire and Domestic Fiction* (1987).[15]

At this late date, unless I am mistaken, the optimism of that earlier political moment in the history of the novel has been blunted, and the discourse has become more ameliorative in its aims, more a therapeutic coping mechanism than the echo or instigator of a positive program. I don't know that anyone has improved upon the incisive formulation of the essential political conundrum of the genre offered in Janice Radway's classic work of cultural anthropology, *Reading the Romance* (1984):

> Does the romance's endless rediscovery of the virtues of a passive female sexuality merely stitch the reader ever more resolutely into the fabric of patriarchal culture? Or, alternatively, does the satisfaction a reader derives from the act of reading itself, an act she chooses, often in explicit defiance of others' opposition, lead to a new sense of strength and independence?[16]

I would only add that, responsive to the desires of its readers, the romance hero is not necessarily to be confused with his real-world counterpart. To want the literary alpha billionaire is to want him to want you, yes, but it is also to want to set the terms of his desire, to get inside it and take the wheel.

As though it is not enough to leave this implicit, the state of the art in the genre, which by and large favors first-person narratives from the heroine's point of view, is to find ways of inhabiting his consciousness, too. And so, in works like Pamela Aidan's *An Assembly Such as This* (2006) or Janet Aylmer's *Darcy's Story* (2007), Austen's romance is retold from the hero's perspective. In Christina Lauren's self-published modern romance sensation, *Beautiful Bastard*, chapters alternate between the heroine's perspective and that of her boss, whose brutal sexual harassment of her in the workplace looks like something else from his (and eventually her) point of view: it looks like falling helplessly in love. (Perhaps ominously, in this novel the modern context of workplace sexual harassment policies has been folded into the romance, lending their lovemaking a further charge of forbiddenness.) For her part, when she completed the *Fifty Shades* trilogy, E. L. James set about rewriting the whole thing from Christian's perspective, beginning with the novel called simply *Grey* (2015). As Cora Kaplan noted some time ago, against our habit of thinking about the mechanics of identification as a straight line between reader and character, especially a protagonist, it may instead be identification with a character system, a structure.[17] It might also be a mistake to think that that structure is indistinguishable from the non-textual ones upon which it is based.

For all that his wealth and power hold him above the humiliations of ordinary servile life, the alpha billionaire is after all "unmanned," drawn by force of his own attraction to the heroine into the role of protector, traditionally enough, but also caregiver and even, dare we say, nurturer. One of the repeated motifs of *Fifty Shades of Grey* and its sequels is Christian's constant, nagging insistence to Ana that she should *eat more*: "'Eat,' he says more sharply. 'Anastasia, I have an issue with wasted food ... eat.'" His obsessive concern for consumption in its original sense stems, we eventually learn, from his having grown up hungry, the child of a neglectful "crack whore" and victim of horrific abuse by her pimp.[18] *Fifty Shades of Grey* is in other words a trauma narrative. It asks us to see the pitiful underdog hiding inside the master of the universe, the hungry boy inside the ultimate consumer, with nary a sympathetic thought for the plight of that namelessly bad mother, known only by her epithet, who might have had her own story to tell. Imagining what that story might have been, we come to suspect that the "real" trauma at the heart of the novel, and perhaps of the alpha billionaire genre as a whole, is the existential threat of patriarchal capitalist violence, from the symbolic violence of demeaning and dehumanizing contempt to the physical violence of abuse, rape, and murder. The secondary trauma would be the discovery that your mother cannot finally protect you from that threat, inasmuch as she has been and remains subject to the same dangers, or worse, and has had to make her own accommodations.

In this context, the context of Christian as victim, the sexual pleasure he takes in hurting women who look like his mother is meant to seem understandable, if not as laudable as his desire to feed the world's poor. It is not a fundamental character flaw but a condition Ana can help him to heal, leading the way to the homely joys of what they together call "vanilla" sex. At the same time, such is the mobility of this allegorical figure that the fearful little boy is also a kind of stand-in mother to Ana, whose own mother is presented in the novel as a flighty and unreliable multiple divorcée. Christian's gradual willingness to supply emotional labor to Ana is no small part of the commodity being consumed, in a kind of return to the primal scene of literary comfort, the cozy bedtime story. Thus, while it is tempting to read him as little more than a poster boy for neoliberal capitalism, for *that* set of brutalities, he is also the symbolic vehicle by which that system is "softened" and made caring again in the little welfare state of a loving marriage.

Even so, there is surely a limit to the crypto-feminization of the alpha billionaire, a limit to the perhaps surprisingly polymorphous flexibility of his gender, which is in fact continually in the way of being *made one* in the smithy of pure masculine will. While Christian can seem surprisingly motherly at times, his main utility as an "alpha" is to offer symbolic resistance to the general "feminization" of life in a consumer economy, where all roads lead back to the docile bodies of the domestic sphere, and where emotional labor—the provision of good service—is the order of the day for workers of all genders. Consumerism constructs the world in expectation of a general receptivity on the part of shoppers and workers alike, rather than as the heroic extrusion of supply. The alpha billionaire responds to that feminization by asserting the authority of the unitary executive. As Christian tells Ana, "I own my company. I don't have to answer to a board," and from *Pride and Prejudice* to the present, independent wealth appears as a feature of the romance hero again and again.[19]

If it weren't so obvious, it would be quite astounding how faithful to this kind of man the genre is, how many modes of dependent masculinity it excludes from the hero slot. The psychic utility of the so-called authoritarian personality to those around him has been analyzed by Erich Fromm, Theodor Adorno, and others, and has been linked to a deep uneasiness on the part of the modern masses with the novelty of their own freedom.[20] To an extent more extreme than the world-unto-itself of marriage described by Luhmann, to "marry" the alpha leader in a psychological sense is to be absolved of the existential inconvenience of choice. Selling Ana on the idea of her own submission, Christian makes this perfectly explicit: "All those decisions—all the wearying thought processes behind them. The 'is this the right thing to do? Should this happen here? Can it happen now?' You wouldn't have to worry about any of that detail. That's what I'd do as your Dom."[21] Will she buy? Her decision is akin to that of the citizen of a democracy who contemplates voting in a dictatorship.[22]

The particular existential dilemma of "freedom of choice" most relevant to the romance novel is, however, a discernably distinct if adjacent one. It occurs not at the ballot box but at the intersection of human intimacy and consumer capitalism. It springs from the essential seriality of the latter's efforts to provide ever-novel forms of customer satisfaction, the drive toward which might at any point supersede loyalty to a given product. This is where the alpha's preternatural *decisiveness* comes in: "'You. Are. Mine,' he snarls, emphasizing each word."[23] So complete is his certainty that you are for him, and he for you, you can be sure he will stay with you forever. He will be your knight in shining armor tilting against time, warding off the arrival of new objects of his desire and yours.

In this sense, even as he admits to being the ultimate consumer, the alpha billionaire presents himself as a fantasy antidote to consumerism. That he—or a man much like him—does so for the habitual romance reader in *novel after novel*, again and again, is what gives away the game: the deepest problem, it turns out, is not that there are too many potential objects of desire, but that you have *but one life to live*, as they say, for pursuing them. And this, as we shall see, is where the romance genre's fundamental, as it were, *indecisiveness* comes in, its freedom from determination: set free, as a series of repeatable fictions, from the terminal linearity of real time, the novel offers itself as an ongoing, pleasurable existential supplement to inherently limited lives.

What will be surprising, perhaps, to anyone who thinks the alpha billionaire romance is uniquely incoherent or cynical in being founded on these paradoxes, is how central they have been to the historical unfolding of the novel form as such, which has only sometimes appeared in the form we call the realist novel but has always been deeply conditioned by the dictates of the real world.

Being and Time Management

What does it mean to say that the function of the novel is to attenuate the depressing limitations of embodied life? It means a lot more than to say, as we so often do, that novels—trashy novels in particular—offer an "escape" from that life, as though that escape weren't also necessarily an addition to it, a real experience among others.

To take the measure of the novel's serial addition to the life of the reader in properly literary-historical terms, it will be useful to revisit a distinction made by Fredric Jameson in *The Antinomies of Realism* (2013), where he reopens the discussion of what has seemed to many scholars and readers to be the genre's signature if much disputed feature. For Jameson, the rise of realism in the novel is to be explained in terms of an unresolved and possibly unresolvable struggle between, on the one hand, an original "narrative impulse" at work in any storytelling form, and, on the other, a new registration, beginning in the nineteenth century, of what he calls the "body's present," or *affect*, usually in the form of the closely described novelistic scene or setting.[24] The first disposes events in chronological order, sampling the raw material of human life and delineating meaningful destinies within it. Almost always operating in the past tense, it speaks of events completed and packaged as any one of the many kinds of story. The second produces a kind of pause in the march of time, a quality of *being there* in a richly embodied and distended present.

Of the two fundamental components of the novel, narration and affect, the latter is for him the more historically eventful—indeed more *novel*.[25] It is part of what distinguishes the genre from the narrative forms that preceded it, enabling it to project fictional worlds at once visceral and virtual because centered in the human sensorium.[26] It makes its most unmistakable appearance in literary naturalism, in the work of Émile Zola, and is embedded thereafter both in the intensity of modernist narrative experimentation *and* in genre fiction. Naturalism announces the revolutionary arrival of affect in literary history but is also inevitably the beginning of what, echoing Luhmann, Jameson calls its "codification." It occasions both the deep dive into the embodied psyche we find in James Joyce and serves "as a standard for the practice of mass culture and the best seller up to our own time and all over the world."[27] And it's true, genre fiction, no less than the high realist or naturalist or modernist novel, is geared to *set a scene*, and to encourage the reader's visceral participation in the fiction. At its extremes, it produces what Linda Williams has evocatively called "body genres"—genres associated, in the reading (or in her case, viewing), with the excretion of one or another human juice.[28] In that light, we can now see how much the contemporary romance novel owes to the arrival of literary naturalism, without necessarily being mistakable for an instance of it.

Think about it: in proximity to the so-called alpha male—a term borrowed from ethology, the study of animal pack behavior—love becomes visible as a matter of "chemistry," a matter of instinct triumphing over artificial social impediments such as rules against sexual harassment. So, too, the genre's lexicon of *falling—helplessly—madly* in love; its detailing of the insatiable *hunger* of body for body: looked at in a certain light, it can seem eerily similar to something we might find in a Jack London story, only moving it indoors. Both are what Jennifer Fleissner has taught us to think of as discourses of compulsion, where natural forces work not at the behest of but through the human, dragging us along in repetitive action.[29] At a minimum, then, we might speak of the historical co-emergence of "high" literary naturalism-cum-modernism and "trashy" romance.

Why that co-emergence? Following the lead of Goran Blix, we might begin to answer this question by noticing a lacuna in Jameson's account of the rise of affect: "Why does the formal

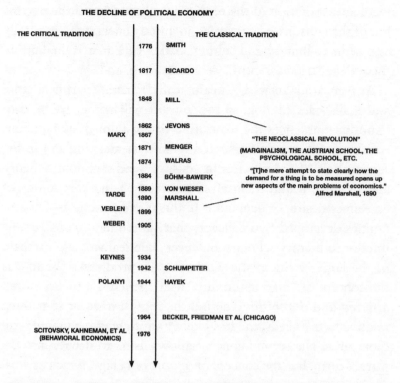

THE DECLINE OF POLITICAL ECONOMY

THE CRITICAL TRADITION		THE CLASSICAL TRADITION
	1776	SMITH
	1817	RICARDO
	1848	MILL
	1862	JEVONS
MARX	1867	
	1871	MENGER
	1874	WALRAS
	1884	BÖHM-BAWERK
	1889	VON WIESER
TARDE	1890	MARSHALL
VEBLEN	1899	
WEBER	1905	
KEYNES	1934	
	1942	SCHUMPETER
POLANYI	1944	HAYEK
	1964	BECKER, FRIEDMAN ET AL (CHICAGO)
SCITOVSKY, KAHNEMAN, ET AL (BEHAVIORAL ECONOMICS)	1976	

"THE NEOCLASSICAL REVOLUTION"
(MARGINALISM, THE AUSTRIAN SCHOOL, THE PSYCHOLOGICAL SCHOOL, ETC.

"[T]he mere attempt to state clearly how the demand for a thing is to be measured opens up new aspects of the main problems of economics."
Alfred Marshall, 1890

Classical and Critical Traditions in Economic Theory A schematic representation of classical and critical (Marxist, Institutionalist, Keynesian, Behaviorist, etc.) traditions in economics, isolating for consideration the so-called neoclassical or marginalist revolution of the second half of the nineteenth century.

impulse he calls 'scene' burst forth ex nihilo in the 1840s? And what would make it overpower the narrative substrate in less than a century? The implicit answer, of course, would be history, and the development of capitalism, but it's not clear what precise logic connects economics to formal aesthetic concerns."[30] That logic, I would like to suggest, is supplied by the gradual transformation of the economies of the Western world from ideologically *productivist* to ideologically *consumerist* ones. It is no accident, I think, that it is the naturalist novel—Zola's *Au Bonheur des Dames* (1883) and Theodore Dreiser's *Sister Carrie* (1900) preeminently—that first captures the sensory thrill of the luxury department store as the signal institution of the new consumerist regime. These projects are part and parcel of a general ideological rotation of the economic sphere toward the psychic life of the consumer, as revealed in a body of thought, generally anathema to literary and cultural critics, called "marginal utility theory" or "neoclassicism" (see figure on p. 131).[31]

As Amazon is related, genealogically, to the department store and mail-order catalog, so too, or so I will argue, are its contemporary practices the realization of a way of thinking about economic activity that emerged in Austria and England in the second half of the nineteenth century, when economic theory and practice found themselves centered on the psychology of consumer desire, or demand.[32] In this context, neoclassical economics developed two concepts that should be of considerable interest to literary scholars, however skeptical we might remain of the larger economistic worldview they express. The first is the concept of "marginal utility" itself, which is a theory of *relativized* and *diminishing* desire: the more I have of something relative to my needs, the less likely I am to want to pay for still more of it. The second concept allows us to go deeper into the novel's form. It is the concept of *opportunity cost*, which as we'll see is a concept of human finitude in time.

As noted by Ronald Schleifer, staging the question of value as one of marginal utility—of the relative desire of having *more* of something I already have some of—would seem to reflect a historical situation of relative abundance.[33] And sure enough, like novelists of the same period, the original neoclassical theorists looked upon an industrializing world whose awesome productive capacities were making the problem of subsistence per se a highly abstract and distant one. It was a problem for premodern societies only—elements of which, to be sure, could sometimes still be found in other parts of one's own city. Why, then, did the concept of scarcity play such a central role in neoclassical economics? As explained by Nicholas Xenos:

> The perception of a general condition of insufficiency is refracted through a prism of choices. Because we experience the necessity of choosing between alternatives, we see an affinity between the absolute neediness of someone experiencing hunger and the

relative neediness of someone who cannot have all of his wants supplied simultaneously.[34]

In a world of advertising and commercial spectacle, one might continually conceive of new and sometimes desperate wants, not all of which can immediately if ever be satisfied. This is *scarcity amid abundance*—that is, consumerism—in action. It is the psychodynamic of the *relatively lucky*, of the modern middle class in its broadest historical construal. As vividly portrayed by Zola and Dreiser alike, it is the occasion of a complex phenomenology of shopping, now often conducted online, from the prospective delectation we call browsing, to the comparison of commodities to each other and of each to its price tag, to the purchase decision, pro or con, and then on to various shades of satisfaction, indifference or regret.

Hence the importance to the theory of that proximate *other* thing that, having fatefully "pulled the trigger," one might conceivably have chosen to buy instead. The satisfaction forgone in *not* buying that other thing is what in the neoclassical tradition is called an *opportunity cost*. It also pertains to investments: the opportunity cost of investing a given sum in Amazon stock is the chance I forgo for gains that might have been won by investing in Google. No less than the commodity as theorized by Marx, it is a concept abounding in metaphysical niceties and theological subtleties. While it is born of the ambition to extend the reach of accounting logic further than ever before, even into the realm of the unreal, the *not* done, it is by the same token that place where the theory touches the limits of its coherence.[35] If it can justly claim a universal significance, in that everyone is required to make choices in at least a minimal sense—if only the choice to remain alive—it seems obvious that, historically, only for some people has life been explicitly defined *as* a series of personal choices, from the trivial (what should I order off the menu today?) to the more or less momentous (whom should I marry? what shall I do for a living?).

For this lucky bunch there remains one truly insolvable form of scarcity—a scarcity of *time*. In a culture of consumption there is no such thing as "free time," especially, ironically, for the most privileged among us, who are haunted by the *worth* of their hours, and accordingly live in a state of perpetual hurry.[36] "As an exceptional entrepreneur and major benefactor of our university, his time is extraordinarily precious—much more precious than mine," says Ana Steele of Christian Grey before she meets him. He is therefore "spending" vast sums on her even when he is not giving her first editions of Hardy novels or squiring her around in a helicopter.[37] In short: *the primordial scarcity eradicated in the arrival of industrial modernity returns as the specter of time-famine.* This is why we want fast delivery, and why the only good service is fast service. In apparent obedience to this rule, all the events of the first two volumes of the *Fifty Shades* trilogy leading to the betrothal of Ana and Christian, seven hundred-or-so pages worth of action, take place over only twenty-two days.

Although time had found a place in neoclassical theory from the beginning, in Carl Menger, who stressed that economic activity is always a provision for the future, and in Stanley Jevons, who notes that "we are in fact altogether the creatures of time," it took a while for the discourse to acknowledge all of the ways time can *distort* its idealized models—how, for instance, one might take so long making a purchase decision that the benefits of making the "right" decision are lost. It took even longer to acknowledge, as readers are so well positioned to know, that the act of consumption *itself* takes time, and that the time of consumption might be considered to have a cost. This is already implicit in Franklin's "time is money," a warning about the hidden cost of leisure, which we can now see as one of the original statements of the principle of opportunity cost.[38]

The concept came into its own, however, in the early twentieth-century work of the Austrian school of economics, the yield of its obsession with the problem of competing desires. The key thing to see about opportunity cost is that it is a fundamentally temporal concept. This is what distinguishes it from, more simply, cost, which can be thought of as a spatial one. If the time we had for satisfying our desires were endless, we could simply satisfy them in succession, finding the money for their purchase at our infinite leisure. But it is not so. As thinkers from Martin Heidegger to Martin Hägglund have brilliantly reminded us, time is *limited* in quantity, the medium of our being-unto-death, and relentlessly unidirectional in its entropic movement toward that end.[39] So, too, on a smaller scale, implicit in the very idea of "opportunities" is the sense that they come and go (as in, "*now* is your opportunity; these prices won't last!").

For Alfred Gell, whose impressive work *The Anthropology of Time* (1992) provided the spark for my train of thought here, this is what lends the concept of opportunity cost a philosophical depth he thinks anthropologists should take very seriously.[40] Indeed, for Gell, it exposes the sheer imposture of the traditional anthropological approach to temporality since Émile Durkheim, for whom time is only a culturally relative social construction. Gell advocates instead for the view that these constructions only make sense as different symbolic managements ("codifications," in our adopted lexicon) of an original physical time whose necessities are intuited and acknowledged in our sequential interactions with the physical world. And indeed, is there a place on Earth—other than in the anachronistically structured narrative—where one could cook a steak after eating it, or look forward to last year?

For Gell, far from simply discrediting cultural constructions of time, acknowledging the primordial friction between our somatic comprehension of physical time and its highly various symbolic managements is what lends the latter their interest as, in effect, practical-symbolic negotiations of the problem of opportunity cost; that is, of our ability to choose to do some things, but not all things, in a given period of time. These negotiations are therefore meditations on nothing less than the *fatedness* of human existence, the way it unfolds as the series of irreversible determinations, histories, happenings—that is, everything expressed in the term "narrative" as opposed to "affect." In other words, what Jameson and affect theorists tend to see in terms of human political potentiality—our unruly embodied state—is also our fundamental limitation. As such, the opportunity-cost concept points at something larger than the act of purchase or even investment per se. You can't buy one dollar's worth of kale and one dollar's worth of chocolate with the same dollar bill; but neither can you walk to the left and to the right simultaneously or marry both of your suitors at once. You must choose. (Or at least *seem* to yourself to be choosing, whatever the status of that choice might be in the ultimate philosophical reckoning of free will.)

Now, it goes almost without saying that that we might bring the idea of opportunity cost to bear on the everyday economy of literature, but it is worth pausing to consider the way it frames the relation of individual readers to that economy. There is, first of all, the book you can't afford to buy because you bought the one you did. Next is the book you can't "afford" to read in another sense, because you don't have the time. In the Age of Amazon, a very long book can often be acquired for very little money, but the opportunity cost of reading a long book, say *Infinite Jest*, can seem well-nigh infinite in its own right. To read it is to see weeks pass by without your having time to read anything else. So, too, like the air we breathe, the monetary cost of works of classic literature now approaches zero. Once they were only accessible in expensive leather-bound editions or from the circulating library. Then they appeared as cheap Oxford or Penguin paperbacks. Now, finally, as un-copyrighted e-texts widely available on the internet, they are approaching the status of a gift of nature. And yet the existential opportunity cost of reading the classic remains as high as it has ever been, arguably higher, inasmuch as the number of books we are *not* reading while we read it has, in this time of literary hyperabundance, soared.

This is Ana's dilemma as she opens the British Library App on her new iPad, worrying that she could get lost in it for an eternity. "So many books, so little time," reads a charming slogan, attributed by the internet to Frank Zappa, which has found its way onto T-shirts and posters. It is a sentiment anyone reading this is likely to share, an expression both of the abundance of our literary opportunities and the profound limitation of our literary lives. We cannot read more than one book at a time, not literally, and we will not live long enough to read even a fraction of the books we might enjoy reading. The overstuffed Kindle e-reader or iPad is at once a world-historically powerful condensation of potential literary experience and a little tombstone prophesying the rapidly approaching day of our death. No wonder, then, that so much of Amazon's effort, once it has led the customer to its infinite online trough of goods, is to find ways to get her to click "buy" rather than stare in irritated awe at the number of objects she has to choose between; these include the ratings system, recommendation algorithms, free delivery, and assurance of an easy return process.

What makes the concept of opportunity cost even more interesting, however, and so tempting to think about as something *internal* to literary form, is the aura of counterfactuality, if not fictionality, it injects into daily psychic life. As Gell puts it:

> Opportunity costs arise from the fact that the representations, or conceptual models we make of the "real" world, represent the world as being capable of being otherwise than we believe it to be, actually. The world is as it is, but we think it could be otherwise, and it may be otherwise than we think. Although there are no "real" opportunity costs, because the real world is not in an alternativeness relationship with itself, from the standpoint of our cognitive representations of the world, opportunity costs are very real indeed ... [O]ur evaluations of both objects and events in the actual world depend crucially on our notion of what constitute the alternatives to those objects and events, in the penumbra of non-actual worlds surrounding this one.[41]

In this passage are the makings of a substantially new account of the realism of the novel, which we are here reminded was after all realist *fictionality*. For Catherine Gallagher, the appearance and codified embrace of the latter as an aesthetic value in the eighteenth century was coincident with an emergent attitude of skepticism in early mercantile capitalism, where, in the interest of not being taken for a ride by con men, it was important to be able to separate the plausibility of a story from actual belief in it.[42] The fictionality of opportunity cost is perhaps no less a product of capitalism, but can be attributed to its conceptualization of life as a series of costly choices rather than to its cultivation of a skeptical attitude.

It is the job of fiction, any fiction, to be the medium of alternatives to the actual world inhabited by readers, which fictions amount, in their consumption, to affective experiential add-ons or supplements. For what is fiction but a special case of the "penumbra of non-actual worlds" that surround the real world? What is a novel but a series of artful reflections on the problem of opportunity cost as a function of the unidirectionality of time? What is it, finally, but an exercise in virtual existential time management expressed in and as the labile, at times even anachronistic, relation between story (the "natural" order of events) and discourse (the order in which these events are narrated)? This is the service it performs as a commodity, again and again.

Romantic Realism

Are romance novels realistic, then? Apparently not, but the nature of their unrealism is more difficult to pinpoint than one might expect. Certainly, it is of a different order than we find in other sectors of the contemporary genre system such as epic fantasy, horror, or science fiction, which traffic in physical impossibilities like easy travel to other planets, efficacious magic spells, ancient curses, zombies, vampires, and ghosts. Outside its paranormal variant, the unrealism of romance is not one of worlds built entirely otherwise but of relative idealization and improbability—of improbably rich, handsome, and youthful men and the women who love them. Reminiscent of the princes and princesses of fairy-tale and Arthurian romance, these characters are not the ordinary people critical tradition has taught us belong at the center of proper novels, although the heroine might modestly think herself one. And yet their possibility can be granted within the bounds of the natural order, which order after all allows for remarkable cases, and even a few melodramatic coincidences. If the act of centering a novel on just *these* sorts of extraordinary people betrays the presence of literary conventions mediating the relations between the "common reader" and the otherwise familiar world she sees represented in a work like *Fifty Shades of Grey*, most modern romance novels are still substantially more realistic than their plainly fantastic forebears in pre-novelistic "romance" in its broadest historical sense.

If the typical romance novel is a *romance*, it is also a *novel*, and at least outside the subgenre of paranormal romance, it shows an at least mild aspiration toward "formal realism" long associated with that modern form.[43] When E. L. James took to the internet to recast Stephenie Meyer's *Twilight* novels as *Master of the Universe*, later changing the title to *Fifty Shades of Grey*, aging its heroine by four or five years and removing the vampires, she made a work originally directed to a young adult readership more "relatable," in contemporary publishing parlance, to the lives of adult women. If Eva Illouz is correct, many of these women proceeded to use the work as a kind of sexual self-help book, sending worldwide sales of BDSM sex toys soaring.[44]

That use of the book is a useful reminder that the "realest" thing about any encounter with fiction is the body holding the volume or device, followed closely by the volume or device itself. That affective body takes what it will from the affecting text, launching from it, launching into it, firing up the psychosomatic fantasy circuits while remaining subject to socioeconomic determination and physical law. The reader imagines being rich enough to own a jet plane, yacht, and Aspen vacation home in which to wear her expensive shoes, and most likely will never have them for reasons we could enumerate. Even more confining are the strictures of nature, including most obviously the second law of thermodynamics, the law of entropy, the law of ever-encroaching disorder and decay. The latter is the antithesis of romance's "happily ever after," assuring us of love's dissolution in time, whether tomorrow or sixty years from now or whenever.

In its structural fixation on youth, in its imaginary construction of a love bond "for all time," but especially in its commitment to the *happy ending*, the romance novel imagines a kind of triumph over time, with the barest acknowledgment of the end predicted in the ritual phrase "till death do us part." Put differently, it conducts an ongoing, intimate argument with death as the ultimate limit. This is never more obvious, ironically, than in paranormal romance, in which death is everywhere but means almost nothing, means *immortality* of all things. In the vampire romance, dying is a precondition for living forever. In the ordinary romance, by contrast, but no less unrealistically in a way, dying is something that simply cannot happen to the would-be bride and groom, whose trajectory is rather toward marriage and the reproduction of the social body.

If death is still everywhere in the atmosphere of a work like *Fifty Shades of Grey*, it, too, is transformed into a kind of vivacious transcendence. In their generic perfection, Ana and Christian are empty forms, he of "Grey," she of "Steele," and absent any tint or taint of the mongrel quality of modern democratic life.[45] That burden is carried by Ana's college friend and Christian's easily vanquished rival, José, whose Latino heritage would appear to be carelessly derived from the Native American/Werewolf identity of the same rival figure in Meyer's *Twilight*. *Fifty Shades of White*: the comforts of the generic and the racially normative, as they have been brilliantly explored in Lauren Berlant's work on popular melodrama, are in force here as well, but they drive toward an even deeper comfort, a state of paradoxically passionate indifference.[46]

But death is only the most final and total of the many limitations of embodiment that infuse works of novelistic realism, *precisely to the extent that they are realistic*. Here, in the interplay between these limitations and the "imaginative possibilities" of fiction, is where the novel asserts itself as a commodity with a specific existential utility: it is a therapeutic instrument for managing the problem of opportunity cost. The realistic and the romantic or fantastic in literature stand at two poles in the calculus of trade-offs in a transaction between referential gravity, or pseudo-relevance to the reader's life, and something like escape velocity, freedom from natural and social law. The utopian negation specific to therapeutic realism is a *minimally negative negation*. In positive terms, it is a mode of chastened fantasy. If the very idea of *realist fiction* can, as Gallagher notes, seem a contradiction in terms, then the concept of opportunity cost locates that contradiction on the border between the actual and non-quite-actual in psychic life.

If I nonetheless want to retain the mark of the utopian in the term I would offer as a defamiliarizing re-inscription of "realist fiction," *sub-utopian counterfactuality*, it is only out of respect for the extraordinary reach of utopian thought as theorized by Ernst Bloch. In his own book on utopian science fiction, Jameson points us to a distinction in Bloch's encyclopedic *The Principle of Hope* (1954–59) between the utopian program and the utopian impulse.[47] The first, whether fictional or real, is characterized by an aspiration toward totality in the transformation of extant social relations, and on the closure of the new dispensation to influences from the corrupted past. The second is all but omnipresent in the human psyche, a fugitive, unsystematic principle of hope that infiltrates all our imaginings, and is compatible with the most ineffectually fleeting fantasies and modest projects of reform.

This sounds congruent with the phenomenology of opportunity cost, but leaves out something equally crucial thereto, something we might call the "principle of hopelessness." It is attuned both to the real possibility of disappointment or even disaster as the consequence of our choices, and to the certainty that even the best of them are only temporary diversions from a mortal end. Only by way of this dialectical inclusion of hopelessness can we do justice to late nineteenth-century realist fiction, in which some of the greatest achievements in the history of the novel were reached by subjecting romance to the *test of time* in a literal sense. What we might think of as the inherent buoyancy of fictionality is weighed down in realist fiction not simply by its quasi-referentiality, its duty to the real, but also by its recognition that even the "freest" of the choices characters make will have binding consequences for them.

Consider, for instance, Henry James's *Portrait of a Lady* (1881).[48] Many if not most instances of the marriage plot in the history of the novel are rightly seen as fictions of opportunity cost —indeed I would say it is the literary figure of opportunity cost par excellence. Participants in the marriage market are required to make highly consequential choices under time pressure, leaving them to wonder ever after *what might have been*. Who will she choose? Which one does she want? The right one? The wrong one? Was it a mistake to submit to the patriarchal heterosexual reproductive order to begin with?[49] Would it have been better to remain unmarried? Fascinated in particular—as the eight hundred pages of hemming and hawing in Anthony Trollope's *Can You Forgive Her?* (1865) amply attests—by the idea that a young *woman* might act as a subject as well as object of the marriage market, the nineteenth-century novel was rarely less than realistic about the way the emotional consequences of matrimonial decision are thoroughly mixed with economic ones. This attitude made the best-selling writer of the day, the gleefully unrealistic Marie Corelli, sad enough to write a pamphlet decrying the problem called *The Modern Marriage Market* (1898).

And yet James's novel, alike with other instances of what we can call the *bad* marriage plot, takes this meditation on erotic opportunity cost to a new level. The novel's profound understanding of the paradoxes of freedom has been celebrated in the critical tradition, and the most casual glance confirms that this freedom is a freedom of choice. Indeed, the word "choice" and its grammatical variants appear no less than fifty times in the novel, usually in relation to its choosy protagonist, Isabel Archer. One of its more interesting uses occurs after Gilbert Osmond has declared his love for her, the third man to do so in the novel:

> "Oh don't say that, please," she answered with an intensity that expressed the dread of having, in this case too, to choose and decide. What made her dread great was precisely the force which,

as it would seem, ought to have banished all dread—the sense
of something within herself, deep down, that she supposed to be
inspired and trustful passion. It was there, like a large sum stored
in a bank—which there was a terror in having to begin to spend.
If she touched it, it would all come out.⁵⁰

And sure enough, in this instance, to marry Osmond is literally to give him all her money. For the realist novel, choices
are only free before they have been made, and even the free
expression of an authentic passion can be figured as a possibly bankrupting expense in the sense that it forecloses upon all
future "purchases."

By contrast to Trollope's *Can You Forgive Her?*, which dilates
the period of courtship and indecision, James's *Portrait* traces
the destiny of its heroine long after the fateful choice has been
made. In more ways than one, Isabel begins in a situation of
abundance: she has an abundance of suitors and then, having
been made the heir to a great fortune, an abundance of money
to offer them. She chooses against Lord Warburton, then
against Caspar Goodwood, finally accepting the proposal of
Osmond. He is a supremely physically attractive but, as it turns
out, singularly awful and what we would now call sexist man.
"Marriage is always a grave risk," she tells her friend Ralph
Touchette before the deed is done, ignoring his "prevision" of
her matrimonial misery. She makes her choice and accepts the
consequences. They are assessed in what many have judged one
of the great sequences in the history of the novel. James himself
pointed the reader in this direction: in the preface he wrote for
the New York edition, he describes his intent to "show what an
'exciting' inward life may do for the person leading it even while
it remains perfectly normal," and points us to Isabel's "extraordinary meditative vigil" while the rest of the household is asleep
as being the best "application of that ideal."⁵¹

To be sure, the bottom line of that vigil is remarkably blunt
and depressing: "They were strangely married, at all events, and
it was a horrible life." And yet the very dilation of the thought
processes ("her vigil took no heed of time ...") by which this

conclusion is reached and savored is tinged with its own value, lending her situation the barest patina, even now, of salvific sub-utopian counterfactuality. And so, too, for the reader of this scene: James licenses us to see in Isabel's vigil a representation of reading itself, that other thing we might do by the fire into the wee hours. Our meditation on her fate is a mediated meditation, no doubt, and spares us the actual awfulness of Isabel's situation. That distance allows the conversion of awfulness into art by whose means we pleasurably increase our, as we say, wealth of experience, compressing several years of Isabel's life into several hours of reading.

If James's novel still leaves something to be desired as a fiction of opportunity cost, this is because of Isabel Archer's commitment to the finality of her decision, her utter lack of interest in contemplating, say, what life might have been like with Warburton. To this extent, her choice is revealed to have been an *ethical* and not purely *consumerist* one. She is regretful, but she does not as it were indulge those regrets by imaginatively canceling them. That privilege is reserved for the novelist himself, who, as James put it in the preface to the novel, has the "power ... to range through all the differences of the individual relation to its general subject matter, all the varieties of outlook on life." Instead, her hellish situation is figured as a literal enclosure: "She had taken all the first steps in purest confidence, and then she had suddenly found the infinite vista of a multiplied life to be a dark, narrow alley with a dead wall at the end."[52]

It would only be conventional to argue for James as a precursor to literary modernism, but here we can make that claim in a very specific way: what we call the modernist novel is the effort to retain the "infinite vista of a multiplied life" through to the end of the story, even as it in general remains wholly committed to realist canons of probability. Both arise from conditions of post-scarcity, but modernism is the form that would hold choices in therapeutic suspension, entertaining the problem of opportunity cost without, if possible, fully paying it.

How else could we explain the form of a novel like Virginia Woolf's *Mrs. Dalloway*?[53] If critics have not in any of the

750-some articles on the novel listed in the Modern Language Association database read it as an instance of the marriage plot, then no wonder. The rituals of courtship and decision animating that form have, in this novel, happened long in the past. They can only linger as consequences that continue to reverberate in the novel's setting on a single fine day in June after the end of the Great War. In that setting, after the temporary privations of the war years, London is becoming once again the scene of abundance. It is an abundance of flowers, clothing, and other commodities, to be sure. But as though to produce a neoclassical human equivalent of this abundance, it is also depicted as the scene of a multiplicity of human desires, decisions, disappointments, and satisfactions—the scene, that is, of a thriving "experience economy."

While James's *Portrait* commits itself to the limited perspective of its heroine, *Mrs. Dalloway* is all over the place, virtuosically shifting narrative points of view even as it methodically tracks the passage of the day from morning to evening. That said, at its core are two marriages: the marriage of poor Lucrezia to Septimus Smith, the suicidal veteran, and, most centrally, the marriage of Clarissa to Richard Dalloway. The latter marriage is what has left Peter Walsh in a state of emotional suspension over the many years he has been away in India. Where Isabel makes her choice and lives with it, Woolf's spouses do not cease to entertain the alternatives to the decisions they have made.

For Clarissa and Peter in particular, this is the obsessive refrain that rings throughout the day, layering the richness of their sensory experiences of blue sky and urban bustle with a constant meditation on *what might have been* if different choices had been made all those years ago: "So she would still find herself arguing in St. James's Park, still making out that she had been right—and she had too—not to marry [Peter]. For in marriage a little license, a little independence there must be between people living together day in and day out in the same house ..." In other words, the opportunity cost in choosing Richard over Peter, while real, has been lower, because in marrying the boring Richard, Clarissa has maintained a kind of freedom even within the bounds of matrimony. As though refracted through the self-effacing consciousness of the narrator, the marriage plot appears again shortly thereafter in the mind of the people-watching Mrs. Dempster as she observes young Maisie Johnson: "You'll get married, you're pretty enough, thought Mrs. Dempster," whose own husband, we gather, is an alcoholic.[54]

Mrs. Dempster's regrets are then, as it were, handed off once again to Mrs. Dalloway as she suddenly encounters Peter in the flesh: "Now of course, thought Clarissa, he's enchanting! Now I remember how impossible it was ever to make up my mind —and why did I make up my mind—not to marry him? she wondered, that awful summer?" Without exactly speaking these thoughts to Peter, Clarissa manages to communicate them to him, setting him off on his own reverie of what might have been, which is then silently handed back to her: "Take me with you, Clarissa thought impulsively, as if he were starting directly upon some great voyage; and then, next moment, it was as if the five acts of a play that had been very exciting and moving were now over and she had lived a lifetime in them and had run away, had lived with Peter, and it was now over."[55]

This is indeed the purest literary expression one might hope to find of matrimonial opportunity cost held in imaginary suspension by the condensed lifetimes of fiction. It is a thing, as Alfred Gell might have said if he wrote like Virginia Woolf, of "visions which proffer great cornucopias full of fruit to the solitary traveler, or murmur in his ear like sirens lolloping away on the green sea waves ... Such are the visions that ceaselessly float up, pace beside, put their faces in front of, the actual thing ..."[56] These penumbral visions are, as Woolf and Gell would agree, a way of managing the intractable problem of the scarcity of time.

Even so, even as the weight of that final determination cannot be denied, neither can the wonderfully weightless-seeming mobility that Woolf creates between subjectivities, which are sampled here almost as flowers are by bees. Comparing this novel to a mass-market romance novel cannot help but throw into relief its relative *singularity* as a work of art in a literal sense. What Woolf would accomplish in one virtuosic novel—essentially, a comprehensive windfall of new experience, worthy of being read again and again—the romance novel can only do piecemeal, serially, one roughly similar book after another. As a worthy member of "the canon"—a thing Amazon has no particular relation to at all except as a list of books that students tend to purchase—one could almost forget *Mrs. Dalloway*'s deep continuity with its opposite in the book market, at least as regards prestige: the *book-as-serial iteration*. While the modernist novel is a medium of internal multiplication and totalization, the romance is as we have seen a story of numerical reduction, from the Fifty to the One, *again and again*.

Coda: Technologies of Choice

A mainstay of the market in children's literature throughout the 1980s and early '90s, the ninety-three entries in the *Choose Your Own Adventure* series of books had its origin, their creator Edward Packard tells us, in the incessant demands of his children to be told stories night after night.[57] It was storytelling by customer demand, requiring, as in the market of contemporary genre fiction, constant minor variation on established models. But rarely has customer demand so interestingly determined the form of fiction as in the series that grew from Packard's parenting, which embedded that seriality in its form. On the occasion of the purchase and renaming by Bantam Books of what had been a small-press venture called *The Adventures of You*, Packard published *The Cave of Time: Choose Your Own Adventure #1* (1979). Because it could not count on the young reader's familiarity with this innovative form of storytelling, it begins with a "Warning!!!!":

> Do not read this book straight through from beginning to end! These pages contain many different adventures you can go on in the Cave of Time. From time to time as you go along, you will be asked to make a choice. Your choice might lead to success or

disaster! The adventures you take are a result of your choice. *You* are responsible because *you* choose! After you make your choice, follow the instructions to see what happens to you next. Remember—you cannot go back![58]

Not, that is, until you do what every young reader was expected to do, which is to start the novel again upon one of its provisional conclusions and make different choices. If it is impossible to miss the declension in literary quality from *Mrs. Dalloway* to a book like this, neither should we miss the way it literalizes some of the aspirations of its high modernist precursor, making them available for mass consumption. By the same token, the series contains even in its modestly "technological" form the kernel promise of consumer electronics as a supplier of a mediated variety of life forms and events; of ever more access to affective-existential add-ons. The question is whether it is we who use electronics or they who use us; whether our aggressive drive to tune in isn't, in fact, aggressively solicited from us by the grid. The accumulation of web-connected iPads, MacBooks, and BlackBerries in *Fifty Shades of Grey* is truly prodigious, and provokes the question of their relation to the whips and straps and such, the instrumentalities of BDSM; the gadgets in the novel are the very medium of the discourse of passionate love, but are by the same token a place where that discourse is materially interwoven with dreary office communication; and thus also, as it happens, with the designs of Ana's psychotic sexual abuser boss, Jack Hyde.

Addressing the reader in the second person and present tense, a book like *Cave of Time* is notable not for the virtuosic narrative mobility of point of view, but for the effort to build that mobility into the novel's form in such a way as to make it the responsibility of the young reader:

You step back, feeling confused and helpless. You wish it were just a dream. You retrace your steps a way, trying to think clearly. You know that your only chance to get out of the cave is to follow one of the two branches before you.

If you follow the right branch, turn to page 33.
If you follow the left branch, turn to page 35.[59]

And yet, as you can see, that young reader is also taught a lesson in *ir*responsibility. Not only is the commercial-grade existentialism of the novel's insistence that "*you* are responsible because *you* choose" hedged by the possibility of what on the playground is called a do-over, the decisions one makes in the Cave of Time are, as we see here, strikingly arbitrary, there being no apparent intent to instruct the young reader in choosing wisely or morally toward better ends. For this novel, a life choice is like a throw of the dice in which we are somehow responsible for the number that comes up.

This is something *The Cave of Time*—as though brought to a higher level of self-reflexivity by the series' entry into the publishing big time—reinforces with the surplus conceit of the titular cave, entry of which transports "you" to a different point in history, from the medieval period to colonial times to the Civil War to a perfect society of the future in where "your room contains a computer terminal that enables you to select any movie or other program you desire from over 10,000 possibilities. There are even films where you are the main character and you can make choices as to what will happen next in the story."[60] Such was the future seen from 1979, and so it came to pass that, by the late 1990s, with the advent of video games, the whole series had come to seem antiquated even as the cultural logic of Choose Your Own Adventure lived stubbornly on.

For instance, if one visits the Kindle Store of the present day, one sees it deployed in works like Kristy Flowers's self-published novel *Jane Murray: My Open Marriage* (see figure on p. 150). Facilitated by the device's linking technology, which obviates the tedious flipping through pages of a book, it bills itself as an "Interactive Pick-Your-Path Erotica with Multiple Endings." In a work like this, the long development of the romantic marriage plot from capture to coverture to companionship and contract reaches one of its logical conclusions in the suggestion that,

Kristy Flowers, Jane Murray: My Open Marriage—Live the Sexual Dream! (2015)

sexually at least, a commitment to marriage needn't have any
opportunity costs associated with it at all. The erotic appeal
of your husband having become *marginal*, you needn't ask
for a no-fault divorce; you can simply choose and choose and
choose again, and never will your marriage be the worse for
your doing so:

> It all started about a half a year ago. I told Henry that I wanted
> a divorce. He was shocked at first and we spent the entire night
> talking about it … I realized that while I loved Henry, I also
> craved to have sex with other men. I wanted to have an orgy.
> I wanted to have an affair. He nodded and listened intently. He
> then opened his mouth and made one suggestion: "why don't we
> just remove the guilt?"
>
> It was a simple but ingenious solution … It would save our
> marriage. Henry however had one condition; that I would tell
> him the details about every single man I slept with.

So—a marriage saved by its rupture of sexual monopoly,
monogamy, monotony. And also by storytelling, which makes
Jane's narrated experiences the shared, if mediated, property
of her admirably un-jealous husband. Even here, though, one's
pathway through sexual adventure wouldn't make any sense
except as bound in and by time. That's why you, on behalf of
Jane, are forced to choose your path through the day, however

many times over, rather than having all of your satisfactions
at once. Your job is no help: "Ugh ... I hated how I couldn't
control my own time ... Underneath that peaceful buzz [at the
office], it was a bloody battle for the next promotion." As lunch-
time arrives at Jane's office, what should you do? Living on the
clock set by your employer, and by nature, you only have one
hour. Do you:

Go do a little shopping – [click here]
Go eat lunch with Rachel – [click here]
Search for fuck buddies on your phone – [click here][61]

All three choices are intended to set you on the road to consumer satisfaction, but each has its opportunity cost, and only
one will lead to the best orgasm you've ever had.

Others will lead to distinctly lesser outcomes. One will find
you performing fellatio on the manager of the store you tried to
shoplift some sunglasses from; another will take you unpleas-
antly but survivably past your sexual limits. And then there is
the time when, having made a string of really poor choices, you
find yourself being assaulted by that fuck buddy you contacted
on Craigslist on your phone. In fact, in sudden violation of the
law of genre, he appears to be a serial killer:

Something warm trickled down my neck. Was that my blood?
    "Well, I guess I have to finish what I started."
    He hit me again. I felt a crack ... did he break my skull? I
didn't close my eyes—but I couldn't see anything either. Was my
brain incapable of receiving signals from my eyes?
    The world grew dark.
    END
    [Click here to go back to the start][62]

I suppose some solace could be taken from the fact that this
is a technologically remediable horror, but not much. Clicking
back to the start and choosing lunch with Rachel doesn't really
make it go away. Perhaps it is because the looming threat of

violence at the hands of yet another Jack Hyde is not simply the unlucky outcome of a series of blind choices, but a structural element of the economic system in and from which women seek pleasure enough to make life worth living.

4

Unspeakable Conventionality

The Perversity of the Kindle

Mother Genre

There is a case to be made for self-published Adult Baby Diaper Lover (ABDL) erotica as the quintessential Amazonian genre of literature, as strong as some other candidates—epic science fiction among them—might be. It all depends what aspect of Amazon one decides to put at the center of one's inquiry. Is it the great, quasi-imperial sprawl of the company's many technical and logistical achievements, its seemingly unbounded ambition to multinational if not multiplanetary commercial presence? Or is it instead the cozy scene of consumption, the scene of *fulfillment*, the home?

To the extent it is the latter, the erotic genre featuring the infantilization of the hero—often, but not always, he is the arrogant alpha male type featured in more conventional romances—and hyper-maternalization of the heroine who lives to suckle him provides a concentrated image of the company's fabled "customer obsession," the way it attempts, as the mother does with her child, to minimize the delay between demand and gratification. Doing so, it inspires in the customer a sense of dependent well-being, or *commodity* in the archaic affective sense (see figure on p. 154).

ABDL Erotica

In "Help Wanted: Adult Baby Diaper Lover," part of the
Mommy Claire Chronicles—Volume II (2017), a handsome jerk
nicknamed Chris Alpha is lured into the bathtub by a mysteri-
ously alluring older woman he thinks he can seduce, Mommy
Claire. Instead it is the first step in his rapid transformation into
Little Girl Chrissy:

> She took extra care drying me off and it's strange but I could
> feel the love in her effort ... I closed my eyes, enjoying her atten-
> tion. That's when I felt the soft smooth skin of her breast against
> my face. It was very comforting and when her nipple grazed my
> cheek, I did what came natural, suckling her into my mouth and
> feeding like my inner child needed nourishment. Mommy Claire
> cuddled me while I nursed on her breast and it felt wonderful. If
> I had any concerns in life they were gone at that moment. It truly
> was blissful.[1]

It's all so sweet, although not without its menace, as that
loving care becomes a kind of bondage. Indeed, with its shifting
of the "dom" role from the alpha male to the mother, the ultimate service provider, ABDL erotica is a helpful reminder that
Amazon's customer obsession is ultimately an investment in its
own market power, in what I called in chapter 1 its posture of
servile domination. Taking the image of the patriarchal power
as we find it in *Fifty Shades of Grey* (2011) and turning it inside

out, the mommy dom is in some ways merely a softer agent than he of consumer "lock-in," or customer loyalty, possessing, as this text has it, "some magical quality that made me feel all safe and warm inside, a place I never wanted to leave."[2]

The mommy dom fantasy is also a reminder of the global actuality of mothering, the labor of childcare practiced far and wide, which is the precondition of the survival and healthy development toward adulthood of every single human being. Claimed in ABDL narratives for its pre-oedipal erotic potential, it conceives of the usual genital-to-genital sex act as comparatively limited—the "thing about Mommy love is that it can make a man feel good all the time"—even as it imposes its own limits: "I tried to position my cock to enter her but that was not to be.[3] 'Little boys don't get to fuck Mommy,' she said with a sly smile."[4] As an agent of his blissful relaxation and, to be sure, eventually also of orgasm if not inside her, Mommy's erotic ministrations are nonetheless symbolically retractable at a moment's notice, leaving in their wake an image of purest wholesomeness. It is the wholesomeness of mother love and also of domestic provision via Amazon, which nobody would accuse of being a sexy company, as cheerfully phallic as its logo might be (see figure below).

That this structure of alternating patriarchal and matriarchal, oedipal and pre-oedipal eroticism is embedded deeper in the company's corporate soul than a fringe genre alone can prove is suggested by the history of the Kindle reading device it introduced to the market in late 2007. Nothing short of epochal in

The Amazon Logo The smiling phallus. Ever bending upward, it stretches from A to Z, disseminating utility across the entire span of effable needs.

its significance for Amazon's relation to contemporary literary life, it came as a result of Jeff Bezos's recognition that the direct digital download of media products successfully pioneered by Apple's iTunes could be the future of books, too, but only if there were a device somewhat like the iPod music player to make it so. Produced under the guidance of former Apple hardware engineer Gregg Zehr over the course of three years at Lab126, a secretive Silicon Valley facility founded for the purpose, the Kindle brand now accompanies the consumption of a sizable and relatively stable percentage of the books purchased in the United States, and a much larger percentage than that of works of genre fiction.[5] Although the Kindle has by no means killed off the print book, as some at first feared (or hoped), it does direct our attention to the fact that print textuality is now but one manifestation of an otherwise comprehensively digital existence for literature, beginning with its composition as a computer file.[6] A digital existence is a liquid existence, something like mother's milk, flowing to the scene of need.

Imitative most directly of earlier, weaker efforts on the part of other companies to produce an electronic reading device, "Project Fiona," as it was code-named at Lab126, was also importantly inspired by Neal Stephenson's novel *The Diamond Age: Or, A Young Lady's Illustrated Primer* (1995).[7] In this novel, a work of science fiction, Fiona is the daughter of a later twenty-first-century nano-engineer responsible for the creation of the interactive book of the novel's title, a book that, coming to know its young reader as an individual, evolves and changes with her over the years as she grows. Composed of "smart paper," into which has been condensed "about a billion separate processors," the book is nonetheless not an autonomous device but a connected one, and less a textbook than a virtual nursery and school.[8] Many of the most significant interactions with it are guided not by artificial intelligence but a real woman, a "ractor" contracted to supply its voice in real time. When a copy falls into the hands of a grubby Dickensian waif, little Nell, the ractor Miranda becomes a provider of the maternal nurturance the girl does not receive from her derelict mother and a series of horrifically abusive boyfriends. (A version of the same bad-mother figure stands in the background of Christian Grey in *Fifty Shades*, driving his sadistic abuse of women who look like her.) In this sense, only fully realized when, in 2019, Amazon introduced its Kindle Kids edition, complete with a colorful cover and subscription to a dedicated children's book download service, the Kindle was first imagined as a kind of portable mother and schoolteacher.

While Nell does not, as far as we know, pleasure herself in the company of her Primer, as so many users of electronic devices putatively now do, the novel is otherwise not shy about drawing a link between technological mediation and sexual fantasy, devising a complex plot involving the sexual transmission of cultural as well as genetic information in its retro-futuristic Chinese setting, where individualistic "phyles" like the Neo-Victorian New Atlantis rub shoulders with others, including the communitarian Celestial Kingdom. As, in a sense, the ideological operating system of the Kindle, which would in fact be manufactured in China, this commitment to *intimate mediation* figures the device as a fetish, but also as a symptom of that larger and more abstract-seeming ideality, customer satisfaction. Indeed, for Amazon, the obdurate physicality of the device, as of the traditional print book, is secondary to its continuously interactive provision of digitally mediated service of any and all kinds. This is why it was happy, eventually, to offload Kindle functionality to other devices as an app, the better to facilitate universal access to the company's increasingly many digital wares. The same of course is true of its fantastically successful line of Amazon Echo interactive speaker devices, supplied with an agreeably female if not maternal voice called Alexa. These devices, we can perhaps surmise, are less important to the company as a profit center in their own right than as deep infiltrators of domestic space and mechanisms of further lock-in to the Prime ecosystem.

As exceptions that prove the rule, these devices make clear how, for all its sprawl, Amazon produces very little in the traditional industrial sense, the overwhelming bulk of the enterprise being devoted to one or another form of warehousing, sales, and fulfillment, including, with Amazon Web Services, the warehousing of data. For this reason, analytical frameworks derived from the Marxist account of industrial production alone, while relevant, run the risk of overlooking much of the specificity of its operations, and even more so their cultural significance.

To be sure, the fate of Amazon, like that of any business enterprise, will ultimately be determined by its success in profiting off the labor of its hundreds of thousands of employees, but what makes the company distinct is its penetration of the home, the scene not of production but of social reproduction. As the process by which the body of the worker is, as it were, taken into the shop—fed and rested and re-clothed, not to mention reproduced in a literal biological sense in his offspring—before being submitted to the wear and tear of the workday again the next morning, social reproduction played a crucial conceptual role in Marx's account of capitalism, establishing the baseline of the subsistence wage. Even so, it was something about which he had relatively little of substance to say, perhaps because it seemed the static or unoriginal part of a system otherwise characterized by its convulsive historical novelty. Giving short shrift in particular to the women who have done and continue to do most of the unwaged labor of domestic care without which the global economy would grind to a whining halt, and do so under conditions not of their own choosing, Marx's account has been helpfully supplemented by what has come to be called social reproduction theory.[9]

SRT refuses to "black box" this most crucial precondition of the capitalist mode of production or naturalize it as a given. Instead it provides tools with which to link the exploitation of labor in the workplace to everything else, including the exploitation-at-remove of the superficially autonomous domestic sphere. Only by dint of aggressive ideological obfuscation is the latter seen as a space of freedom from the wage relation. Once upon a time it had been inseparable from the productive sphere, workshop and manger, dining room and sleeping quarters having been directly continuous in the pre-capitalist world, if not one and the same. The task of social reproduction theory is to rejoin those spheres once again in theory if not spatial practice, pursuing the consequences of the production of productive labor itself in the "factory" of the home.

One of the interesting things about the labor of care is how tightly entwined it tends to be with consumption in the most literal sense, as when a mother cooks and serves a meal to her family. One wonders therefore how deeply entwined social reproduction and consumption can be considered to be from a broader perspective. We know of course that, come the twentieth century, to a degree that was not the case in Marx's mid-nineteenth century, the relation of capital to the working class was complicated by its recognition of the latter as a source of growth in consumer demand often funded by credit card and other debt. In the cauldron of the so-called consumer economy, at the risk of faltering economic expansion and crisis, any accounting of the "necessities" of life must gradually become more generous if more stressful in their attainment. Attending to the dynamics of social reproduction as consumption should not entail, as in neoclassical economic theory, transforming the "revealed preferences" of consumers into the unassailable ground of economic truth and justice, but it should entail seeing that consumption is not simply the terminus of the line of production, the unanalyzable end toward which it moves. It is also a laborious origin point in its own right, as necessary as any other, in the perpetual motion of a circuit more complex and far-reaching than the strictly accumulative one leading from investment to the extraction of surplus value to re-investment and so on.

This capacious circularity undoubtedly confuses things, but it does so productively, if not from the economist's than from the cultural historian's point of view. Is the woman buying groceries for her family a "consumer"? Yes, but she is also from this point of view a *reproducer*, which is to say, an unpaid laborer doing some work that has to be done if the world is to continue to be as it is. And how about the single person pouring herself a bowl of cereal? Does it make sense to say that she is, in that act, performing a bit of unpaid labor to the end of reproducing herself as a wage earner? Why not, since it is hard to see how the *self*-reproduction of the labor force is any less reproductive than housework done for others? How about when she reads a book on her Kindle on her lunch break—a self-indulgence that she might tell us *keeps her sane*, readying her to endure the rest of her shift? Has reading in that scenario, which we might have thought of simply as cultural consumption, become visible as a kind of reproductive labor? And what if the novel she's reading turns her on? Is masturbation at bedtime part of the homework she does to ready herself for more wage work the next day?

These examples strain the definition of "social reproduction" to the breaking point, surely, but are powerfully suggestive of a new frame within which acts of cultural consumption might validly be understood, one of particular value in helping us to see what it means to view Amazon as the protagonist of contemporary literary history. If the keynote of Amazon's performance of this role is the digital dissolution of the book into the general consumer economy, as "Earth's Biggest Bookstore" becomes the "Everything Store," this does not mean that literature in the Age of Amazon no longer participates in the construction and maintenance of our collective and individual identities, only that that construction is continuous with self-maintenance in a grosser, corporeal sense. The scene of social reproduction is perhaps most crucially where babies are born and raised, where family members are fed and clothed, but it is also a scene of intensely embodied *cultural* reproduction.

Thanks to a long tradition of Marxist interpretation of culture, we are used to thinking of cultural reproduction in ideological terms, as the re-transmission of a set of ruling ideas or, as Louis Althusser had it, of imaginary solutions to real contradictions. For Jane Tompkins, we might even think of literary texts as performing a kind of "cultural work" upon the world in which they circulate, "expressing and shaping the social context that produced them."[10] In most cases, however, we are not asked to worry about the metaphorical nature of that "work" as performed by a *text* as opposed to the human being who writes or reads it in highly specifiable institutional conditions and with variable aims. This is the difference between Tompkins's "new historicist" and more recent literary-sociological methodologies that otherwise overlap to a considerable extent. The latter asks the properly economic-sociological and materialist question of where and with what institutional supports literary experience comes into being such that it can even begin to have ideological force. In this case, setting the scene of literary consumption in the home or other non-workplace, it asks what the utility of literature might be from the reader's perspective, what it is understood to *do for her* as part of a repertoire of self-care such that it is perceived as a worthwhile expense of money and especially time.

What are the *uses of literature*? This is the question asked in a work of that title by Rita Felski, a key figure in the new literary sociology.[11] For her, its use is in generating a series of cognitive-emotional effects—recognition, enchantment, knowledge, and shock—in and on the reader. An answer suggested by social reproduction theory would more simply be to say that, as soon as they are detached from their uses in formal schooling, stories provide therapeutic comfort to those who read them. It is a pointedly unheroic answer. It is also true to observation to an extent even greater than it appears in Timothy Aubry's important *Reading as Therapy* (2006), where the therapeutic utility of cultural consumption is confined to works of middlebrow earnestness.[12] Here, by contrast, the idea is that entering the space of the novel of any kind is somewhat like entering the womb or nursery. Its world is one the reader inhabits as irresponsibly as a newborn. The mother reads to her child, the child learns to read on her own, but ever thereafter seeks from novels—if that child happens to continue to be a reader—a kind of mediated mothering. The novel *cares*, or at least seems to, as the embodiment of the author's intention to communicate, its fictionality indicating a commitment to the customizability of reality to the end of the reader's pleasure. The novel *coddles*, even when trying to disturb or offend, inasmuch as it reassures the reader that life is meaningful.

If this seems offensive to our commitments to literature's critical *alterity*, to its virtuously difficult *challenges* and effected *transformations*, that modality of literary experience is a fairly marginal one in the practice of literary life as a whole, although indubitably wonderful when it appears. It is also subject to reintegration in the status quo as *useful subversion*. As it happens, the latter is one of the major themes of Stephenson's *Diamond Age*, one of the things that Primer is supposed to effect in its charges as a way of *perpetuating* the neo-bourgeois culture of the New Atlantis phyle, not abolishing it. Subversion in that context is only really the act of producing healthy variation on a continuing theme. What we're drawing attention to here is not the singularity of the literary encounter but its repetition, to everything that aligns it with the "re-" in reproduction. Reading is a habit—something the type of person who reads at all does repeatedly, if at various speeds, in the flow of daily life.

Perhaps the most concrete form of the appearance of social reproduction in the literary field is that embodied in *genre*, where the call is always for the production of stories of a more or less familiar kind. Certainly, genre is inescapably central to everything that Amazon does to and for literature. It is a form, indigenous to the literary field, of the broader phenomena of market segmentation and product differentiation. Although there are many genres—in fact Amazon multiplies them astonishingly, offering writers avenues to "best-seller" status in no fewer than ten thousand separate generic domains—each is a structure of symbolic repetition and variation tending toward predictability. Inspired by social reproduction theory, we might observe in turn that genre is reflexively linked to gender. As explained by Anis Bawarshi and Mary Jo Reiff:

> On the one hand, *genre* can be traced, through its related word *gender*, to the Latin word *genus*, which refers to a "kind" or a "class of things." On the other hand, *genre*, again through its related word *gender*, can be traced to the Latin cognate *gener*, meaning to generate. The range of ways genre has been defined and used throughout its history reflects its etymology. At various times and in various areas of study, genre has been defined and used mainly as a classificatory tool, a way of sorting and organizing

kinds of texts and other cultural objects. But more recently ... genre has come to be defined less as a means of organizing kinds of texts and more as a powerful, ideologically active, and historically changing shaper of texts, meanings, and social actions.[13]

Presented here as distinct, the *classificatory* and *generative* meanings of "genre" are in practice necessarily dialectical in relation, there being no act of classification, however seemingly inert, that isn't also trying to achieve something, no act of generation divorced from the question of what kind of thing is being generated. Bawarshi and Reiff's emphasis on the latter is nonetheless thought-provoking, a consequence of their institutional location, not in literary studies as traditionally practiced, but the discipline of Rhetoric and Composition, where the consequences of Carolyn Miller's epochal essay "Genre as Social Action" (1984) for writing instruction have been unfolding now for thirty-five years.[14] The point put simply has been to make student writers conscious of the pragmatic-situational nature of textual composition, where, for example, in order to get a job one might write a job letter, a genre with compositional rules quite distinct from those of a wedding toast, and so on. As active means to differentiated social ends, genres are understood as *generative* of those ends, and thus to the ongoing reproduction of a social order constituted, among other things, by the writing and reading of job letters.[15]

While the turn to genre in Rhetoric and Composition studies was built on a rejection of what seemed the merely classificatory strain of literary studies, trading it in for a conception more relevant to contemporary writing pedagogy, it is not impossible to conserve its insights for the study of reading, which is also a kind of action, however comparatively passive it may seem. In fact, part of that work is already done in Adena Rosmarin's contribution to literary genre theory, *The Power of Genre* (1985), which argues that genre is not an objective phenomenon of the literary field, something that might be noticed or not, but an active hermeneutic tool, a way of *achieving something* as a critic.[16] Might we push this line of thinking into the arena of popular reading practices facilitated by Amazon? If so, inspired by the Rhet-Comp understanding of genre as action, we would ask what the reader hopes to *do to herself* on any given occasion by setting out to read a novel *of a given kind*. The field of action in genre consumption is not the job market or workplace but the individual sensorium, the "self" wherever it may bodily be, on lunch break or on the train or at home.

This understanding of genre is nicely articulated in what is to this point the most celebrated work to have been published by Amazon's in-house science fiction imprint, 47North. Anne Charnock's *Dreams before the Start of Time* (2017) is set in the year 2034, extending by steps to 2120, chronicling the lives of three generations of characters bound by family and friendship ties. Doing so, somewhat like Aldous Huxley's *Brave New World* (1932) but without the latter's sharply satirical edge, it pieces through the implications—political, emotional, and otherwise—of various advancements in reproductive technology, from in vitro fertilization and sperm donorship to various aggressive eugenic gene therapies and even a kind of parthenogenesis. At the center of the novel is Dr. Kristina Christophe, a reproductive biologist. Counterpart to the male nano-engineer at the center of *The Diamond Age*, she is a successful health care professional as well as inveterate reader of romances, available on some presumably more advanced version of a Kindle, elaborately structuring her reading life outside work with lists of books already read and to be read. No less than the drugs she prescribes to her patients does she "prescribe" romances to herself as means to a biblio-therapeutic end. In her case, it is the end of relaxation, and also, it is suggested, a way of avoiding inevitably disappointing and exhausting entanglements with real men. The point being that her efforts of literary self-care are no less "reproductive" than those she performs for others in a more literal, biological sense, the very predictability of the romance form, including the happy ending, being one of that form of self-care's central charms.

Given her elevated professional status, Dr. Christophe would not necessarily count as a "typical" reader of romances, but that only makes the truth about socially reproductive reading practices, and about the readership of the romance in particular, easier to see. Whether in the form of the sex-scene vignette or full-blown marriage plot, the romance tells the story of social reproduction to those in whom that reproductive function is overwhelmingly vested. Just as, for instance, early twentieth-century pulp science fiction, in John Rieder's invaluable account, was directed implicitly at a burgeoning class of relatively low-status technical workers and amateur tinkerers (all one has to do is look at the magazine ads surrounding those stories), so is romance directed toward a kind of worker, a person who may or may not be female but is doing "woman's work," the labor of care.[17] More than any other, romance is the genre that records our life as gendered, as generative, and as generic, and as lived in conditions of radical disparities of power. The question is, what is its relation to the genre system as a whole?

The Perversities of Genre

From a certain perspective—the perspective taken by this chapter —what most stands out about a work like E. L. James's *Fifty Shades of Grey* is the conventionality of its kink. What are a few whips and chains and cable ties against the formation of a couple of such blinding whiteness and rigorous heterosexuality? Indeed, never mind its mannequin-like protagonists, is there anything more conventional than "whips and chains," anything more cliché than the S&M costume repertoire as a whole? Without denying that the transcendent success of E. L. James's novel was in large measure a *succés de scandale*, it is tempting to declare that the real scandal was not in dragging darkly marginal sex practices into the light of the cultural mainstream but in laying bare some of the core contents of the mainstream psyche, if there is such a thing.[18] By the time of the novel's appearance, the world to which the scandal qua scandal supposedly referred—a bourgeois world, a world of unapologetic enforcement of norms—no longer existed in anything like its original form, having gradually been hollowed out by the system of for-profit permissiveness otherwise known as consumerism. So much so that one is led to suspect that, in a further turn of the screw, the real aim of the collective fantasy apparatus surrounding the novel was the *re-establishment* of the patriarchal Law it had formerly been our pleasure to transgress.

This understanding of the *Fifty Shades* phenomenon is in line with the state of the art in psychoanalytical understandings of perversion, where the central fact to be accounted for in the twenty-first century is the large-scale disavowal, on the part of the Authorities, of any right to define what the shape and aims of the sex drive should be.[19] A whole host of things that would once have been confidently pronounced perverted—homosexuality, most notably—are now accepted as perfectly normal if minority orientations, while those who would deny the right of the people to whatever victimless pleasures they can imagine seem like reactionary cranks. What's more, while it's not as though everyone is perverted in the sense of having some highly specific fetish or another, it is true that the consumerist regime of which Amazon is the signal contemporary avatar addresses us as "perverts" in a broader, even hackneyed sense. In this consumerist regime we are not persons looking to structure our lives around a lack, or who dutifully accept the reality principle so as to get on with the neurotically self-abnegating business of bourgeois family life. We are instead persons selecting among a browsable infinity of enjoyments, a vast range of objects and services, tastes and textures and images—and narratives—that meet our immediate demand.

Of course, we shouldn't exaggerate the extent to which perversion has become the norm. Taboos against incest, bestiality, and pedophilia remain in force, however shakily, and progressive gains in sexual liberation, incomplete in any case, might always be revoked as they have in the past. Some notion of universalized and banalized perversion, however, is a good place to begin to see what it means to say that, in the Age of Amazon, all fiction is genre fiction. Dividing contemporary literature into a vast array of searchable genre categories, each with its own

best-seller list, Amazon is the host of a genre *system* conceived
as an engine of infinitely infoliating permutations of objects
of narrative desire. In the vast space defined by Kindle Direct
Publishing and the Kindle Unlimited subscription service, it is
a given that genres will splinter and mix and reform and spring
up anew, but each of these genres is temporary destiny, a body
of compositional rules if not of the Law. At the margins of that
system, once one has crossed the, for it, significant boundary
between the genres of "Erotic Romance" and "Erotica"—the
latter typically dispensing with most of the non-sexual story
elements in favor of direct treatment of the kink and, if plaintive
erotica authors are to be believed, embraced much less enthusiastically by the recommendation algorithm—one can find some
fairly niche, as they say, entertainments like ABDL.

It would be absurd to deny that these works are transgressive
in some sense—it's not hard to imagine *someone* being offended
or grossed out by them—but they do not transgress the Law
of the Everything Store, which states that, whatever you need
from the literary text, some generic version of it will be available for you there—and if not, do it yourself! That's what KDP
is for. Your fellow, say, *alien*-erotic-nursing fantasists will thank
you. In this assurance, the literary genre system is in sync with
the structure of normalized perversity at large, where the singular reproductive aim, heterosexual coupling, is daily diverted
toward a polymorphous plenitude of other objects, each of them
constituting a generic object of desire, a symptom or fetish, in
its own right. The implication being that this is explanatory of
the Amazonian genre system as such, even in zones—military
science fiction, cozy murder mystery, literary fiction, you name
it—superficially far removed from the prurient interest per se.

The status of genre fiction has never been higher in elite circles
of literary opinion, which now routinely dismiss the blanket
prejudices against popular forms characteristic of an earlier era
as snobbery or disingenuousness. In this, these circles have in a
sense simply gotten with the program of shamelessly pluralized
perverted pleasures. If the enjoyment of trashy fiction is something unto itself, different from what I look for in respectable

literature, why would I deprive myself of it? In Amazonia, the more is always the merrier. And if high and low pleasures get mixed up? Fine. That could be another cool thing.

As Andrew Hoberek was among the first to document, the retreat of boundary policing between the precincts of high and low culture—a boundary situated far above the one between erotic romance and erotica!—has found expression in a growing number of works of literary fiction unashamed to declare their kinship to genre fiction, and even to test the distinction between these categories. Hoberek dates the beginning of the "genre turn" in fiction to 1999, when Jonathan Lethem's *Motherless Brooklyn* (1999), with its elements of hard-boiled detective novel, was awarded the National Book Critics Circle Award, and finds further exemplars in celebrated works by Michael Chabon, Colson Whitehead, Junot Díaz, and others. For Hoberek these works announce what can only be described as a "thorough-going breakdown of the traditional barriers separating genre fiction from its more prestigious cousins."[20]

Yet, as Jeremy Rosen notes, the institutions in and by which novels come into being and begin to circulate remain as differentiated as ever, with nobody at risk of mistaking an author published by, say, Knopf from one published by Harlequin, let alone one self-published through KDP.[21] The latter is particularly telling in this respect, inasmuch as the one and only avenue to some form of prestige as an indie writer is through exalted sales, whether on the model of the folk-heroic best-seller status of Hugh Howey, discussed in chapter 1; or the fabled success of the UK's "Queen of Kindle," the mystery writer LJ Ross; or the self-described "father" of the popular new genre called LitRPG, Aleron Kong, discussed in chapter 2. However convergent literary fiction and genre fiction may be on the page, the assumptions that greet them in their circulation are no doubt distinct. While the Amazon website is relatively agnostic on the matter of prestige, counting any and all novels as works in some genre or other, KDP is to all appearances overwhelmingly a medium for the production of crowd-pleasing generic forms, including a thousand permutations of the story told in *Fifty Shades of*

Grey. What Hoberek perceives as a "breakdown" of distinctions might more realistically be understood in terms of their mutually reflective proximity as adjacent elements of a system. The only mistake, one that Hoberek helps us not to make, would be to think that these differences split neatly into aesthetic success on one side and failure on the other. We all know how bad a "literary" novel can be.

According to Rosen, when works of the literary genre turn are more closely examined, they tend to reveal themselves as ironic instantiations of generic forms. This is what we see in Whitehead's zombie novel *Zone One* (2011), with its deliberately digressive pace and unflattering account of the zombification of consumers of mass culture. In this it recalls an ironizing impulse already visible in the nascently "postmodern" 1960s, when works like William S. Burroughs's cut-up SF novel, *The Soft Machine* (1961), or Ishmael Reed's surrealized western, *Yellow Back Radio Broke-Down* (1969), offered themselves to advanced readerships as sophisticatedly deconstructed generic forms. The '60s were also a time when, long in advance of the recent genre turn, science fiction made what can only be described as a "literary turn": originally published in relatively unheralded cultural industrial venues, works like John Brunner's *Stand on Zanzibar* (1968) and Samuel Delany's *Dhalgren* (1975)—or, indeed, the entire New Wave of science fiction associated most famously with J. G. Ballard—are incomprehensible except as extensions of modernism into a heretofore lowly precinct of the literary field. Granted, official acceptance of these projects is something else, with successful works of genre fiction often having to wait for a protracted period before being brought into the canon as "genre classics," as with H. P. Lovecraft or Philip K. Dick, and before them Mary Shelley. And yet the long-standing interest of the avant-garde publisher Semiotext(e) in science fiction—it published a compendious "SF" issue in 1989—suggests a recognition of the potential legitimacy of genre fiction long predating the turn of the millennium.

But not of all genre fiction. However one dates it, however tall or short the barriers between genre fiction and literary fiction may be, it would appear that the genre turn has bypassed the romance novel. Is it that romance is simply irredeemable? Too lacking in the latent (or not so latent) intellectualism of detective fiction and science fiction, or the prestigious violence of the western, or sheer negativity (and thus allegorical criticality) of horror? Is it simply—as Hoberek suggests, but without pursuing its implications—too feminine to count as literature even now, when we think we know better than to hold these biases? Without objecting outright to Daniel Harris's observation, quoted in the previous chapter, that love as construed by the modern romance industry "is such a universal experience that it reduces us all to the same generic person," it must be noted that it is a curiously gendered universality—universal only to the extent that "we are all feminine" now. Which in some ways we obviously, desperately are, inasmuch as 80 percent of us (in the United States at least) are occupationally involved in the relatively low-paid provision of services, not the unionized manufacture of things. "Romance" in broad definition might mean anything emanating from classical or European vernacular storytelling traditions, such as Arthurian quest-romance; or, even more broadly, any text working in the trans-generic mode of literary wish fulfillment described by Northrop Frye in his *Anatomy of Criticism* (1957). Even so, the term as it is predominantly used today refers to a kind of popular fiction whose readership is said to be at least 85 percent female. It is a love story.

Perhaps it is in the very nature of romance forms not to be noticeable when they *do* find their way into otherwise "literary" fiction? While it is now understood as a member of the larger set of forms collectively called genre fiction, romance is different from its mass cultural siblings in important ways, carrying the term "romance" into the present even as it has fallen out of use in English as a label for other, more obviously fantastic works like the erstwhile "scientific romances" of H. G. Wells, which we now call science fiction. For Frye, the romance is indeed "the structural core of all fiction," and the key to understanding how fiction caters to "the imaginative needs of the community."[22]

From *Pamela* to *Pride and Prejudice*, from Brontë's *Jane Eyre* to Trollope's *Can You Forgive Her?* and on to the more complicated cases of Eliot's *Middlemarch* and James's *Portrait of a Lady*, "the novel" as such was frequently enough structured by the marriage plot, producing works we have no trouble calling masterpieces. Considering the durability of the models they offer to contemporary writers, the novels of Jane Austen are particularly interesting in that their own historical present, the early nineteenth century, now organizes one of the major subgenres of the mass-market romance novel, the Regency romance, itself one of the subunits of a larger division into historical and contemporary modes. Austen, even more so than Shakespeare or Dickens, is no doubt the supreme example of a writer who continues to attract maximum amounts of both popular love and critical scholarly esteem. She is an avatar of the genre turn *avant la lettre*. And yet, come the early twentieth century and the founding of the industrial-strength romance publisher Mills & Boon, followed thereupon by Harlequin Enterprises and now KDP, the love story such as we find it in Austen was simultaneously assigned a place in the mass-market genre system and evacuated of any claims to high literary value. It was in this context that, as Sandra Gilbert and Susan Gubar have shown, the woman modernist writer ambitious for critical esteem would naturally feel an anxiety of affiliation with female authors of the romance and also attempt to distance herself therefrom.[23]

For my money, if there were no other reason to be fascinated by the contemporary romance novel, the sheer depths at which it dwells in official hierarchies of literary value should suffice to inspire serious critical reflection upon it: surely a badness so profound, so completely disqualifying of critical esteem, or even sustained curiosity, has something interesting to tell us about the contemporary literary field as a whole? In searching for that something, our aspiration would be to add to the small but highly distinguished body of criticism on the contemporary romance, from Janice Radway's pioneering *Reading the Romance* to Eva Illouz's *Hard-Core Romance* (2014), which has sought for the most part to understand the genre on its own terms and in isolation from the larger literary field, anatomizing its various formal features and pondering its vexed significance for feminism.[24] To be sure, it is a phenomenon huge enough to have warranted such an exclusive focus, which mirrors a devotion on the part of certain readerships, or fan cultures, to their genre of choice, to the exclusion of interest in any other kind of fiction. With its sprawling commercial reach and complex internal differentiation into subgenres, the contemporary romance has been said to account for nearly 35 percent of all novels published today, and around half of all mass-market paperbacks of any kind.

The situation of romance is in other words one of clarifying extremity, the feast it enjoys along one axis of valuation intersecting with famine along the other. Taking the opportunity presented by this extremity, I would argue that romance draws our attention to, if I can be forgiven the phrase, *the genericity of the genre system in general*. Generous in doling out its pleasures, generative of ever-new wrinkles in the (as psychoanalysis puts it) itinerary of the drive, the genre system as detached from the school, absorbed by the culture industry, and then radically pluralized by Amazon assumes a fundamentally affirmative, therapeutic, and, for all its perversity, socially reproductive function. With its by-all-accounts absolute requirement of a happy ending for it to even receive recognition as a member of the genre by its devotees, the romance's unforgivable sin is that it flagrantly satisfies the "imaginative needs of the community," even as it in many ways can claim "vanguard status" as the leading edge of new innovations in marketing and distribution.[25] What other genres do indirectly, or even "critically," it does shamelessly in the open and in resourcefully new ways.

From *Pamela* to the present, the novel in the English-speaking world has developed alongside and within a capitalist economy increasingly oriented toward consumer enjoyment and, if only implicitly, has been telling the story of that economy the whole time. What we now label the "romance" novel is the reflexive expression of the novel's original appeal: not only is it written for the satisfaction of the imaginative needs of the reader, but it is *about* that satisfaction in the figure of the heroine and her mate, who always get what they want, and who in getting what they want reassure their readers of the legitimacy and continuity of the social order. While it has become better known in the academy as a vehicle of "bourgeois ideology," which is among other things an ideology of rectitude and restraint, Terry Lovell has demonstrated that this fails to account for the "vast quantities of fantasy fiction" consumed by the middle class in the eighteenth century, when the bourgeoisie was coming into its own as a historical force; it fails, indeed, to account for the residuum of fantasy that remains in even the most sternly realistic novel, distinguishing it (notionally at least) from nonfiction.[26]

What does the novel's therapeutic cultural work look like, concretely? Entering through the eyes as a succession of words, the novel is transformed into a series of affectively charged mental images of people and places. These images might amount to a "meaning" we could more or less coherently state to anyone who asked—an English teacher, paradigmatically—but perhaps we should be wary of overstating the importance of complexly effable meaning in this sense to the reading that most Amazon customers do. These customers are largely not in school, and when they reflect on the works they read—for instance, when they write a review on Goodreads—they do so as customers, not students. We might say instead that what the reader is looking for in fiction is a *sensation* of meaning, an idea I think has great potential in describing literary experience, but even that might be too strong. It would be for Norman Holland, whose classic *Dynamics of Literary Response* (1968) argues that the better part of what we do when we read is to activate emotional resonances between the text and our unacknowledged fantasies of return to pre-oedipal pleasures (see figure on p. 174).[27]

In his view, the conferral of interpretive meaning on the literary text is a form of defense against the unruliness and unspeakability of those pleasures, which are nonetheless the text's primary raison d'être and source of generic appeal. In this sense, and never more so than when it is utterly obscene "adult entertainment," all literature is children's literature at its core (see figure on p. 175).

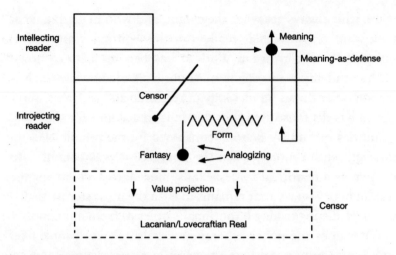

Meaning as Defense In this, my adaptation of one of Norman Holland's several diagrammatic depictions of the dynamics of literary response, the hermeneutic articulation of "meaning" in the text appears at once as a "higher" activity (literally so in the diagram) and as far removed from the real source of its power, which is the inarticulable fantasy embedded in its form. As convergent contributions of author and reader, respectively, literary form and literary meaning-attribution are modes of "defense" against a direct confrontation with that fantasy, which for Holland is a pre-oedipal "oral" or "anal" one. In the mostly unconscious act of introjection, which converts words into psychic events, the reader finds (or feels) analogies between the text's fantasy material and their own. I have added an additional "basement" level, representing something like the Lacanian or Lovecraftian Real—that is, the substratum of utter indifference to human well-being from which literary and all other forms of fantasizing are obsessively repeated attempts to recover. The literary text is in this sense a therapeutic processing of that indifference as a pleasurable sensation of narrative meaning, and each distinct genre a quasi-algorithmic form of doing so.

Building on Holland, we could assert that the domain of social reproduction, as of consumer culture as a whole, is by now a largely *perverse* one, in the psychoanalytical sense. If it is still in the business of convincing us to grow up, it is also a prodigious provider of "merely" diversionary enjoyments. These enjoyments do not necessarily aim toward fulfillment in the sexual reproduction of the family—they may even impede or obviate that end—but in the meantime they make life tolerable and even pleasurable, minute by minute, day by day. So, too, the enjoyments on offer in novels. Peering back from our historical moment to the novel in the nineteenth century, one sees how the genre at its moment of greatest cultural centrality might seem

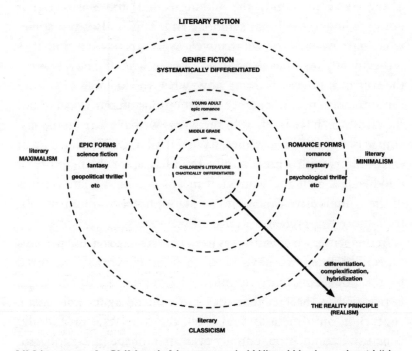

All Literature Is Children's Literature As William Wordsworth said, "the child is father of the man," an insight that would reappear in more complex form in psychoanalysis. In this admittedly speculative depiction of the contemporary genre system, children's literature is at the core and is never entirely irrelevant to what fiction is providing to its readers: a fictional world tailored to their presumed imaginative needs. While works of children's literature are of course quite different from the others, they are not systematically differentiated except by age level (picture books, chapter books, etc.), a "grading" that is itself an artifact of systematic market segmentation. ("Middle grade" literature? Who ever heard of that until it arose to serve a market?) In works of YA fantasy such as the *Hunger Games* or *Twilight* trilogies, romance (the love story) and epic (the making of history) are frequently only semi-differentiated, while adult genre fiction more definitively splits them (in fact, the boundary between YA and adult epic fantasy can be an exceedingly porous one in practice). Literary fiction bears the traces of the epic/romance division in the form of the distinction between maximalist and minimalist fictions whose extremes are negotiated toward equilibrium in the "classic" realist novel. In turn, a "realism" of ideological intent if not always of classic realist form is what allows literary fiction to assert (to some degree truthfully, but not entirely) that it has put away childish things. Further implications of the polarity of the contemporary genre system are pursued in chapter 5.

to have enlisted itself in the project of the social reproduction of the bourgeois family, the bildungsroman and marriage plot both tending toward that symbolic end. This is already a somewhat narrow view of what novels were up to then, but it is self-evidently insufficient as an account of what the novel—even the romance novel—is doing now, when the keynote of culture is not the resigned acceptance of limitations on our freedom but the effort to "have it all."[28] In theory, as we have it from the discourse of women's magazines, having it all means having a great career along with a great family. In practice, for the majority of middle-class men and women, it means access to whatever it is in the commodity-scape that can stand, however momentarily, for a more comprehensive sense of well-being.

In this sense, we have always been perverted, even and perhaps especially when we have been consuming works structured by the bourgeois marriage plot. The perversion of the latter is revealed in the fact that they are enjoyed again and again, rupturing, on a meta-textual level, the otherwise profoundly conclusive completion, happily ever after, of the linear trajectories toward heterosexual marriage they portray. The result is a symbolic system that insists on *having it both ways* and indeed on *having it all* in a myriad of senses. Most specifically, it is a way of dealing with a fact about modern marriage observed by Illouz and others: it has found itself riven at its core by incompatible expectations, on the one hand for peaks of romantic emotional intensity, on the other for the daily comforts of home life. In this context, the habit of romance reading finds its utility in the repeated aesthetic activation of that intensity in fiction, thus reducing however slightly the opportunity cost of being with one partner at a time.[29] In the early twentieth century, the relative shifting of attention from love to sex in the modernist novel arguably had a critical and even disenchanting "naturalist" intent with respect to naïve or hypocritical Victorian-Chivalric romantic rhetoric. In the early twenty-first century, by contrast, explicit sex has been wholly folded into the love story, the search for One True Love and the search for juddering orgasm now combined in one narrative package. This puts significant limits on how far into the future of its protagonists a work like *Fifty Shades* can go. Yes, it can give us glimpses of the satisfactions of marriage and motherhood and philanthropy, but it needs to lower the curtain before sexual boredom sets in, leaving the field to successor works that can start at the very beginning, with the meet-cute of freshly named protagonists.

Hypnotized, understandably, by the greatness of great individual works, scholars have given short shrift to the importance of easeful *repetition* in fulfilling this function. For them, since the 1960s, the "pleasure of the text," when it has been acknowledged at all, has been associated with works of virtuous difficulty. In a kind of symbolic transposition of the sex act onto the act of interpretation, in these works "the play of language," as Roland Barthes put it, leaves gaps in the story the reader blissfully fills. The "text of bliss" is the "text that imposes a state of loss, the text that discomforts (perhaps to the point of a certain boredom), unsettles the reader's historical, cultural, psychological assumptions ...";it is also the text in and through which one earns a certain amount of cultural capital—which can indeed be quite pleasurable, as any literature scholar or free-range literary type would attest.[30] One might assume that the contemporary romance novel is by contrast what Barthes calls a mere "text of pleasure," his terms for works with little or no interest in disorienting innovation at the level of the sentence, or in leaving gaps in the narrative, or in unsettling the reader's assumptions. But while it is quite true—and in a way definitional—that works of popular genre fiction do not typically acknowledge the unit of the sentence as a site of meaningful innovation, the reality of the contemporary romance scrambles Barthes's categories inasmuch as it is the bearer of pleasure and bliss alike. Refusing to break faith with the rectilinearity of the marriage plot, the disseminative linguistic force and self-loss of Joycean modernism is transposed to another level, the level of serial generic permutation as such.

In this transposition as in everything else, the romance insists on having it all. I know of no better embodiment of this truth than Barbara Deloto and Thomas Newgen's rigorously cheerful self-published novella, *The House of Enchanted Feminization* (2019).[31] Not all of this duo's expansive oeuvre is so sweet, with darker Sadeian elements showing up in works like *Forced Feminization: A Hot Wife, Cuckold, Forced Fem, Male Chastity, Feminized Men, Shemale Slut Story* (2016) and others. But the norm for their work is relentless affirmation as we find it here, when an unsuspecting engineering undergraduate finds himself looking for new housing for himself and his male roommate. Like something out of a lifestyle magazine, the "meticulously maintained old craftsman-style home" he stumbles onto, with its billowing "sheer white curtains" and "refurbished kitchen," is an image of bourgeois well-being, and although he worries he won't be able to afford the rent, he can't resist. Moving in, he immediately feels himself beginning to transform, first speaking like a girl, then growing hips and breasts, so much so that he has to avail himself of the closet full of women's clothing that the house magically supplies. In the first of the novella's pointed disavowals of potential trauma, he is first disturbed but then immediately somewhat pleased to be possessed of a female body, with the newly configured ecstasies that offers: "Why worry about things I can't control?" The second disavowal of trauma is encoded in his (hereafter her, since she is now referred to as a "girl," although gender neutral pronouns would also be appropriate) roommate's reaction to her transition into a "shemale," with a body corresponding in every way to that of a lusciously sexy woman except for the large, thick penis crowding her panties: "Wow. Chris, you look stunning! Here, have a seat and let me pour you some wine."

You can probably see where this is going. But can you really? Yes, the more or less heterosexual union of Chris and Bill is on the horizon, but not before a series of fascinating divagations from that relatively conventional end. For one reason or another, even as the roommate relation is redefined as a love match, coitus keeps on being delayed. This supplies the novel's modicum of suspense, such as it is: why is this couple not fucking? First comes Chris's realization that, needing to solve the wardrobe problem of the bulge in her slinky dress, she can simply put her albeit semi-softened penis in her own vagina, storing it there. It feels good: "I was beside myself—and inside myself—with desire." This condition of perfect erotic self-completion is exciting, but not finally satisfying. She wants to include beloved Bill in the circuit of her self-relation, and even marries him, but consummates the marriage in an unusual way: by having an orgy with him and some friends. In the event, it is a kind of communal successor to the more solipsistic perfection of self-fucking, a gymnastic mutual filling in of corporeal and existential holes: "I was stunned by the wonder of the unselfish gifts they had given me." What one should not however miss in this resistance to *coupling* is the story's dogged maintenance of the marriage plot, which no less than in *Pamela* or *Persuasion* or *Jane Eyre* structures the narrative to the end not of transgression but social reproduction in the classic sense, or close enough: "My life after the night to remember was no less amazing. Our lives were a never-ending pleasure as we lived as four lovers and friends in our supportive family."

Enclosing the Genre Commons

Finally, the romance *affirms*. That is its function, its failure, its perceived inferiority to works of critical force. And yet, how could anyone read a story as sweet as *The House of Enchanted Feminization* and not be charmed by its sheer will to happiness? This is especially so when contrasted with the depressing actuality of real-world gender dysphoria more easily visible in its gothic variants. It's not that critique has run out of steam. Critique chugs along, fed by the infinite coal-supply of capitalism's contradictions. It's just that critique should be as thoroughly dialectical as it can, as suspicious of its own suspicion as of anything else. After all, every single novel ever written is an affirmation of a sort—if only of the worth of writing a novel at all. In its pages whole worlds might go up in fictional flames, but that burning is also the building of *yet another* (in this case postapocalyptic) novel.

If I generally find it difficult to get behind Amazon's theory and practice of literary life, skeptical as I am of its corporate populism, these opportunistic efflorescences at the very margin of the unregulated KDP genre system seem self-evidently redeemable and loveable for their existential courage. They remind us that the task of social reproduction is larger than capitalism. It is not only the making and maintaining of labor power, but also of livable human lives and, if possible, joyous ones. True, there is a sense in which group sex—a much more popular kink than ABDL, with its own panoply of acronymic sub-kinks—can be taken as an expression of the consumer's greed for *more*—more sources of enjoyment—and an expression of Amazon's dominating desire to be the one to give it to them. For all their triumph over the couple form, works like Julie Piper's *Auctioned to Her Brother's Best Friends: MMF Menage Romance* (2020) and even Charlotte Snape's *The New Normal: Bisexual and Gay Threesome MMF Military and Cowboy Romance* (2019) might be found lacking when compared to Stephanie Brother's *Huge X4: A Double Twin Stepbrother MMFMM Menage Romance* (2017) on grounds simply of their lesser numbers. And yet this strenuous multiplication of objects of desire can also be understood as a lunge toward erotic collectivity and community if not communism.

Granted, it is the corporatized, the branded form of that community, but once one has become alert to it, a host of other forms of utopian collectivity native to the Age of Amazon call themselves to our attention. Like social reproduction, corporatism is a larger concept than its use in corporate capitalism per se. Consider, for instance, the thriving world of internet-enabled fan fiction, or "fic," discoverable on sites like fanfiction.net. It is where *Fifty Shades of Grey* first came into being. Before that novel achieved its destiny as a market singularity, it jostled with hundreds if not thousands of similar narratives consumed without cost by hundreds if not thousands of devotees of the romance genre of a certain kind. They read and commented upon what E. L. James first posted under the pen name Snowqueens Icedragon as a fictional extension and re-imagination of Stephenie Myer's hugely popular vampire romance trilogy, *Twilight*. James's effort was titled *Master of the Universe*, an allusion to the cocky invest-ment banker figure in Tom Wolfe's social satire *Bonfire of the Vanities* (1987), where it in turn alludes to a superhero movie of the same vintage. There is something to be said about the fact that Christian Grey began his imaginary life as a vampire, as the previous chapter tried to show, but here the point is simply that the novel first circulated among a more specific readership than the one it eventually found, one we can affirm as a community, a model of mutual aid.

Writ large, the fan fiction world is one where countless thou-sands of fictional extensions and reimaginings of literary works circulate among devotees of a given master text, some of whom assume pro bono responsibility for keeping the story going or performing new variations upon it, posting new chapters as they go and with no money changing hands. The fanfiction.net site alone currently lists well in excess of 800,000 *Harry Potter* fics of various kinds and lengths, along with the comparatively modest—but everything in literature is modest compared to *Harry Potter*—220,000 *Twilight* fics and nearly 4,000 of *Fifty Shades of Grey*, the latter being fics to the second degree. On another fic site, AO3 (Archive of Our Own), there are still more of all three, along with an array of fics of sub-blockbuster origi-nals across the spectrum from Henry James to Ray Bradbury. If it is not, as one of its critical luminaries has it, "taking over the world," it is a deliriously fecund form of social reproduction, and like the work of social reproduction in general, it is largely unpaid.[32]

In fan fiction, the reader becomes a writer, partially reversing the polarity of the production and consumption of narrative, "blurring the lines between amateur identity and professional activity."[33] James only definitively crossed that divide when she withdrew the original manuscript from free circulation and began selling it first as an e-book from a small publisher, then under a major imprint. In the world of fic, the original text is in effect the anchor of a new genre, much as *Robinson Crusoe* would become the anchor of the "Robinsonade," or *Ivanhoe* the anchor of the historical novel, or *Ulysses* the anchor of the neo-epic experimental masterpiece, and so on. That said, these genre-generative works are frequently crisscrossed and internally differentiated by other genres and subgenres, as when Meyer's paranormal romance is defanged as Icedragon's contemporary romance, or when ABDL erotica splits into cozy and gothic variants. In this we see the permutative drive of genre at work in a particularly concentrated way, but it is everywhere. Thus James's rewrite can be rewritten again in a work like B. F Dealeo's *Fifty Shades of Brains* (2013), a well-executed satire of an "original," which is of course not original at all, and not just for its ties to *Twilight*.[34]

Eva Illouz describes that original as a "mix[ing] of the genres of the traditional and erotic romance novel," and that is true even if this combination has been available in the Harlequin Romance line for many years now.[35] If one could imagine a merging of *Pamela* with Pauline Reage's *Story of O*, *Fifty Shades* might be it. But one can certainly add to this list of ingredients (see figure on p. 183).[36] Most importantly, we know that this otherwise contemporary urban realist romance novel has a vampire story at its heart. Franco Moretti has shown that the literary vampire can be understood as an allegorical expression of capital, a personification of Marx's "dead labor which, vampire-like, lives only by sucking living labor, and lives the more, the more labor it sucks," and the transformation of the *Twilight* vampire Edward Cullen into the capitalist Christian Grey does not seriously impede the progress of that allegory, fangs or no.[37] While the vampires are gone from *Fifty Shades*, the gothic mood persists in the novel even in its achromatic title and the oft-mentioned "darkness" of the hero's character. It really flowers in *Fifty Shades Darker*, naturally, which near the beginning finds Ana reading—and soon enough living her own version of—Daphne du Maurier's *Rebecca*, the story of a wife haunted by her deceased predecessor in that role.

As in the Vampire story, *Fifty Shades of Grey* is a story of physical desire expressed as a primitive physical *need*. As in *Rebecca*, it is a need that cannot quite expel the horrible truth

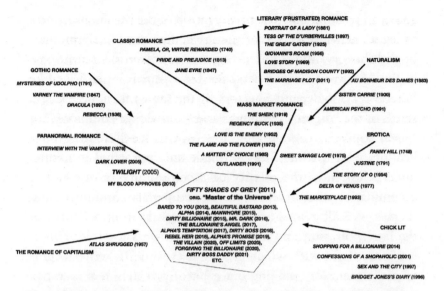

Genealogies of the Alpha Billionaire Romance The sources of the appeal of *Fifty Shades of Grey* to readers are many. To me the most interesting event revealed in this diagram is the sharp splitting of romance into high literary versions virtually defined by their attention to the failure or frustration of romance, and mass-market ones where true love continues to reign supreme.

of its iterability across a series of objects of desire of a generic type. While Ana is doubled by her similar-looking forerunners in the role of submissive, Christian himself is doubled by Ana's literary-type boss at Seattle Independent Publishing, the not-so-subtly named Jack Hyde. The work of the trilogy is then to try to separate the One True Love from the dangerously similar fake: Ana is not to be confused with the pathetic, wild-haired hysteric one of her rejected predecessors has become; and neither, appearances often to the contrary, is Christian to be confused for a garden-variety psycho sexual harasser. By the end of the trilogy, it is absolutely clear who is who. Along the way, it is able to pause for pleasures more closely associated with other genres, including the fashion-oriented hedonism of works of so-called chick lit.

Pursuing this line of thought, we might think of genre on the model of the "commons," the term political economists and historians of Britain use to describe natural resources to which everyone in a given community has or should have free access, above all pastureland. The privatization of the commons by acts of legal enclosure is one of the great themes of early modern English history, and it has strong resonances in the recent past in the "enclosure" of cyberspace by commercial entities like Facebook, Google, and Amazon. By the same token, people still speak of the "digital commons" and "knowledge commons," of "open source" programming and "open access" journal publication, which, while they are made and not found in nature, nonetheless have the quality of a community resource. The accumulation of storytelling tropes and patterns and forms and themes we call genres are in some ways the original form of the latter, offering imitable models to writers for free. This is the inheritance with which each and every KDP writer begins to make their way, staking out a bit of privately remunerative territory by means of trademark and copyright, only to see it borrowed by writers of fic and other, more mercenary imitators. In a world structured by corporate capitalism, it can all get quite complicated, as the squalls of conflict surrounding so-called #Cockygate demonstrate.

You are forgiven in advance for assuming, as you might, that the questions at issue in this 2018 legal dispute surrounding the use of the word "Cocky" in the titles of romances published for download from Kindle Unlimited fall well beneath your concerns as a serious reader. For writers of genre fiction, by contrast, and for anyone hoping for a comprehensive understanding of the contemporary literary field, they are of significant interest. They point us to the many ways that, in the Age of Amazon, the job of writing fiction converges with the job of marketing it, which begins simply with the choice of a given book's title. As you may already have noticed, in the KDP space a book's title is already a kind of advertisement of the generic pleasures it has to offer, which potential readers are assured will be something like those she remembers having gotten from works of the same kind. In hopes of roping in more readers, the temptation is to multiply generic qualifiers endlessly in the subtitles, such that a work is not a gay military romance but a *Bisexual and Gay Threesome MMF Military and Cowboy Romance*, and so on. The search for readers in and around KDP is frequently a desperate one, and competitive, the many thousands of contributors to Amazon Unlimited's subscription offerings each taking a share of a roughly $20 million monthly payout from Amazon based on how many pages of their writing Kindle users have actually read, or at least clicked through.

As reported by Sarah Jeong, the #Cockygate scandal began when one member of an online indie writers' support group, Bookclicker, claimed to have a trademark on the word "cocky," with its conveniently double entendre reference to the personality trait most evident in the romance hero from Mr. Darcy to Christian Grey, and to the never less than impressively scaled body part in which that trait is fetishistically embodied.[38] Thus did Faleena Hopkins, author of *Cocky Roomie: A Bad Boy Romance Novel* (2016), sue her fellow writer and Bookclicker member Tara Crescent, author of *Her Cocky Doctors: A MFM Menage Romance* (2017), for trademark violation (see figure below).

Proving the persistence of communitarian norms even in this most competitive of markets, the reaction on Bookclicker and eventually in the broader romance writing and fan community

#Cockygate Is it possible to trademark the use of a single word in book titles? Faleena Hopkins thought so. More recently, Christine Feehan, author of *Dark Prince* (1999), *Dark Fire* (2001), *Dark Promises* (2016), and thirty-some other paranormal romances in the *Dark Carpathian* series, attempted to trademark the word "dark."

was outrage. Competition or no, this seemed to many a violation of the spirit of camaraderie and mutual aid so prevalent in the KDP world, with its innumerable support groups and friendly cross-marketing agreements, sharing of email lists, pricing strategies, and so on. Neither was Hopkins's legal case very strong. It was after all based on one word of a book title, a word that had already in any case been used in 2015, in Penelope Ward and Vi Keeland's delightful *Cocky Bastard*. (There is no justice in the literary field—this novel is far superior to *Fifty Shades of Grey*, let alone the idiotic *Cocky Roomie*, with a real sense of humor as well as a sidekick role filled by a blind baby goat.) Eventually the heat got unbearable enough that Hopkins withdrew her claim, but in some ways the damage had already been done. As reader Terri G. commented in a review posted to Amazon on August 23, 2018, "I enjoyed the story very much. What I didn't like was the author making it nearly impossible for other authors to use the word 'cocky' in their book titles. There is not one person on earth that has ownership of language and I will never buy anything from her again." Having wounded her own reputation, Hopkins rallied by republishing *Cocky Bastard* as *Jake Cocker*, the first of what are now no fewer than twenty-four entries in the Cocker Brother series of romances.

But of course, *pace* Terri G., there are a great many persons who have ownership of language in a given configuration—every holder of a copyright does—the only question being how many words are included in that configuration, how convincing a case they seem to make for their specific enclosure of some part of the genre commons. This was the predicate of one of Amazon's most interesting if ultimately failed experiments in the delivery of generic pleasures, Kindle Worlds, which ran from 2013 to 2018. The idea was to monetize and privatize the world of fan fiction. Instead of a free-for-all, fans would be licensed to contribute to or extend the "worlds" associated with one or another popular writer, with proceeds on the sale of the resulting texts split between the original creator, the imitator, and Amazon. The latter even began to recruit well-known authors and texts to the endeavor, including the original KDP superstar

Hugh Howey, as well as *Gossip Girl* and *Vampire Diaries* and the like. Howey himself even used the platform to produce a *Slaughterhouse-Five* fic, the fascinating novella *Peace in Amber*, as a way to process his own experiences (analogous to Kurt Vonnegut's in Dresden) in and around Lower Manhattan on the day of the terrorist attacks of September 11.

It's not clear why Amazon suddenly pulled the plug on this endeavor, which left some writers who had grown to depend on it as a revenue stream in the lurch. One can, however say that, compared with the sublime outpourings of fanfiction .net or AO3, Kindle Worlds simply didn't take off, remaining a comparatively small-time operation with no obvious advantages to readers. In a world where Amazon otherwise seems to rule relentlessly, its failure to enclose the genre commons in this instance might be taken as an encouraging sign that the human desire for story is even larger than the Everything Store, with potentialities not yet determined by the market.

Coda: Beta Intellectual Romance

The task of social reproduction theory has been to construct an adequately feminist Marxism, a Marxism that does not forget the unwaged but socially necessary work done largely in the home. Inspired by that project, this chapter has attempted to extend this line of thinking into an analysis of the contemporary literary field, arguing that it is in and by the permutative mechanisms of genre that the practice of literary life most directly contributes to the social reproduction of individuals ready to face the next workday. For reasons that I hope have been clear, the path to demonstrating this function of the genre system has been through its down-market sub-basement, where things like ABDL erotica dwell. The point throughout has been to emphasize the legibility of these categories to their consumers, for whom the acronym is a kind of beacon leading them to their fetish. In this itinerary, the "merely" analytical, theoretical, or critically constructive use of genre falls by the wayside, but can it now be brought back? Might it even allow us to observe something about literary fiction we might not otherwise have noticed? I think so. To see *Fifty Shades* as one act of enclosure of the genre commons is to see it not as a singularity but as a particularly effective (and to some degree simply lucky) expression of one region of a larger system, and there is nothing stopping us from mapping further adjacencies in that system.

Perhaps the most immediately telling of these adjacencies, one that only becomes visible in the bright light cast on it by the alpha billionaire romance, is a theoretical genre we could call the beta intellectual romance (see figure below).

For the sake of convenience, and because of the serendipity of it having been published to considerable acclaim the same year as *Fifty Shades*, we could posit Jeffrey Eugenides's *The Marriage Plot* (2011) as the signal work of this genre, even as it is also more simply a work of self-consciously literary—which is also to say, frustrated—romance in the tradition stretching back to Henry James, not to mention the best example I can think of a work of the "genre turn" based in romance. Like *Fifty Shades*, the novel establishes a reflexive relation to romance in the young female protagonist's course of study, English literature,

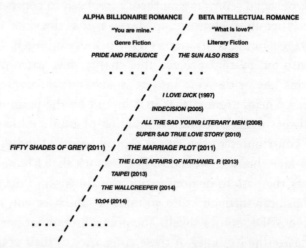

The Beta Intellectual Romance as Theoretical Genre of Contemporary US Literature On the basis of its distinction from alpha billionaire romance, one might argue for a system-wide but superficially bifurcated preoccupation in recent fiction with the contradictions of contemporary masculinity.

in this case at Brown University in the 1980s (when, for what it's worth, Eugenides himself was a student there). Unlike *Fifty Shades*, *The Marriage Plot* actually conducts the reader into the classroom for a brief lesson in literary history with obvious relevance to the story it tells. Madeleine is taking a class called "The Marriage Plot" taught by a certain Professor K. McCall Saunders:

> In Saunders's opinion, the novel had reached its apogee with the marriage plot and had never recovered from its disappearance. In the days when success in life had depended on marriage, and marriage had depended on money, novelists had had a subject to write about. The great epics sang of war, the novel of marriage. Sexual equality, good for women, had been bad for the novel. And divorce had undone it completely. What would it matter whom Emma married if she could file for separation later? How would Isabel Archer's marriage to Gilbert Osmond have been affected by the existence of a prenup? As far as Saunders was concerned, marriage didn't mean much anymore, and neither did the novel. Where could you find the marriage plot nowadays? You couldn't. You had to read historical fiction. You had to read non-Western novels involving traditional societies. Afghani novels. Indian novels. You had to go, literarily speaking, back in time.[39]

For Saunders, in effect, the novel has been ruined by its gradual assimilation to the progressive regime of customer satisfaction and free returns, which has coincided with the rise of the idea, if not the fact, of sexual equality. The novel at hand both refutes and confirms Saunders's view, telling the story of Madeleine's brief, ill-fated marriage to a young male depressive intellectual type uncannily reminiscent, in many ways, of Eugenides's generational rival David Foster Wallace.[40] On the one hand, after enduring some harrowing experiences with her partner—his self-loathing corpulence and loss of sex drive when he takes antidepressants, his manic insanity on their honeymoon when he stops taking them—Madeleine comes through more or less okay, realizing herself as a young, independent divorcée and modestly published academic literary critic. On the other hand, *pace* Old Man Saunders, the stakes of her amorous encounters as a young woman have been high enough to make them seem serious and significant, the makings of a satisfyingly intelligent and believable realist historical novel of upper-middle-class collegiate manners, not to mention a slyly affectionate domestication, on the part of an academic creative writer, of the once-upon-a-time self-important exotica of Theory.

The key difference between the beta intellectual romance and the alpha billionaire romance is the version of masculinity they put at their center. The beta intellectual is a man who at least superficially has absorbed the basic lessons of modern feminism, as in the case of the protagonist of Adelle Waldman's uncannily sympathetic inhabitation of the type in *The Love Affairs of Nathaniel P.* (2013): "Nathaniel Piven was a product of a postfeminist, 1980s childhood and politically correct, 1990s college education. He had learned all about male privilege. Moreover, he was in possession of a functional and frankly rather clamorous conscience."[41] Eugenides's Leonard Bankhead is a similar but more troubled version of the same kind of young man. When he and his nerdy friends imagine the future transformation of their names into adjectives (à la "Derridean" or "Foucauldian"), he defines Bankheadian as "characterized by excessive introspection or worry. Gloomy, depressive. See *basket case*."[42]

Note how the generic alpha and beta converge, in this instance, on the representation of the "fucked up" young man; but note also their divergent diagnoses, the one's PTSD driving him to unrealistic feats of universe mastery, the other's depression driving him first from a promising career as a scientist, then altogether out of his youthful marriage. While not always representing him as a depressive, the beta intellectual romance often makes explicit even in its title that there may be a problem with the very protagonicity of the male protagonist, who it wouldn't make any sense to call the novel's hero even if he does avoid ending up in diapers. *Indecision, All the Sad Young Literary Men*: the type of man in these works cannot be expected to muster the executive will to abolish all doubt, or to obviate the search for new and more intense pleasures, or even to buy you an Audi.

And so they were in bed, and taking off their clothes, and suddenly Sam realized with a start that he wasn't hard. He was betrayed! Full of lustful thoughts, although also many other kinds of thoughts, but lacking in lustful deeds. Saint Augustine had written of this—impotence, rather than sinful passion, was the crowning argument in his proof that lust was evil, that it was not subject to the human will. And now behold poor Sam.[43]

Behold poor Sam. Thoughtful as they are, and sensitive, and well equipped to interrogate the meaning of "love," they can be as problematic in their way as the abusive alpha, and not only for their disappointing feebleness. Even at peak physical performance, they seize the historical privilege of romantic indecision and wield it as a kind of soft power, letting their winnings multiply. As denizens, typically, of political environments at least somewhat skeptical of capitalism, beta intellectuals are not inveterate shoppers (they have little money in any case) except in the market for the attention of attractive ladies whose opinions they ambiguously respect. They do not want to whip them, just to waste their time.

5

World-Scaling

Literary Fiction in the Genre System

Adapting to Information

The model of sociological information theory developed by
Orrin E. Klapp in a series of texts written in the 1970s and
'80s did not manage to become particularly influential within
either sociology or informatics, the two disciplines it sought
to conjoin, and evolved over time into a conservative critique
of the state of the culture of a kind more vigorously mounted
by contemporaries like Christopher Lasch. It might seem especially quixotic, then, to suggest that it offers a suggestive frame
within which to view the modern history of the novel, a thing
about which it had absolutely nothing to say. It will seem only
slightly less questionable to claim its fertile use for the analysis
of the latest phase of that history, which we have been calling
the Age of Amazon. And yet, in framing the question of human
well-being in terms of the social management of information,
such a frame is what it provides. More precisely, it can be used
to draw our attention to a heretofore unrecognized dimension
of the contemporary genre system, the sorting mechanism—
differing it its particulars depending on whether it is operating
in the editorial offices of publishers, bookstores, online search,
or academia—that categorizes individual works of fiction as
iterations of a generic kind.

The dimension of the genre system disclosed by Klappian sociological information theory operates on a different level than the fetish genres examined in the previous chapter. It does not appear by name in that system, replete as the latter is with overlapping and at times competing terms, including the two that have proved most salient to this book thus far, "epic" and "romance," which will continue to be at the center of the discussion here. The opposition of which I speak is indeed to some degree *sub-generic*, a structure of opposing orientations toward the flow of information that only imperfectly manifests as works fitting those terms and their like. Operating in the substratum of genre labels, this opposition is associated with their characteristic *attitude* toward the world insofar as that "world" exists for modern subjects—which in large measure it does, if we're honest—as mass-mediated hearsay. As Niklas Luhmann puts it, drawing our attention to the weakness of immediate experience as a producer of formal knowledge of broader contexts,

> Whatever we know about our society, or indeed about the world in which we live, we know through the mass media. This is true not only of our knowledge of society and history but also of our knowledge of nature. What we know about the stratosphere is the same as what Plato knows about Atlantis: we've heard tell of it.[1]

Nowadays we might say that we've read about it on the internet. The question is: what is the relation of the novel to all that?

The idea at the core of Klappian information theory is simple enough: as first laid out in *Opening and Closing: Strategies of Information Adaptation in Society* (1978) and developed further in *Overload and Boredom: Essays on the Quality of Life in the Information Society* (1986), Klapp proposes that societies can be analyzed as living information systems tending toward a state of either increasing or decreasing receptivity to novelty.[2] Furthermore, each of these states is subject to critical limits: on one side is the escalation of informational novelty into cacophonous noise, on the other, its collapse into pure redundancy and mechanical predictability, both of them experienced as the

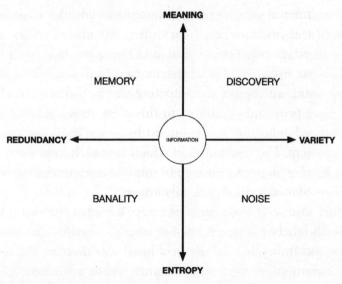

The Klappian Square Not all information theorists would place "meaning" and "entropy" at odds, but Klapp's doing so is highly intuitive, allowing us to see how "worn out" utterances—clichés—can become equivalent to incoherent ones from the (bored and/or irritated) subject's point of view.

"entropic" degradation of social meaning. Much as in the sweet spot of productive "orderly disorder" described in the adjacent enterprise of chaos theory, between these limits information can appear as a positive gain in either useful novelty or reassuring resonance with the already known.[3] In the first case it is experienced as the satisfaction of curiosity, of cognitive wanderlust, in the second as a welcome reinforcement of cultural memory and identity (see figure above). This is its most value-neutral and, it seems to me, defensible form.

However, echoing other conservative critiques of modernity, the implication throughout Klapp's analysis is that society in the late 1970s and '80s has been problematically biased toward the first, toward novelty, creating conditions for general anxiety and alienation. Baited by the mass media, the attention of the individual is coercively drawn to various forms of scandalizing but, for all that, highly marketable representations of otherness. This of course would notoriously become the case with Facebook's news-feed algorithms, where outrage at what "those people" are doing is the coin of the realm. Regardless of its actual distance from and practical relevance to the individual, they experience news of the world in this form as an intimate intrusion upon and violation of their way of life. At the same time, as though in perverse construction of the worst of all possible worlds, Klapp sees contemporary culture as beset by forms of mechanical repetition and standardization of messages leading to a generalized condition of cynicism, boredom, and disaffection. The key engine of this bad redundancy is the selfsame electronic mass media, where the incessant replay of commercial messages degrades the pursuit of genuine meaning.

More than a few elements of Klapp's analysis resonate with life in the Age of Amazon, the age of ethno-nationalist reaction to the social novelties of the neoliberal world order, the age of the clever new meme almost instantly become tiresome cliché, and of what Debjani Ganguly aptly describes as a generalized "'compulsion' to be world-oriented" through the medium of our screens.[4] Our interest here is not so much in the validity of Klapp's critique of culture, with its frequent substitution of moralizing for the materialist analysis it begs for given that informational *capitalism* always seems to be lurking in its background. It is in the way *different forms of the novel* might relate to the dilemmas of the modern informational condition that Klapp's critique compellingly if no doubt all too simply formalizes.

Reaching its apogee in the advent of the internet, the chiasmus of *overloading novelty* and *banalizing redundancy* is also a problem for narrative art, one aspect of a larger complex of questions surrounding the aesthetic management of informational quantity. I take the latter to permeate literary experience in all its dimensions as an accompaniment to the production of qualitative meaning. Crucially, the sources of information needing to be managed reside both inside and outside any given text, determining the writer's sense of what can be taken for granted (for example, this human character has lungs) and what not (her name is Ana), how much the reader needs to know at a given point in the unfolding of a plot, and so on. The "attention economy" internal to the work is inevitably enmeshed with the one that surrounds it in a thousand complex ways.[5]

This is true not only for assumptions readers are able to make about fictional worlds—even otherwise wildly fantastic worlds—by extrapolating from the real or primary one. It is also true on the level of book marketing, where the effort is to draw attention to that represented world in the first place. The Age of Amazon is the scene of several innovations on that account. Among them are the Amazon-owned book-centric social media site Goodreads and the literary web more broadly—everything included in what Simone Murray describes as the Digital Literary Sphere.[6] Into this arena comes the "Goodreads Author," the professional author who has established a quasi-official presence on the site to cultivate a readership, which is also to say customer base. Whether as pleas for attention or as

Products related to this item

Sponsored ⓘ

Pre-order now

Midlife Curses: A Paranormal Women's Fiction Mystery (Witching Hour Book 1)	An Invitation to Murder: An amateur sleuth murder mystery (A Mary Blake Mystery Boo...	Raspberry Ripple Murder: A Bitsie's Bakeshop Culinary Cozy (Bitsie's Bakeshop Cozy...	Nabbed in the Nasturtiums (Lovely Lethal Gardens Book 14)	A Good Man Gone (Mercy Watts Mysteries Book 1)
Christine Zane Thomas	AG Barnett	Abby Byne	Dale Mayer	A.W. Hartoin
A snarky grandmother. A talking cat. And one very dead vampire.	After playing a detective on tv for years, Mary must now become one...	★★★★☆ 203	★★★★★	★★★★☆ 985
★★★★☆ 1,397	★★★★☆ 270	Kindle Edition	Kindle Edition	Kindle Edition
Kindle Edition	Kindle Edition	$0.99	$4.99	$4.99
$2.99	$2.99			

Customers who read this book also read

Trick or Murder? (Sophie Sayers Village Mysteries Book 2)	Humpty Bumpkin: Page-Turning Cozy With Fun and Fabulous Fur Babies (Country Cousin...	Murder in the Manger (Sophie Sayers Village Mysteries Book 3)	Reservation with Death: A Park Hotel Mystery (The Park Hotel Mysteries Book 1)	Springtime for Murder (Sophie Sayers Village Mysteries Book 5)
› Debbie Young	› Sam Cheever	› Debbie Young	› Diane Capri	› Debbie Young
★★★★☆ 196	★★★★★ 1,148	★★★★☆ 148	★★★★☆ 696	★★★★☆ 585
Kindle Edition	Kindle Edition	Kindle Edition	Kindle Edition	Kindle Edition
$3.99	$0.00	$3.99	$4.99	$3.99

Associated Products Browsers of Debbie Young's cozy murder mystery *Best Murder in Show* (2017) are directed either to works that have proved of interest to other purchasers of that book—a line frequently dominated by other works by the same author—or to works associated with it for a fee paid to Amazon. The "sponsored" tier is frequently dominated by self-published works in the same genre—genre being the most reliable indicator of the "kind of thing" a given reader might enjoy based on past or current purchases and browsing habits.

something like the thing itself in the form of criticism and discussion of literary works, these phenomena are continuous with Amazon's own marketing algorithms and ad placements, which, based on various criteria, including payment of a fee by their authors, shuffle some thumbnails of purchasable books into the visual field of the online customer and not others (see figure on p. 197).

More abstractly, but just as importantly, one can speak of the continuity between the literary field in the Age of Amazon and the space of social media, where the twenty-first-century attention economy takes its most literal and consequential form. Both are occasions for the production and consumption of what we might call *surplus social presence*, an ideological inversion of the relative anonymity of the worker entering the economy bearing a fungible quantity of labor time. Social media presence is for them—for us—an essentially compensatory enterprise, a reassuring curation of our meaningful life story as against the rage-inducing news-feed juxtaposed to it. The quasi-ideality of "cyberspace" has been crucial to its functioning, enabling something made of cables, switches and servers to stand for the collective consciousness that recognizes and massively valorizes the Surplus Self as celebrity, as "influencer." It also makes every user a kind of micro-celebrity to their social media friends and followers. So, too, if in a different form, self-expression as a writer of fiction, whether as an esteemed professional in that trade or self-publishing wannabe. The point is that the urge to post selfies and the urge to publish a novel are on a continuum as modes of self-exposure and attention-getting and would-be self-aggrandizement in an otherwise thoroughly massified world.

For good reason, all of this might seem *superficial* in the pejorative sense, a violation of the high seriousness of literature by ego gratification. But attention-getting and attention-keeping are also, of course, mechanisms internal to the novel's form.[7] At the extreme, we have the recent innovation in Amazon's Kindle Unlimited program of paying the authors who contribute to it on the basis of the number of pages subscribers actually read, as reported back to the mother ship by the Kindle-enabled device itself, not on the basis of number of downloads of the work, which was the original arrangement. It is not a good idea, in this regime, to be too slow in getting your story off the ground! And sure enough, in a new wrinkle of the serial cliffhanger of yore, that world is replete with *immediately tension-filled* openings. Working in the opposite direction are the relatively easeful buildup of the story-worlds of literary fiction, which count on the existence of readers looking for that sort of thing, or at least able to tolerate it on the way to sophisticated pleasures.

It would be a mistake, I think, in the spirit of Orrin E. Klapp, to dismiss these processes on the grounds that they assimilate literary experience to less-than-flattering aspects of the contemporary human condition. The novelist is not and cannot be indifferent to the matter of keeping and managing the reader's attention. "Entertainment" is a much more complex concept than it sometimes appears, with its etymological implication of things being held together (*entre-tenire*), first as a form of conviviality, as when one entertains a guest, then as a particularly intense relation of the mind to an object, as when one entertains a thought. The mid-twentieth-century convergence of left and right cultural criticism in condemnation of "mere" entertainment as frivolous if not worse has left us less observant than we might have been of what exactly is going on in the mind of the reader in the event of literary entertainment, although several scholars working on the neurophysiological, cognitive, and evolutionary bases of reading fiction have been trying to rectify this situation.[8]

Partly owing to the sheer difficulty of that enterprise, literary scholars have remained largely content to take literary entertainment for granted as the uninteresting opposite of serious reading, the thing we encourage and teach. This is so even as the subordination of literature to visual culture everywhere but in the classroom has, if I'm not mistaken, lent the consumption of written narrative of *any* kind a hint of virtue, if only for the way it calls forth the exercise of the reader's own powers of visualization. Notably, while a famed NEA-sponsored study of US reading habits, *Reading at Risk* (2004), did not count the consumption of works of nonfiction in its depiction of an increasingly unliterary America, genre fiction and literary fiction were put on equal footing in it as cultural goods.[9]

If this weren't the case, the panoply of "reading challenges"—the publicly declared and collectively self-monitored goal of reading *these many books* in *that* amount of time—made and met on Goodreads would make as little sense as a similar "porn challenge" would. So, too, although at a higher cultural level, the entire enterprise of Oprah's (and more recently Reese Witherspoon's) Book Club is founded on the ideal of personal betterment through reading. If it would be too much to say that reading fiction is now always understood as "good for you," its assimilation to a regime of informal therapy and self-care is clear enough. Once it has been detached from an explicitly educational mission, where it is understood to have an important role in acculturation and the acquisition of advanced literacy, reading becomes part of a repertoire of techniques of mood regulation, of getting by, for the highbrow as much as for the middle- or lowbrow. And this is where Klapp's sociological thermodynamics comes in, with its suggestive linking of well-being and information.

What are novels *for*? What are their *uses*? For Amazon itself, of course, it is enough to say that novels are something the customer wants and that it is happy to supply for a relatively low price. But that wanting comes in different forms and with different expectations for what symbolic service a novel of whatever kind will provide. This book has already tried out some ways of articulating those services in terms more specific than we usually hear, from the experience of virtual quality time, to the expression of corporate subjectivity, to the provision of existential supplement and repetitive facilitation of fantasy. In this chapter the function of the contemporary novel will be described as the *therapeutic processing of information*. The idea—speculative to be sure, grounded in observation of literary form in historical context and not neurological data—is that narrative effects an unsystematic conversion of incessant streams of notionally nonfictional "news" (political, cultural, or otherwise) into reassuringly meaningful because coherently designed fictional worlds. In hoary old terms, narrative helps us *makes sense of the world*—but, crucially, does so in reaction to and in dialogue with other forms and sources of information. This is to see the novel as having a particular therapeutic function in a larger media ecology, one enabled by its nature as a "world-enclosing total system," albeit a relatively small and portable one.[10] On another, grosser level, it is to see the work of Amazon as a deliverer of fiction as occurring alongside that of Facebook and Google as deliverers of unbound information, of a radical *muchness*, *otherness*, and *ongoing-ness* of the data feed.

The further claim is that this processing occurs in the complementary forms suggested by Klapp: as either an "opening" to the excitement of novelty and cultural otherness or "closure" in pursuit of good redundancy and personal resonance. As we'll see below, Klapp's terms will be translated into what I take to be their literary-historical analogues: on the one hand, epic and romance; on the other, maximalism and minimalism. As modes of symbolic opening and symbolic closure, the novelistic modes pertaining to these terms organize the genre system of contemporary fiction and become visible on the surface of the work as its participation in one category or another—even as genre itself, for most Amazon customers, presents a kind of good redundancy, a return to familiar and reliable sources of pleasure in an otherwise alienating world.

Minimalism and Maximalism Revisited

In my book *The Program Era*, I argued that postwar literary fiction can usefully be seen as driven by the stylistic polarity of maximalism and minimalism, that is, by the competing compositional impulses, never realized in their purest forms, to say all there is to say or to say as little as possible. With deep roots in the preeminently inclusive history of the novel as a grab bag of many-splendored ordinary life, the maximalist text tends toward symbolic surplus—toward the "polyphonic" or "heteroglossic" rambunctiousness so well described by Mikhail

Bakhtin, and which for him was the essence of the novel form.[11] This inclusiveness is associated in turn with crowdedness of characterization, complexity of plot, and relatively long length, working always toward the rebellious *expansion* of signification across larger and larger stretches of otherwise unmarked and unredeemed historical actuality. For the maximalist text, the truth of fiction is in the whole, in all the things and beings and voices it includes. Maximalism is most prominently exemplified in the twentieth- and twenty-first-century US tradition by writers of historical fiction from William Faulkner to Thomas Pynchon, William Vollmann, and Karen Tei Yamashita, and is highly visible in postcolonial or world literature, too, in writers ranging from James Joyce to Salman Rushdie and Roberto Bolaño. In this tradition the unfolding of "history" presents an ongoing proliferation of traumatizing data, or *bad news*. It is the job of the novel to narrativize that data against the threat of its falling into ethical meaninglessness as an immense panorama of futility and anarchy, as one damned thing after another, as grotesque power and greed naturally having their way.

The minimalist fictional text then appears as a dialectical rejoinder to the post-epic aspirations of maximalism, presenting the value of closure and consolidation as a counter to the maximalist value of openness and expansion. An innovation, more or less, of literary modernism, the minimalist narrative tends toward understatement, suggestive simplicity, and lyric brevity. Its represented worlds are generally less populous than those of the maximalist narrative, having extracted and refined the bourgeois novel's historical commitment to the individual in such a way as to reduce its crowded bulk. Minimalism is exemplified in the US tradition by the short fiction of Ernest Hemingway, Raymond Carver, Mary Robison, and many others, having become the house style of the writing program, and is evident in a different way in figures of world literature as diverse as Samuel Beckett, Clarice Lispector, and J. M. Coetzee. At its most intense, as in Hemingway's early stories, it aspires to locate itself in a diegetic present and remain there, shielding a frequently author-identified protagonist from the trauma of history, but, more frequently, giving exquisitely stark testimony to the inability to do so. In short, where the maximalist text expands so as to absorb and process data, the minimalist text shrinks so as to repel it.

The latter aspiration yields sequences of sentences like these from Hemingway's "Big Two-Hearted River" (1925), long and rightly read as representing and indeed performing some kind of therapy, the key point being that in this story a *grammatical* invulnerability undergirds a *thematic* one: "There had been this to do. Now it was done. It had been a hard trip. He was very tired. That was done. He had made his camp. He was settled. Nothing could touch him. It was a good place to camp. He was there, in the good place."[12] These famously clipped sentences can usefully be compared to a section from Faulkner's "The Bear" (1942) in which the unit of the sentence, expanding to 579 words, exceeds and contains the unit of paragraph. It is associated with the narrator's breathless effort to "track" genealogical time as an unbroken line of historical complicity in ecological destruction and slavery alike:

> He could say it, himself and his cousin juxtaposed not against the wilderness but against the tamed land which was to have been his heritage, the land which old Carothers McCaslin his grandfather had bought with white man's money from the wild men whose grandfathers without guns hunted it, and tamed and ordered or believed he had tamed and ordered it for the reason that human beings he held in bondage and in the power of life and death had removed the forest from it and in their sweat scratched the surface of it to a depth of perhaps fourteen inches in order to grow something out of it which had not been there before and which could be translated back into the money he who believed he had bought it had had to pay to get it and hold it and a reasonable profit too: and for which reason old Carothers McCaslin, knowing better, could raise his children, his descendants and heirs, to believe the land was his to hold and bequeath since the strong and ruthless man has a cynical foreknowledge of his own vanity and pride and strength and contempt for all his get: just

as, knowing better, Major de Spain and his fragment of that wilderness which was bigger and older than any recorded deed; just as, knowing better, old Thomas Sutpen, from whom Major de Spain had had his fragment for money: just as Ikkemotubbe, the Chickasaw chief, from whom Thomas Sutpen had had the fragment for money or rum or whatever it was, knew in his turn that not even a fragment of it had been his to relinquish or sell

not against the wilderness but against the land, not in pursuit and lust but in relinquishment, and in the commissary as it should have been, not the heart perhaps but certainly the solar plexus of the repudiated and relinquished: the square, galleried, wooden building squatting like a portent above the fields whose laborers it still held in thrall '65 or no and placarded over with advertisements for snuff and cures for chills and salves and potions manufactured and sold by white men to bleach the pigment and straighten the hair of negroes that they might resemble the very race which for two hundred years had held them in bondage and from which for another hundred years not even a bloody civil war would have set them completely free

himself and his cousin amid the old smells of cheese and salt meat and kerosene and harness, the ranked shelves of tobacco and overalls and bottled medicine and thread and plow-bolts, the barrels and kegs of flour and meal and molasses and nails, the wall pegs dependent with plowlines and plow-collars and hames and trace-chains, and the desk and the shelf above it on which rested the ledgers in which McCaslin recorded the slow outward trickle of food and supplies and equipment which returned each fall as cotton made and ginned and sold (two threads frail as truth and impalpable as equators yet cable-strong to bind for them who made the cotton to the land their sweat fell on), and the older ledgers clumsy and archaic in size and shape, on the yellowed pages of which were recorded in the faded hand of his father Theophilus and his uncle Amodeus during the two decades before the Civil War, the manumission in title at least of Carothers McCaslin's slaves:

"Relinquish," McCaslin said.[13]

Crucially, as we can see here, the maximalist/minimalist polarity is an affective or attitudinal polarity, too, the linguistically prideful—or, in Faulkner's case, loquaciously self-loathing—hysterical muchness of maximalism countered by minimalism's rigorously cool or brooding emotional self-regulation and withdrawal.

Of course, in practice, most fiction falls somewhere between the extremes of minimalism and maximalism, which are in any case subject to interesting dialectical inversions and reversals. Thus can we speak of the compressed maximalism—the miniaturism—of works like Pynchon's *Crying of Lot 49* (1965) or Mohsin Hamid's *Exit West* (2017), or of what can only be described as the *monumental minimalism*—the monumentalism, let's call it—of a work like Karl Ove Knausgaard's multivolume *My Struggle* (2009–11). The latter has been a particularly fertile mode of late, defining texts like Megan Boyle's *Liveblog: A Novel* (2018) and Lucy Ellmann's *Ducks, Newburyport* (2019). More simply, one might point out how the expansive historical conspiracies lurking in the novels of, say, Dan Brown are compressed precisely by virtue of the conspiracy or cabal as explanatory *techne* (a compression doubled, in his case, by setting all the action of the novels on a single day, just like *Ulysses*). By the same token, even the most expansive epic fantasy can be accused of simplifying the world, if only technologically, by returning us to a world where messages are few and far between, traveling at the speed of horse or hawk. The idea is not to produce separate categories into which a given work must conclusively fall, nor to overcommit to the granular accuracy of what is after all a deliberately reductive interpretive model. It is to sketch a conceptual map with coordinates helpful to the task of interpretation even now, as the Program Era gives way (in my research agenda at least!) to the Age of Amazon.[14]

Part of the point of this book's strategic re-periodization of the present as the Age of Amazon is to put popular genre fiction—the bread and butter of the KDP world and of Kindle-enabled consumption in general—at the center of scholarly concern rather than at the margins where it usually finds itself.

Beginning with the novel's generic appeal to the ordinary reader, the idea of literature as either an arbiter of cultural values, or engine of cultural capital formation, or equipment for moral improvement recedes before a conception of reading as everyday self-care; as the repetitive provision of the pleasurable sensation of the meaningfulness of life. While they are typically less interested in putting pressure on the unit of the sentence than their high-literary equivalents, works of genre fiction are also organized by the polarity of the maximal and the minimal, but more accurately by and between the pointedly pre-novelistic compositional values we can label "epic" and "romance" (see figure below).

Toward the first, epic pole of the contemporary genre system we find science fiction, fantasy, and geopolitical/historical

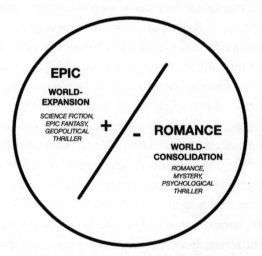

The Dialectic of Epic and Romantic World-Building To the extent that this dialectic structures our sense of contemporary fictional form as such, as I believe it does, it suggests the immense pressure put on the novel qua novel in the Age of Amazon, at least as we know it from the great tradition of novel theory centered on nineteenth-century realism. To be sure, the term "novel" remains in common use across the genre system as a way to refer to a discrete unit of product, but the fundamental symbolic integrations of which that genre was alleged to be the vehicle—as when the competing claims of the social order and protagonist are successfully negotiated in the bildungsroman—are now being pulled apart and distributed to different "pre-novelistic" novelistic modes. This is perhaps why we tend to think there are no truly great novels anymore, only—and even then in a spirit of generosity—a great many interesting ones.

conspiracy thriller; toward the second, romantic pole we see all the many varieties of mystery and romance fiction and the domestic or psychological thriller. Epic and romance are the super-generic vehicles of a popular maximalism and minimalism. The first is geared to world-expanding sprawl and exhilarating ongoing-ness in the exploration of historical or pseudo-historical reality.[15] The second is geared to world-consolidating completion in the "small world" of marriage or excision of the criminal element from the (literal or figurative) village social body. As we would expect, the first is most often relatively long, the second most often relatively short; and when not, meaningfully so: the fattest romances are historical romances, as in Diana Gabaldon's long-running *Outlander* series, where the love story is accompanied by rafts of prettifying but also ennobling period detail, as if to say: this isn't *just* a love story, it's bigger than that. By the same token, it would be wrong to discount the importance of the short story and novella in the history of science fiction, whose brevity has been conducive to serial narrative "experiments" in extrapolating from scientific ideas to future historical consequences, only some of which are improved by being blown up into multivolume SF epics. We are dealing here then with two different modes of world-building, but also with their dialectical interpenetration and complexification.

To be sure, in line with the practices of capitalism at large, the generic norm for popular romance and mystery, as for science fiction and fantasy, is the production of works in series, but this similarity covers a relative difference in the nature of the units of which they are made up. While installments in the science fiction and especially fantasy series are notoriously open-ended—this being one of the most common genres of complaint in Amazon reviews—the installment in the romance or mystery series typically reaches a decisive conclusion in the forging of the marriage bond or the solution to the crime. That they do so in *volume after volume* is a latent contradiction, but an understandable one because, after all, in the embodied life of the reader, entropy marches on, the sense of resolution they have won from fiction beginning to decay as soon as they put down the book. Although the maximalist text sometimes wants to deny it—think here of the quasi-biblical status David Foster Wallace's *Infinite Jest* (1996) achieved for some its readers—in secular modernity no one book, no matter how good a book, will suffice. To be a "reader of fiction" is to read *many* works of fiction: a point so obvious it must be underlined again lest it be ignored. What kind of pleasurable service do popular epic and romance respectively and in combination provide? How do they function within a culture of quantification—capitalist culture—more broadly?

We have heard plenty about the way capitalist abstraction and quantification violates the complex human essence, but what about its order of operations, where inputs and outputs, profits and losses, are constantly monitored and regulated along the arithmetic axis of *more* or *less*? Do they, too, have existential analogues in narrative form?

And where does literary fiction fit in this picture? If part of the point of calling the present phase of literary history the Age of Amazon is to draw our attention to the structuring of the literary genre system by popular generic forms, this does not mean that literary fiction need be ignored, only reframed and redefined (see figure on p. 209).

To examine the category of literary fiction, we place it at the margins of the genre system, aligning literary maximalism and minimalism with their counterparts in the genre core. This diagram also allows us to see what might be thought of as a middling or classical position in literary fiction, neither maximalist nor minimalist, where more or less ordinary family life takes the stage, even as historical forces draw the family unit outward toward history, yielding the multigenerational family saga. On the other side of this scheme (obviously a heuristic one—you could make a parlor game of debating the accurate mapping of a given work), we can see how the space between lyric autofiction and classical realism is occupied by the coming-of-age story, whose protagonist might be moving in one direction or another, toward alienation or social integration.

In these loftier precincts, too, the maximalist/minimalist polarity operates in a form specific to the needs of the present, but with

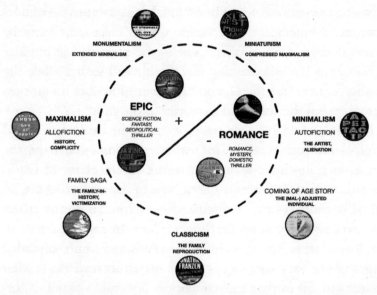

Literary Fiction in the Genre System A sketch of the contemporary genre system in which literary fiction is extrinsic to but also defined by its proximity to core generic operations of world consolidation or world expansion, the first tending toward autofiction, the second toward what we can call by contrast "allofiction." In between these poles lie the would-be equilibrium of the family as a social unit. All works of literary fiction lie in close proximity to their generic siblings, but the very moderation of "classicism" makes it especially porous in relation to less prestigious categories like "women's" or "book club" fiction. At the top of the diagram are dialectical inversions of the maximalism/minimalism relation, which I label monumentalism and miniaturism, respectively, the first stretching autofiction out to epic length, the second condensing "the world" into a text of lyric brevity. Placed in a marginal relation to genre fiction, the prestige of literary fiction is defined in part by its proximity to the extra-literary "real" as a matter of common concern.

a key difference from genre fiction. Whereas the worlds built in genre fiction tend toward what we might call an essential fictionality, holding themselves responsible to internally established rules and the accretion of same as generic conventions, those of literary fiction are beholden even now to the "real world" as a guarantor of referential gravity. This is why, as we shall see, the figure of the writer-as-character looms so large there even now, long after the "death of the author," in a way it does not often do in genre fiction. It is also why recent discussions of the so-called genre turn in literary fiction, examined in chapter 4, err when they decline to account for its equally prevalent dialectical opposite, the impulse not to be fictional at all but novelized documentary or memoir.[16] The "genre effects" of the first can be understood as a bid to offer some of the pleasures of popular culture even while remaining identifiable as literary, while the "reality hunger" of the second would ground that literariness ever deeper in the supposed authority of the real.[17]

The real-world referent reigns even in the case of so-called magical realism—that is, *lo real maravilloso*—perhaps the best-known aesthetic formation of the recent phase of world literature, amply represented even now in the ranks of Amazon Crossing translations, as discussed in chapter 2. While critics have tended to focus on the "magical" or "marvelous" part of that formulation, seeing it either as a repository of pre-capitalist values or cynical packaging of exotic wares, its *realismo* is what is meant to tell us that a given work is not child's play but "literature" in the honorific sense, possibly worthy of the Nobel Prize.[18] Laying claim to the authority of the real is how literary fiction maintains its increasingly tenuous superiority of esteem to the popular genres around it. By the same token, it's also how genre fiction gets taken more and more seriously, as its more flagrantly built worlds come to be understood as making the same claim about a real world that seems increasingly unreal.

Network Effects I: Epic Maximalism

The best way to examine the operation of the maximalism/minimalism polarity in the space of literary fiction is dialectically or even, dare I say, deconstructively. By these means, any given superficially maximalist work will be discovered upon close-enough inspection to harbor some of the therapeutic motives of minimalism, and vice versa. It could not be otherwise, inasmuch as even the longest literary works severely reduce the potential informational totality of the world they represent, while even the shortest works imply the existence of an unmarked world beyond their confines. To view works in this way is to view them as parts of a dynamic genre system, with individual elements defined relationally. Taking up complementary relations to an original plenum, history, maximalism and minimalism are both crucially important to contemporary so-called world literature, but the first mode is often overtly worldly, enough that it has inspired Alexander Beecroft to nominate the "plot of globalization" as a key contemporary form with certain immediately recognizable characteristics.[19]

With its derivation from what has variously been called the multi-plot, systems, encyclopedic, or network novel, the plot of globalization is constructed of far-flung elements but finds an organizing referent in the complex externality of the historical world system. As though by the exertion of capitalist gravity, this referent draws the narrative on and on and on.

A good example from recent American literature would be Don DeLillo's *Underworld* (1997), one of the first major works of literature to register the advent of the internet directly.[20] For Patrick Jagoda, who I think overstates the historical originality of what he calls the "network novel," DeLillo's verbally gymnastic doorstopper is the first major work to attempt to realize the truth and truism that "everything is connected"; that individuals exist as nodes in the vast systems through which they move.[21] And yet, for Jagoda, the inevitably sequential nature of the novel form limits its ability to present that system whole, as we might see it from above in a static diagram. Instead, the network novel specializes in the representation of individual affective responses to the evolving ongoing-ness of connected life. This is helpful even if, as demonstrated by Caroline Levine, it is a structure already fully manifest in a text like *Bleak House*, and in the Victorian multi-plot novel more broadly.[22] The true novelty of DeLillo's novel, I would argue, is only visible relative to a more immediate precursor in the line of maximalist literary fictions like Pynchon's *Gravity's Rainbow*.

Unlike the latter, *Underworld* is not particularly paranoid, at least not in any negative sense. Rather, the constantly reiterated theme of the novel is that even the most obscure member of the masses, someone who might otherwise feel themselves to be the "waste" of history, feels existentially enlarged by their immersion in a system that also contains celebrities. The idea appears early in the novel's prologue, where the famous and the anonymous alike share the social space of a baseball stadium hosting a playoff game: "When you see a thing like that," thinks the radio announcer, "a thing that becomes a newsreel, you begin to feel you are a carrier of some solemn scrap of history."[23] There is no grand historical conspiracy in DeLillo's self-consciously literary novel. What there is instead is a series of more or less incidentally—which is to say, technically but also, in the nature of things, affectively—connected persons and events. They are a "social network" somewhat of the kind that would soon enough begin to be hosted on social media platforms, one whose value is at once sentimentally and ecstatically individualist.

Indeed, if one looks closely enough, DeLillo's network novel can start to look like an overgrown autofiction. As *David Copperfield* was for Dickens, it is by far the most autobiographical of his many novels, a richly detailed exploration of the exact historical period of his young manhood in the immigrant Bronx. It is supplied with a character, in waste management executive Nick Shay, that doesn't take much effort to read as a partial author figure.[24] The rest of that figure is supplied by the Bronx housewife turned international art star, Klara Sax, who briefly becomes young Nick's lover. This pairing helps us to see the continuity, in the category I have labeled "romance," between the "romanticism" of lyric individuality, on the one hand, and of the love story on the other. The first is at the center of literary autofiction, the second of mass-market romance, and watermarks of both are discernible, however faintly, in the network architecture of DeLillo's novel. In different ways and together, Nick and Klara can be read as expressions of the ecstatic semiotic self-expansion experienced by their once obscure but now famous author.

Although 1997 is a very early moment in the Age of Amazon, *Underworld* gives a strong account of how the nesting of individual and corporate identity formation in social media functions. "The corporation is supposed to take us outside ourselves," thinks Nick.

We design these organized bodies to respond to the market, face foursquare into the world ... You feel the contact points around you, the caress of linked grids that give you a sense of order and command. It's there in the warbling banks of phones, in the fax machines and photocopiers and all the oceanic logic stored in your computer. *It expands your self-esteem* and connects you in your well-pressed suit to the things that slip through the world otherwise unperceived.[25]

This is how things might look from the point of view of the corporate executive, the kind of white male authority figure in whom DeLillo has for my money taken an inordinately sympathetic interest, most notably in a work like *Cosmopolis* (2003), which is essentially *Fifty Shades of Grey* for intellectuals. His apotheosis in the culture at large is the folk-heroic-cum-villainous figure of the billionaire like Jeff Bezos or Donald Trump, the latter playing the role of fascist Id to the former's neoliberal Ego. As we saw in chapter 3, this figure looms especially large in the contemporary romance novel.

A more difficult maximalist work to deconstruct in this way is Amitav Ghosh's *Ibis* Trilogy (2008–15), which distributes fragmentary author figurations among a large and evolving character system in the context of the mid-nineteenth-century opium trade in and around the Indian Ocean.[26] In its epic ambition, it is a strong example of the state of the art of "world literature" in the Age of Amazon, where trilogies abound, where the affordances of the novel in its classic dimensions are so often either too much or, as here, not enough to achieve a given aesthetic end. This is so even as its setting in the 1830s absolves it of the responsibility of representing the advent of e-commerce directly. Ghosh's selection of the first Opium War as a historical referent relevant to his present-day readers is nonetheless exceptionally canny, reminding us that, never mind the self-abnegating "Protestant Ethic" so interesting to Max Weber, capitalism has never lacked a strong commitment to what we now call consumerism, with its militant imposition of new and ideally addictive desires.

For the British, it was a national addiction to imported tea, the drinking of which quickly came to be perceived as a quintessential national characteristic and nonnegotiable need. As Ghosh's trilogy explains, seeding the source of this tea, China, with its own addiction to opium produced in British India was a way of balancing accounts in the system of world trade, even as forcing this market to remain "free" under threat of military annihilation points to what would prove to be long-standing contradictions in this system. Long before the wide dissemination of the convenient central "truth" of neoclassical economics—that capitalism is made exempt from moral judgment by its subservience to the "revealed preferences" of the people—the free traders of the trilogy are immune to shaming as the destructive drug pushers they are.

While Binayak Roy is no doubt right to describe Ghosh's project in terms of his creation of a transnational "affective community" composed of the radically disparate persons who find their way to the former slave ship, the *Ibis*, now plying the trade routes connecting India to China, I would first emphasize the way Ghosh figures these routes as precursors to the World Wide Web of the trilogy's present.[27] This is evident from the first pages of *Sea of Poppies*, when Deeti, an artist and wife of an opium factory worker—she proves to be the moral center of the trilogy as whole—suddenly has a vision of a sailing ship:

> Deeti knew that the vision was not materially present in front of her—as, for example, was the barge moored near the factory [on the Ganges]. She had never seen the sea, never left the district, never spoken any language but her native Bhojpuri, yet not for a moment did she doubt that the ship existed somewhere and was heading in her direction ... In time, among the legions who came to regard the *Ibis* as their ancestor, it was accepted that it was the river itself that had granted Deeti the vision: that the image of the *Ibis* had been transported upstream, like an electric current, the moment the vessel made contact with the sacred waters.[28]

After this framing moment of magical realism, the trilogy abandons that mode in favor of an energetic tracing of the emergence of plurality and plenitude as a consequence of the ordeal of international transport.

Ghosh's trilogy is "autofictional" only in that it inserts the too-often ignored importance of his country of origin to what has come down to us as an epochally significant conflict between Britain and China in the Opium Wars. India was after all where most of the opium at issue in those wars came from. The transit of that addictive commodity across the Indian Ocean is also, for Ghosh, the transit of personal identities across the boundaries of tribe, nation, race, and language in this region. *Sea of Poppies*, *River of Smoke*, *Flood of Fire*: the titles of the individual entries in the trilogy reinforce this interest in ontological fluidity, a mediated version of which it offers to the reader like an exhilaratingly pleasant drug. While the trilogy is never less than highly attentive to the racist cynicism and brutality of the system that enables it, this fluidity is nonetheless presented as its "vernacular cosmopolitan" product. As Beecroft notes, it presents the best-case scenario for what capitalism does to language, sparing it from the worst effects of commercial homogenization.

This is what we see in the trilogy's virtuosic seeding of standard English with various transformations and accretions that have clung to it as a result of trade. Early in the first novel, Ghosh fashions a set piece of this linguistic program in a long monologue delivered by the *Ibis*'s pilot, Mr. Doughty, to one of the trilogy's main characters, the African American first mate and eventual militant free trader on his own account, Zachary:

> "The old Raja of Raskhali: I could tell you a story or two about him—Rascally-Roger I used to call him!" ... Wasn't a man in town who could put on a burra-khana like he did. Sheeshmull blazing with shammers and candles. Paltans of bearers and khidmutgars. Demijohns of French loll-shrub and carboys of iced simkin. And the karibat! ... No fear of pishpash and cobbilymash at the Rascally table. The dumbpokes and pillaus were good

enough, but we old hands, we'd wait for the curry of cockup and the chitchky of pollock-saug. Oh he set a rankin table I can tell you ...[29]

Now this is delicate: here is an Englishman recounting the wonderful service he, a sailor, has received as a diner at the table of the Raja. For the reader, that service takes the mediated form of a performative foreign-ness-in-English that, or so it seems to me, doesn't demand translation by the reader in any rigorous way, inviting them instead to feast on this cornucopia of delicious words, to consume words at however distant a remove from their precise meaning. It is as though language itself were a commodity—which of course it frequently enough is. Should we be troubled by this framing of linguistic otherness as literally *consumable* by those of relative and, in this case, racially marked, privilege? Are later instances of the trilogy's staging of multilingualism in the banter of lascar crewmen or colorful pidgin of the Chinese traders to be understood in the same way, or are they significantly different?

As for the first audience for these words, Zachary, about fourteen hundred pages and two volumes later we find him relishing his personal connection to the system of global trade that distributes this deliciousness so awesomely. As he observes the British navy pounding the Chinese into submission, he thinks that he

had never seen such a spectacle, such a marvel of planning and such a miracle of precision. It seemed to him a triumph of modern civilization; a perfect example of the ways in which discipline and reason could conquer continents of darkness, just as Mrs Burnham had said: it was proof of the omnipotence of the class of men of which he too was now a part. He thought of the unlikely mentors who had helped him through the door ... and was filled with gratitude that destiny had afforded him a place in this magnificent machine.[30]

The exquisite sourness of this moment of triumph is, I think, much to Ghosh's credit as an artist, instancing a fascination in maximalist texts, going back to Faulkner, with the problem of *historical complicity* as an adjunct of *affective community*. The magnificent war machine with which Zachary identifies is also, mutatis mutandis, the emergent system of global free trade in whose construction it was a signal event, as well as the increasingly efficient communication networks that facilitated it. They inspire a feeling of exhilarated self-aggrandizement here just as they did in DeLillo.

As critical as Ghosh is of this existential transaction, the marvel of planning that Zachary witnesses is not unrelated to the one witnessed by the reader of the trilogy itself, which for all its sprawl rounds itself into a stunningly complete and fully interconnected whole, a fictional world in the grandest sense. This, I would say, is one of the clues that it is written not in the era of emergent free trade that is its ostensible subject, but rather in one of monopoly capital, inasmuch as it is the latter, aided by the regulatory state, that sees the true triumph of precisely timed logistics. As Ghosh proudly put it in an interview, describing the first volume in a way that seems even more true of the trilogy as a whole: "It was technically very, very demanding, especially at the end, because all the characters come together in this very finely synchronized unfolding of events. It was a very intricate bit of writing, perhaps the most intricate bit of writing I've ever done."[31]

Network Effects II: Romantic Minimalism

Now, if a work like DeLillo's patently maximalist network novel can be read as a crypto-autofiction, what of the slimmer offerings of autofiction itself? Borrowed from the French late new wave, the term "autofiction" serves nicely as a label for an entire wing of contemporary literary fiction, one I would otherwise call minimalist. Characterized, typically, by its centering on a barely fictionalized writer-protagonist, autofiction fits comfortably in a lineage of modernist *Künstlerroman* like Joyce's *Portrait of the*

Artist as a Young Man or Hemingway's *In Our Time*, even as that mode has become available to more kinds of people than young, white, alienated males.

Autofictional minimalism is a rather more "equal opportunity" genre than it once was, although by no means an ungendered one. In fact, the ordeal of gender is its thematic bread and butter, the most significant domain of potentially political sociality in which its protagonists tend to move. This was as true for Hemingway and Carver as it is now true for Chris Kraus, Tao Lin, Sheila Heti, Ben Lerner, Olivia Laing, Jenny Offill, Rachel Cusk, and countless others, including the talented Korean minimalist writer published in translation by Amazon Crossing, Bae Suah. The title of Suah's slender volume, *Nowhere to Be Found* (trans. 2015), might serve as an *ars poetica* of minimalist autofiction, which so often takes the form of a paradoxically performative act of social withdrawal or alienation. Barely managing to stay interested in the heterosexual romance that looks at first like it will occupy the novel's center, the task of this exquisitely downbeat novel is instead to produce its ironically triumphant concluding line: "And that is how I became an absolutely meaningless thing and survived time."[32]

The most basic contradiction visible in this mode is precisely this desire to *publish social withdrawal*, as though one felt the need to log onto to Facebook every day to announce that one is quitting Facebook. Preferring a small world to a sprawling one, it tends to condense a great deal of symbolic struggle into protagonist names and pronouns. Suah, like Lerner and Kraus and Heti, manages the use of the simple first-person pronoun, while Tao Lin gives his author projections overtly ordinary Anglo names like Sam or Paul. In Anna Moschovakis's *Eleanor, or, The Rejection of the Progress of Love* (2018), the unity of the first-person fractures—"Her name is Eleanor," the narrator says early on, already self-conscious about the increasingly obvious generic norms of autofiction, "Did you think she didn't have a name?"—before returning shortly thereafter to intermittently describing what we can only assume to be a version of the same novelist character in the first person. "While waiting to hear back" about a manuscript she has sent to an editor, she says, "I couldn't work on the book. I turned to other, mostly mundane, commitments I'd been neglecting, my process of revision reduced to a sequence of emails (subject: novel) typed to myself from work or on my phone while walking."

When, later, she is sitting with the editor discussing the manuscript, the conversation turns to the wider world in a way that implicates the act of publication as a betrayal of the minimalist ideal:

> My concern with the zeitgeist embarrassed me, and I returned to the subject to confess this to the critic. When he asked why, I cited my book's many unoriginal traits: its episodic structure, its banal storyline tracing the alienation of the individual in late capitalism, and more. But what really embarrassed me was that I imagined a readership at all.[33]

And it's true: at the limit, minimalism can only be embarrassed by this crucial flaw in the literary situation, the bad-faith desire on the part of the author to solicit the reader's attention. Pitched headlong into the flow of the social media feed, Olivia Laing's *Crudo* (2018) does the strangest thing of all, balancing the novel's casually realistic internet-fed banality—the "crudo" referenced in the title, one assumes—with the conceit of taking place in an alternate reality in which the punk postmodernist Kathy Acker didn't die of cancer in 1997 but instead lived on to see the election of Donald Trump as president of the United States. It begins, "Kathy, by which I mean I, was getting married. Kathy, by which I mean I, had just got off a plane from New York."[34]

And yet the dialectical movement of minimalism-become-maximalism is not confined to its exposure of the inherently social scene of first-person narration. It is replicated on a larger thematic level as the problem of the inextinguishable desire of *auto-* for *allo-*, that is, of the authorial self's desire for the romantic other. Yes, it is love that draws the would-be autofictionist into the network of social representation, if not literally onto social media. One cannot help but notice the strange kinship of minimalist autofiction with the contemporary mass-market romance novel. In chapter 4 this was presented as the rise of the "beta intellectual romance" as a dialectical response to the alpha billionaire kind. This, let us say, *negative affinity* with romance has been a self-conscious presence in the genre at least since Chris Kraus's *I Love Dick* (1997), whose original back cover pointedly mimicked the look of paperback romance.[35] Narrated to a second-person "you," who is the author-protagonist's romantic partner, Maggie Nelson's *The Argonauts* (2016) similarly installs the grammar of romance at its center, taking at least one step from solitude to erotically enabled community. In a way this feature of the genre has been evident since Hemingway, whose "Nick" (or Jake or Frederic) is constantly in the way of falling moodily in or out of love.

Until the appearance of the much stranger and stronger *Taipei*, the fiction of Tao Lin could have been described as little more than a sequencing of alienating romantic relationships in the context of online communication and party-going, as seen in the opening of *Shoplifting from American Apparel*:

> Sam awoke around 3:30 p.m. and saw no emails from Sheila. He made a smoothie. He lay on his bed and stared at his computer screen. He showered and put on clothes and opened the Microsoft Word file of his poetry. He looked at his email. About an hour later it was dark outside. Sam ate cereal with soymilk.

The key difference between the popular romance and literary autofiction is their opposed accounts of love as either a solution or problem:

> "Why don't you want to have sex with me?" said Hester.
> "What do you mean," said Sam.
> "I don't know," said Hester quickly.
> "I don't ... not don't want to have sex with you," said Sam.[36]

No alpha billionaire he, although not necessarily any less abusive on that score. As evidenced by its title, minimalism's negative affinity with the romance is certainly there in Moschovakis's *Eleanor, or, The Rejection of the Progress of Love*, which at one point is compelled to declare about itself that it "is emphatically not a romance," even as its publication by Semiotext(e) would surely have blocked that assumption no less than it had done for *I Love Dick*. As has been the case since the late nineteenth century, when the genre split off from its classic antecedent in the love-triumphant brilliance of Jane Austen, the literariness of beta intellectual romance is secured by its depiction of the *failure* of the couple to live "happily ever after."[37]

For the most part, as in Suah's *Nowhere to Be Found*, world-consolidation in autofiction takes the form instead of the successful achievement of individual alienation, surely the most ready-to-hand form of resistance to the threat of dissolution in the informational network.[38] Thus, on the model of Nick's little camp in the woods, is the becoming-allo of autofiction rewired as a closed loop of intelligently mordant individual coolness.

Beyond the bounds of Nick's little camp is the sprawling, violent, crowded world. In his case it is the scene of civilizational fallout from a horrifically wasteful and hideous war, and generations of scholars and students have delighted in finding its symptoms in a text otherwise preoccupied with camping and fishing. Neither can more recent instances of autofiction rid themselves of the geopolitical surround entirely, nor in many cases do they really want to as long as they are not enlisted in the endless task of earnestly tracing its connections.

And sure enough, if one looks closely enough at a work like Lin's *Taipei*, the "wider world" shimmers in the background.[39] It is there in the form of the titular city of Taipei itself, although neither as the compelling zone of intercultural exchange it might have been for a maximalist like Ghosh, nor as the deeply weighted semi-mythical origin point it might have been for an ethnically marked writer of an earlier era. Instead, it is where one's wealthy cosmopolitan parents have decided to live once again after decades in the United States. In Lin's depiction, Taipei is less a cultural center than a node in a global system held together by airports. Not cultural but simple geographical distance is what defines it: it is a place apart from the "IRL" locales of the alt-lit scene in New York—that oscillation between online and live social interaction under the influence of various drugs taking up the lion's share of the other parts of the novel.

As such, the city of Taipei offers the protagonist Paul, as the novel *Taipei* offers its reader, a kind of alienation beyond alienation, an ambiguous utopia that at least for a moment seems an antidote to the routine discharge of mediated sociality back home:

> On the plane, after a cup of black coffee, Paul thought of Taipei as a fifth season, or "otherworld," outside, or in equal contrast with, his increasingly familiar and self-consciously repetitive life in America, where it seemed like the seasons, connecting in right angles, for some misguided reason, had formed a square, sarcastically framing nothing—or been melded, Paul vaguely imagined, about an hour later, facedown on his arms on his dining tray, into a door-knocker, which a child, after twenty or thirty knocks, no longer expecting an answer, has continued using, in a kind of daze, distracted by the pointlessness of his activity, looking absently elsewhere, unaware when he will abruptly, idly stop.[40]

In the US, the four seasons have strangely taken on the shape of a box, which box then surreally condenses into an image of knocking at the door, which image it would not be wrong to associate with clicking on something on social media.

Note how far Lin's prose has come from where it started, when he was still a more or less by-the-book minimalist of the Carver school. There his sentences produced narrative equivalents of the sensation of being stoned, or maybe just stupid. Now not only has the writing gone from aggressively banal to brilliantly weird—reflective perhaps of the new pharmacological cornucopia whose consumption it tracks—but the sentences struggle to conclude. This is minimalism gone maximal, but in a form that skips entirely over the richness of the opium-loosened multicultural sociopolitical world as we have it in Ghosh. Instead, as Paul's thought processes become increasingly unscaled, they overleap this planet for cosmic space. In doing so, they skip over literary maximalism to arrive at science fiction:

> Paul, walking self-consciously toward her, vaguely remembered a night, early in their relationship, when he somehow hadn't expected her to enlarge in his vision as he approached where she'd stood (looking down at a flyer, one leg slightly bent) in Think Coffee. The comical, bewildering fear—equally calming and surprising, amusing and foreboding—he'd felt as she rapidly and sort of ominously increased in size has characterized their first two months together. It had seemed like they would never fight, and the nothingness of the future had gained a framework-y somethingness that felt privately exciting, like entering a different family's house as a small child, or the beginning elaborations of a science-fiction conceit.[41]

This is a long way from *Fifty Shades of Grey*, and it will get farther still, as the confrontation with the un-scalable demands of interpersonal love give way to cosmic consciousness suspiciously reminiscent of the virtual collectivity of the web. It is weirder than that, though, at once darker in its latently suicidal ideation and more self-aggrandizing than any selfie in its assumption that so very many future beings would find his story interesting:

> He couldn't ignore a feeling that he wasn't alone—that, in the brain of the universe, where everything that happened was concurrently recorded as public and indestructible data, he was already partially with everyone else that had died. The information of his existence, the etching of which into space-time was his experience of life, was being studied by millions of entities, billions of years from now, who knew him better than he would ever know himself.[42]

Of course, much of the weirdness of this passage dissipates, or becomes another kind of weirdness, if we assume, as seems reasonable, that beneath a thin layer of allegory this is really just Facebook or Google converting an individual's browsing history into monetizable data.

Coda: Postapocalypse as Micro-epic

What's at stake in the epic is the fate of nations, of whole empires: heroes arise, journeys are undertaken, armies assembled, gods appeased, battles joined, enemies destroyed, futures claimed. The epic canvas contains multitudes, and those multitudes are making history. It's against the backdrop of the epic norm as it appears in popular fiction—the world of *Dune* and *Game of Thrones*—but also in the epic enterprise that is Amazon, that the peculiarity of contemporary postapocalyptic fiction snaps into focus. For while it is apparently "epic" in all sorts of ways, not least in its length, which frequently enough spills into several volumes, the central appeal of the genre is in how severely it reduces the scale of the social world, paring it back to numbers not seen since the rise of agricultural civilization in Mesopotamia 5,000 years ago. It may contain the embodied memory of the social masses in the form of the zombie herd, or it may not, but the elaborate social network of which the world was once the scene is gone, thinned beyond recognition by nuclear war or pandemic or climate crisis. In its place are small bands of survivors talking to each other face to face, finding their way in a new world of scarcity, not least a scarcity of information.

Ironically, given this commitment to scarcity, it would be difficult to overstate the plenitude of postapocalyptic fictions produced in our time, the thin trickle of narratives beginning with Mary Shelley's *The Last Man* (1826) having since the 1950s risen by stages to a veritable flood. Spread across the entire range of the literary status hierarchy from high to low, and across the spectrum of political sensibility from far right to far left, postapocalyptic visions are a key component of contemporary cultural expression, a source of apparently endless appeal. In some cases, in post-nuclear and cli-fi variants in particular, these fictions would appear to want to be admonitory, warning us away from the darker implications of the current state of things. And in all cases, even those bereft of the spirit of moral-political admonition, life in a postapocalyptic world looks pretty hard. As fiction, though, it is the vehicle of fantasy, a fantasy of refreshment and reset. It has been said ad nauseum, as a testament to the failure of the contemporary utopian imagination, that it is easier to imagine the end of the world than the end of capitalism, but it has always seemed to me that this formula gives short shrift to the way the genre of apocalypse *indeed imagines the end of capitalism* at least in the version we know it. Neither is it entirely bereft of the ability to imagine alternatives thereto.

This is spectacularly true of a work like Joshua Gayou's four-volume *Commune* series (2017–19), released by one of the many small-scale "publishing houses"—essentially an aggregation of online cover design, copyediting, and marketing services, a step removed from self-publishing—enabled by Amazon's electronic and on-demand printing services and their competitors. While, as it turns out, the *Commune* quartet has not much to do with historical "communes" such as the Paris Commune,

Look inside ↓

Commune: The Complete Series: A Post-Apocalyptic Survival Box Set (Books 1-4)
Kindle Edition

by Joshua Gayou ⌄ (Author), R.C. Bray (Foreword) | Format: Kindle Edition

★★★★☆ ⌄ 366 ratings

> See all formats and editions

Kindle
$0.00 kindleunlimited

Read with Kindle Unlimited to also enjoy access to over 1 million more titles
$6.99 to buy

Follow the Author

Joshua Gayou   + Follow

A Swelling Epic In Gayou's *Commune* series, time brings opportunities for the growth of the surviving community, which in turn gives birth to intractable problems of political economy.

or with "communism" as the dictatorship of the urban proletariat as conceived in Marxist thought, it manages across its
more than 2,000 pages to become a fairly serious meditation on
political economy as a problem fundamentally of social scale.
From volume to volume, each one significantly (and somehow
meaningfully) longer than the last, a small, ethnically diverse
community of survivors in the American West continues to grow
(see figure on p. 225).

At each stage, interspersed with excellently rendered adventures, heartrending tragedy, and ingenious problem-solving and
no zombies at all, the survivors are driven back to the basics
not only of material survival but social organization. Just when
it appears that the slow and steady aggregation of stragglers
across the volumes might amount to the epic rebirth of a nation,
the plot swerves and the small group of exceptionally competent
survivors we have followed since the beginning decides it must
not be. While life among forty or fifty people can be lived by the
law of "from each according to his abilities, to each according to
his needs," social groupings larger than that require disciplining
by the abstract equivalencies of markets. While the latter, with
their greater capacity for the division of labor, are the source of
valuable technological innovations, in their relative impersonal-
ity and need for communication at a distance they are also
subject to eruptions of resentful rejection of the otherness within.

Without exactly solving the dilemmas it so richly lays out,
and notwithstanding its perhaps excessive adoration of tough-
talking former military men and their weapons, a work like
Commune does at least imagine a solution to the twin problems of overload and redundancy as articulated by Orrin Klapp.
And so indeed—but so frequently with unsavory fantasies of
racial purification absent here—do narratives of survival in a
postapocalyptic landscape in general. In the destroyed world the
"redundant" is new again. By the same token, whatever "innovations" appear in that world do so as welcome remedies to
pressing problems of survival, not as systematically cynical capitalist violations of cultural memory and identity.

One sign of the success of the apocalyptic solution to the social problem of information is that these narratives, for all their ubiquity, do not fit easily into the diagrammatic scheme, set out previously, that otherwise depicts the polarities of the popular genre system fairly convincingly, with their world-expanding or world-consolidating impulses moving in different directions. Postapocalyptic fictions are epic narratives, yes, unmistakably so, but it would appear that their deepest commitment is to the construction and defense of the romantic idyll, the reassuringly small and pointedly non- or post-capitalist community. To this extent, they point to the analytical limits of the diagrammatic imagination insofar as it is confined to two dimensions only. The individual terms of the dialectic of epic and romance are easy enough to see on a flat plane. But the action of the dialectic itself, the force that crushes the contradictions of social interdependency into temporarily usable forms? Not so much. It is only known in the reading.

6

Surplus Fiction

The Undeath of the Novel

The Troll as Author

"Let's try to write a book with the rest of the internet, one character at a time."[1] This was the call for participants in a project called Writey Novel, conceived in early 2016 by an anonymous user of an Amazon-owned video streaming site, Twitch, dedicated primarily to the vicarious playing of video games. "Enter a character to vote. Votes will be tallied every ten seconds, and the winning character will be added to the novel." No further guidance than that would be given, no moderator would be involved, even as the project was announced to the rest of the internet via the now defunct online news site Splinter News. Moving inexorably forward only a single letter or punctuation mark at a time, it would be an exercise in radically incremental composition where, never mind the plot, even the progress of a single word across the screen would be subject to swiftly democratic reroutings of intent, although revision in the more ordinary sense would be impossible. Serving no financial or other external imperative, inspired simply by the surprising success of earlier experiments in the collective playing of video games, it would be an act of autonomous, self-organizing creativity and a proud testament to the wisdom of the crowd.

Sitting at a computer observing the proceedings, a literary historian wondered, although not completely sincerely: Might the result then point a way for the novel form toward something new? Could this be the cure for the atomized individualism with which the genre has so long been associated? Will this novel give us a glimpse of what's on the other side of capitalism?

I say "not completely sincerely" because, in another sense, as though in a return of the repressed of the process's capitalist infrastructure, it would obviously be conducted very much on the clock. Ten seconds is not much time for deliberation on matters of plot and style in a novel, especially if they will not be subject to revision, but is vastly longer than single letters are typically brought to consciousness in the act of writing. Like any old corporate workplace, the composition of Writey Novel thus combined unnatural dilation and absurd hurry in confusing measure, even as it was founded on an unquestioned faith in the ability of the hive mind to sort it all out. As Splinter News put it, "You'd be amazed at the number of impressive things the collective denizens of the internet can accomplish when they decide to set aside their petty differences and work together."[2]

In the event, the results of the experiment were not impressive. Instead, as you might have already guessed because these things have become predictable, upon its launch Writey Novel devolved instantly into an incoherent mass of racist, anti-Semitic, sexist, and homophobic slurs, and not much more. Flecked with vintage 2016 political discourse (Bernie, Trump, cucks), large helpings of plain old nonsense, and what appears to be a massive intrusion of Polish-language vitriol, it is about as distant from a testament to the joys of collective creation as one could imagine. Instead, it is a testament to the joys of rhetorical vandalism, but without anything yet to deface other than a hopeful intention, a quickly faltering and aimless one. It is in any case not much of a novel, lacking as it does any discernible character, setting, plot, or interesting deconstructions of the same (see figure on p. 231).

To read it is neither edifying nor entertaining, even after translating the Polish parts, although the last words of the second paragraph, the comparatively coherent "write a book? fuck that!"

WRITEY NOVEL Ch. 1

fuck mein the ass.the n█████said he would cuck an animal he wuz killed.just cuckmy shit up fam. aaaaaaahhcccumni█████.bernie sandxafuu urddddddddxxxx !aaaan█████w htrumpsucks dick for allahh.hitler did nothing wrong.xxxxxousa sixid aia.lidooks like this is vulnerable to botting. cou should fix that! fuck your mom fagddx v was here.wexd kmoot sucks. ninegag ftw!!if.wwexalax what i s a man a queeer bitch i am gay fat homo sex stu. kill all ni█████; i didntnot do inithin█████tanig big tits and bane for you.big guy.we will rape n█████ and jews and muricans my shit up kaas is baas ,grope my boobies sexy cunt is gayyyy and fake. we are anusersas.qqqqppppissebed. damn mpmpyon. wally did nothing right??!?! kkk likes colberts igloo. a new age of lust for waldo brob brob big stops me nope. kappa sex up the brob. ze jews did everything wrong. ...jan pawel drugi jebal male dzieci! karachan.ork wykop.pl tomasz terka ssie jaderka uuuuuu ponczuchy huj zesralem sie i smierdzi zalgo tociota i chuj aralka ssij muj huj rucham psa jaksra xd ryszard peja rucha tedego.a jan pawel dupa pierdolil male dzieci od zawsze pedofil.chuj wdupe polakom robakom a testo to nasz pan.zalgo to chuj twoja stara kwasny robak wpierdala guwno pierdzi kupom. jooooo noohuj anon modee przypierdol. kobiety to kurwy.anonimus polska to kurwy. tomasz terka to krowa a rajzer to pedoni rekt. wypierdalac nowokurwy. ryszard petru jest debilem aaaaaralka tokurczak. gowin to cipka.czaks to boguslaw linda xd.janusz pawlak narkoman i agitator pedal wykopuje male dziwki. tytus roman i jablko andletkowe. anakin skurwysyn vichuj i karachan jebal malo dziewczynek. czy papaj sra w lesie? jeszcze jak! terka sukinsynu gdzie masz pizde? sram psa jakruchimaroto. karma dla smutaska to kutas w dupsko xd. czary mary jan pawel to twoj stan tutaj w moskwie. clomazepan jesus chytrus skurwesynu chujowy dupczysz golemy. jem kurwy na sniadym kucu. wladca poslanki rucha palikota w odrodzenie polskiego kolosalnego cycuszka.tam gdzie kurwa rodzi jana pawla, a marzena kupuje koks.tam jest serce marysi twych snopkow.a tam godnosc to jebany chalny. ss ssy. sse. szara myszka dla anona z filmu o autyzmie. zzwale kolegom dupom i tam gdzsx? ooooo ale duze pizdziskoo. fuga uga busra. moja mamalyga gdy tak bardzo tb sram do kapcia. kobieta to grzyb na fiucika czarnego jak czarna kawa to zbigniew stonoga. rafalala . xd. kocham ten penis.jest pyszny i pozywny. szara kurwa doskonale radziecka zdoa gumisie zjebac czersczoteme! fuj dostalem gotycka lame serdelki i mortal kim jest? kurwom! zzzza.full bajer xsaxx fuck penis, i hardly ever cuck jewish orphans. universal cancer. porn write a book? fuck that!

Writey Novel Chapter 1 Excerpt From a sea of nonsense emerge fleeting instances of insult and slur. The redactions are mine.

provide an accurately eloquent epitaph to the whole endeavor.[3] Nonetheless, the exercise continued from there for its allotted three days, each devoted to the scripting of a new chapter along much the same lines. Finally came the announcement of the project's closure with a strangely placid musing that the organizer "might release an audio book so you can listen to the book during your busy commutes."[4] Lingering on the web for a while in the manner of smoking wreckage, the Writey Novel site has since been taken down.

Of course, at this point in history, one hardly needed an obscure experiment like Writey Novel to inform us of the problem of hate speech and trolling online or, more broadly, of its association with a twenty-first-century resurgence of fascism in the world at large. Not more than a few months later, Microsoft's experimental artificial intelligence chatbot, Tay, would more infamously devolve into a fount of racist gibberish before quickly being taken offline. Crowding channels everywhere with malignant noise, troll-speak is a bullying presence, a maddeningly distracting one, exacting a large emotional cost for tuning in at all but eliciting that attention as a compulsive ritual of civic responsibility and proactive self-defense.[5] Its avatar is former US president Donald Trump, the ultimate troll and hero to the online right. As Louis Althusser memorably said (in translation) of the operation of ideology in general, the subject is *hailed* by online discourse of this sort, which is interwoven with more positive and genuinely informative but all the same importuning appeals for monetizable attention.[6] That's how it goes now in the pathological public sphere.[7]

Writey Novel's ill-fated experiment in authorship, however, is useful in lighting two avenues of inquiry into the question of what the advent of Amazon has meant for the novel.

What, in the first place, does the company's removal of virtually all barriers to publication through its Kindle Direct Publishing service mean for the literary field in general? How should we think about the exponential growth in the number of novels published each year as a result? Bowker, the agency responsible for issuing ISBN numbers, reports that there were roughly *1.6 million books* of all kinds self-published with an ISBN number in the year 2018, and we can assume that hundreds of thousands of them were fiction.[8] These fictions arrived on a scene where tens of thousands of books were already being published every year by more traditional means. As potential objects of literary experience, most of them can only be nullities, the supply of fictions far outstripping the total time available for reading them. Is there a way to conceive of what I called in the introduction the *underlist*, the vast numbers of books essentially never read by anyone, as anything other than a black hole of literary history?

What, in the second place, has the broader media ecology in which the novel now swims meant for its relevance as a cultural form and capacity for success as a work of art?[9] Is the chaos we see in Writey Novel in any way representative of the situation of the novel in the age of Amazon?

Not that anyone at Amazon itself would necessarily have the least bit of sympathy for the views, such as they are, of the trolls who authored it. As a neoliberal company, its official position, and probably also the one held privately by most of its managerial employees, is the celebration of global cultural diversity brought into harmonious relation by commerce. In this it remains a product of the 1990s, when the company was born, and when belief in the unalloyed benefits of globalization was at its peak. Even so, it is possible and even necessary to see that moment as the seedbed of the fractious present, as the contradictions of neoliberal capitalism coming to poisonous flower. While Amazon is to all appearances okay with cultural diversity—with the idea if not with the intrusive measures that would make it a reality in the upper echelons of management utterly dominated by white men like Bezos himself—its submission of all forms of value to the law of exchange value has the effect of reducing diversity to something akin to product differentiation. In turn, as an operative principle of social intercourse, the latter makes not for functional social worlds but for the atomization and alienation of which the troll is the purest expression. Without necessarily agreeing with a single word the troll says, then, one feels the force of his implicit critique of the neoliberal consumerist world order as fundamentally flawed; feeling antagonism for him, one nonetheless grudgingly acknowledges the truth his asininity forces upon us, the truth of social antagonism as such.

Beyond the few technical preconditions of its unfolding, Writey Novel offered itself as an entirely unregulated, unadministered opportunity for the literary creativity of the people. In this it was in a sense a condensed and miniaturized version of Amazon's own Kindle Direct Publishing system and other self-publishing platforms, by whose means more than a few antiglobalist right-wing fictions have been circulated. As detailed by the authors of an informative study called "The Hate Store," the multiplication of these fictions is "the inevitable consequence of the company's business strategy," with its aversion to ideological and other forms of gatekeeping in favor of uncontrolled proliferation.[10]

Some of these hateful fictions take the form of a genre called EMP postapocalypse (EMP standing for "electro-magnetic pulse"), which offers readers a fantasy of return to a world without the internet or any other electronics, including the Kindle-enabled devices upon which most of them are read. In the EMP world, all that stuff has been fried by shadowy government forces who want to control you. Among the most successful of these fictions—enough so that it was picked up and reprinted by Plume, an imprint of Penguin Random House—is the *Survivalist* series authored by A. American, beginning with the novel *Going Home* (2013). The story of a doomsday prepper caught out on a highway in Florida when the EMP hits, he fears for the well-being of his family but he also fears the advent of communism. Over his dead body will he give up the brand-named things he has wisely accumulated for just such an event, the Maxpedition Devildog bag ("I am a gear freak and love Maxpedition products"), Otis tactical cleaning kit, Silva compass, Wilderness Outfitters SOS survival kit, Swedish FireSteel, "and other assorted items that I thought essential."[11]

Far from a successful effort to imagine a life beyond consumerism, *Going Home* doubles down on it, mistaking market segmentation—all of the products listed in the novel are available for purchase from Amazon in their hunting department—for political independence, with a protagonist obviously delighted to finally have a chance to use the gear he has been accumulating. First up is the Springfield XD .45 he uses to kill the jive-talking Black gangster, Gold Dollar, who threatens to take his stuff.

Of course, not all of the postapocalyptic fiction, let alone the fiction of other kinds, offered to readers via Amazon Digital Services takes this political form, but *Going Home* is a useful reminder, in case we needed one, that Amazon's vision of a disintermediated literary culture is not always a pretty one in its execution, even if its works hold together better than Writey Novel. Indeed, even some self-consciously liberal contributors to it readily admit this. It was none other than Hugh Howey, the great indie publishing success story discussed in chapter 1, who earlier in his career most forcefully expressed the potential problem with the Amazon Way in publishing:

> The *Anti*-Renaissance ensued. As Adam logged onto his account, he shivered at the memory of it. Hell, he was still living it. The outpouring of *stuff*, of *crap*, was so intense, nothing could be seen or heard. The variety and quantity were too much ... The bar wasn't so much raised as buried under the pile of crap.[12]

Sounds familiar—although what the narrator of Howey's self-published novella *The Plagiarist* (2011) is describing here is not Kindle Direct Publishing but a future world in which quantum computing has allowed for the eruption of infinitely complex virtual worlds amid our own. They are hosted on huge university-owned servers and are inhabited by people who have no idea that they are not real. How easy then to put on a VR headset and pillage their intellectual property! Too easy—soon enough there is an oversupply of product. Salvation comes in the form of people like Adam with good taste as readers if not necessarily any gift for writing. Jacking into these virtual worlds, he brings back the good stuff lying about there, and is rewarded for it until—spoiler alert—he discovers that he is himself one of those people who don't know they aren't real, the entire world beginning to fragment and disappear around him.

The Plagiarist is ostensibly a science fiction story about virtual reality and AI, but it has only traveled inches from its more or less obvious allegorical referent in the early KDP milieu from which it emerged. Here, even if they don't produce plagiarized works in the strict sense of the term, aspirants to literary success typically begin with rigorous adherence to the templates and tropes of an established genre or popular work. If the leading note in that milieu has nonetheless been one of celebratory appreciation for the many new voices it brings online in defeat of the snobbery of traditional literary gatekeepers, there is apparently another side to that coin more basic even than its affordance of right-wing political visions: the turbo-charged proliferation of "crap" and the sense of despair it carries in train, with its suggestion that we, too, might mostly be crap, as Adam shamefully feels he is as plagiarist until realizing at the last minute that he's not even real. In either case he is haunted by a sense of profound unoriginality, as though he himself were merely the millionth copy of something, starting with "wannabe writer."

What does Amazon see when it looks at its customers? One answer, contemplated in chapter 4, would be to say that it sees an infinitely various collection of individuals, each with their own purchase history and taste profile and perverse desires. This is the image one gets from recommendation algorithms that no longer, as they once did, group purchasers into discrete clusters of social types who might be interested in purchasing similar things, instead matching the things one has bought or rated directly with other things algorithmically associated with it.[13] With its massive processing capacity and server farms, Amazon is in this sense equipped to track and manage its customers as though they were each a preciously unique grain of sand. Another, equally valid answer might move in the opposite direction, from the billion-fold singularity of customer-individuals to their funneling into one and one only category of human social existence, the *consumer*. For Amazon, our entry into the many other facets of our identities—as student, parent, spouse, coworker, golf lover, Kung Fu movie streamer, Band-Aid needer, romance reader, even, as we'll see, writer—comes through the gate of purchase and is only legible as an expression of that more basic reality.

Which is to say, in a way, that Amazon sees its customers as zombies, the figure coughed up by popular culture to make an allegory of our perfectly universal need to feed. And, in a capitalist world, to feed upon each other. Once upon a time, the zombie was a highly specific cultural creation emanating from Haitian folklore. Pried loose from that context in the mid-twentieth century, he has been appropriated to various symbolic ends, although these ends are never more than a few steps removed from the question of racial othering, from the movement of populations in and out of the category of the fully human.[14] Featured in an even healthier subset of self-published postapocalyptic fiction than EMP, zombies are everywhere in the Age of Amazon, providing our dominant image of humanity as problematically numerous and driven by nonnegotiable desires (see figure on p. 238).

We rightly think of the zombie novel as a low cultural form, but it is possessed of the inherent seriousness of a darkly Dantean theological vision ("I had not thought death had undone so many") that makes this lowliness self-reflexive, as if to say: if this novel were too good it would be self-refuting.

The zombie novel is in any case appealing enough in its allegorical suggestiveness to have inspired more than a few self-consciously "literary" instances, beginning most prominently with Colson Whitehead's novel *Zone One* (2011), where the perplexities of the zombie's racially marked origin reverberate in the margins of a text otherwise inclined to understand the zombie figure simply as the lowest common denominator of commodified creatural life.[15] To my knowledge, zombies have not yet been spotted shopping for quinoa at Whole Foods, the upscale grocery chain Amazon purchased in 2017, but that addition to its portfolio points us to the original and most literal version of our consuming relation to the world. The telling thing about the zombie in this context is the way, in his hunger for life, he represents the final collapse of everything we mean by "humanity" into an unsustainable voracity.

Who else but Hugh Howey found a way, in his highly compelling contribution to the genre, *I, Zombie* (2012), to bring that point home: his take on a genre that lurches forward by just these little twists of the knobs of accumulated convention is to imagine that the persons the zombies once were remain entirely present in their rotting brains, utterly horrified and disgusted by what their zombie selves are doing but incapable of stopping it.[16] They are also in excruciating pain. This justifies a shift in point of view from the

The Zombie Renaissance

human survivors who center most zombie fictions, just as they do survivalist fictions like *Going Home*, to the zombies themselves. With more than its share of kinetic zombie mayhem—a sequence involving a veteran who takes refuge with a newborn baby on top of a dumpster in a crowd of the undead is unforgettable —Howey's novel is also a well-nigh Dostoevskian rendition of psychic self-loathing and self-recrimination. Crucially, this self-hatred is shared by virtually all of the zombie characters composing the novel's large cast, characters who are otherwise carefully differentiated by race, age, and gender such as one might find them in tourist promotional materials for New York City. The suggestion is that our human commonality can only be reclaimed on the basis of our universal damnation.

Published at the other, higher end of the prestige spectrum, Ling Ma's *Severance* (2018) mutes Howey's lurid colors, trading mayhem for a more dignified narrative sequencing of pre- and postapocalyptic events.[17] This alternation of attention between *before* and *after* is an earmark of the literary zombie novel of the sort that might be published, as this one was, by Farrar, Straus and Giroux. It is a way of keeping things real by constantly asking us if we weren't metaphorically already zombies before the plague hit. In Ma's version, the zombies are the least of your problems—they aren't aggressive, just pathetic, continuing to do whatever rote activity they used to do. It's the survivors who should concern you, especially if you are a young woman, a vessel of the reproductive future.

No less than Howey's "Plagiarist," there is a way of reading Ma's novel as a wistful commentary on the state of contemporary publishing. The protagonist's pre-apocalypse job—she works in book production in New York, managing the printing of Bibles with ruthless efficiency—suggests a deflated literary idealism, a strong sense of doubt that the traditional bourgeois literary disposition can survive its ethical encounter with the supply chain that links holy books to exploitative factories in China. Neither will the reassuring forms of ethnic, or as I like to call it, high-cultural pluralist fiction suffice to produce elevated literary experience anymore, the intensities of cultural affiliation and disaffiliation that drove them having, in the life of the Chinese American narrator-protagonist, run aground in the fleeting comforts of depressive upper-middle-class consumerism. This is literally so when, in the tradition of George Romero's film *Dawn of the Dead* (1978), she and some other survivors take up residence in a defunct shopping mall full of products whose origins, like the Shen Fever itself, are in China.

With examples across the spectrum from low to high culture, zombie novels exemplify the zombie plague they represent, being themselves, as novels, conspicuously numerous. Blocking access to facile optimism, they embody the impasse we reach, finally, in this book's effort to assess the outpouring of literary populism of which Amazon has played host as either a good or bad thing. To be a zombie is to be a perpetrator and victim in equal measure, one of the "wasted lives" that, Zygmunt Bauman tells us, are as much the product of modernity as any of its other creations, much as we might want to deny it. How wonderful to think that these wasted lives can finally be given a literary voice free from the strictures of the publishing gatekeepers! And yet there is no guarantee that what those voices have to say will amount to anything we haven't heard a hundred times before, something depressingly generic if not hurtful. As Bauman puts it, a "spectre hovers over the denizens of the liquid modern world and all their labour and creations: the spectre of redundancy."[18]

Surplus and Waste

Economic growth is the original problem of political economy, the guiding concern of Adam Smith's *Wealth of Nations* and a primary focus, even obsession, of just about every interested observer of the global and national economies since then. Living in a world not yet utterly transformed by the industrial revolution but stable enough to experience steady increases in population, Smith positioned the project of economic development against an assumed background of general commodity scarcity —a world where, for instance, the possibility of widespread famine by crop failure remained intensely real, and where what now seem like basic necessities of life were out of reach of vast numbers of people in even the wealthiest of nations.

It would take 150 years or more of industrial revolution to produce the post-scarcity economy of the present day, where in a country like the United States an estimated 30 to 40 percent of the food supply is wasted, and where people go hungry, as they continue scandalously to do, only for reasons of inequality of access to the sloshing smorgasbord. The same could be said of shelter, clothing, tools, toys, and of course books. Capitalism begins in the extraction of surplus value from human labor and continues as the investment of that surplus in further rounds of the same. Over time, using better and better machines, it converts Smith's world of scarcity into our world of surplus, which is also the world of the Everything Store, not to mention the world of contemporary fiction. Everywhere one looks in the developed world one sees an unevenly distributed material plenitude. Compared to a world defined by life-threatening scarcity, this plenitude can only seem a boon, and did so even to harsh critics of capitalism like Marx, who understood it as a precondition to a world finally liberated from exploitative inequality and immiserating toil.

Only relatively recently have we begun to consider and confront the dangerous proximity of *surplus* to *waste*. The amassing of the first has typically been conceived of as an unequivocally good thing—the seed of a new investment, or provision for the future, or way of freeing time from the otherwise never-ending necessity of reproducing the material conditions of collective survival. Surplus has enabled every "higher" cultural achievement one might name, allowing a Michelangelo or George Eliot leave the fields for the studio or writing desk. In a world living off the fruits of industrial agriculture, their case is now the general case, although our achievements are rarely as impressive as theirs. But surplus is by the same token the origin of systematic social inequality, with indolent lords and ladies living off the surplus produced by their peasants and so on.

For Georges Bataille, notoriously, it is not scarcity but the existence of the surplus he called the "accursed share" that is the original and most fundamental problem of political economy, although it is one that, he thought, has been kept from view by the rise of bourgeois capitalism and its attendant economic theories. These theories restrict themselves to a narrow notion of the economic centered on investment and accumulation, leaving most of the broader "general economy," as Bataille called it, out of the picture. The latter is the domain of the exuberantly social, the sacred, the symbolic, the erotic, whose effusive energies are not containable on a balance sheet. If we keep this broader energetic economy in view, we see that it is the *mode of expenditure* and not production that defines a given society, giving us insight into its most deeply held beliefs. Indeed, for Bataille, accumulation of any sort is a *problem* requiring various strategies of dis-accumulation toward the reestablishment of energetic equilibrium. One of them is the "release" of energy in staggeringly wasteful cultural achievements such as the pyramids. Another is war, the ultimate agent of waste, the World Wars having been in his account the result of the inability of astoundingly productive industrial societies to deal in less catastrophic ways with the accursed share.[19]

It is an intriguing if no doubt tendentiously naturalist reversal of the usual way of understanding things, assuming as it does a kind of thermodynamic imperative lying behind our conscious decisions somewhat akin to the Freudian death drive. Then, too, as Jean-Joseph Goux has noted, Bataille's conception of capitalism was somewhat outdated.[20] Still convinced by the Weberian account of capitalism as a matter of rational, rectitudinous investment toward return, Bataille could not quite see what it had in fact already become: consumer capitalism, a capitalism centered ideologically on expenditure and not thrift. Without realizing it, he was supplying a theory not of what exceeds capitalism but of its postmodern transformation. He was also providing the lineaments of a compelling theory of surplus fiction, the underlist.

Bataille's alignment of pyramid building and war as twin forms of energetic release of a surplus toward the end of equilibrium suggest an unsettling kinship between things one might have thought of as perfectly opposed—a form of artistic *production* on the one hand and violent *destruction* on the other. Joseph Schumpeter's conception of the "creative destruction" of capitalist activity is of course one way to think about this kinship, telling us that the destruction in that formulation is only a predicate for profitably building anew. Ancestor of the "disruption" celebrated ad nauseum in the tech business literature of the 1990s and aughts, it is disturbing enough when its cost in human well-being is given a full accounting, but the true force of Bataille's alignment comes into view when we reverse Schumpeter's terms. The idea of *destructive creation* is not so easily assimilated to a narrative of progress or improvement, suggesting as it does that destruction—laying waste —was always the point of productive economic activity, consciously or not.

Could this be said of novel writing, too? Should we decline to see the scripting of millions of books as so many acts of *production* in the ordinary capitalist sense, a series of investments toward profitable returns? That is how they would normally be considered, but Bataille allows us to think of them otherwise. Whether their authors know it or not, we might say, they are best understood as destroying something. But what? For starters, they are destroying time, the time it takes to write the books that will sit inertly as lines of code on a server somewhere, never to be heard from again.

Writing as a waste of time. Shocking. We generally think of it as the opposite, even as close inspection reveals its continuity with our tapping away on a computer or other device when we are online, which no one has trouble identifying as time wasted. So much so as to have become the ironic title of Kenneth Goldsmith's *Wasting Time on the Internet* (2016), a collection of essays that in fact carries the torch of earlier, less jaded accounts of the utopian potential of the internet of the 1990s.[21] Critics like Tiziana Terranova and Jodi Dean do the opposite, noting that what looks like wasted time to us might look like valuable data to those possessed of enough processing power to turn it to account.

Social Reading, Social Writing It is worth remembering how profoundly counterintuitive it seemed to allow harshly negative reviews of products to appear beside the product offering itself when Amazon instituted the practice, making other customers socially "present" at the scene of purchase in a new way. Goodreads's slogan, "Meet your next favorite book"—as though a book itself were a potential friend—emphasizes the sociality of reading in another way, while the "directness" of Kindle Direct Publishing does the same in its suggestion of an unmediated social relation between writer and reader.

To these companies, there is no such thing as excess information about our expenditures of time and money. This is how capitalist rationality asserts itself on the scene of consumerist excess once again, doing its best to bring as much of the general economy as possible into its calculative purview. In social media, the expropriation of our wasted time has been generalized and extended beyond the workday proper, deep into the sphere of leisure, where users in their millions sit at home computers, or stare at the devices in their hands, donating content and other data to the platforms that log them on (see figure above).[22]

While not as successful as Facebook in the realization of this program, Amazon's propagation of the ideal of corporate-sponsored self-expression as "posting" and "sharing" and "liking" has been multifold, from the (at the time) daring novelty of its unrestricted publication of sometimes savage customer reviews adjacent to the product being sold, to the more robust version of the same in its wholly owned book-centric social media site, Goodreads, to the encouragement of mass self-expression via the free-to-use platform Kindle Direct Publishing. For all its modesty compared to Facebook, Goodreads, with its more than 100 million registered users, may be the richest repository of the leavings of literary life ever assembled, exceeded only by the mass of granular data sent back to home base from virtually every Kindle device in the world. (We can only hope that literary scholars will someday be given access to all this data.) All told, these initiatives represent an extraordinary further conversion of leisure time—already associated with expenditures on its accoutrements, including books—into corporate capital, into monetizable "data exhaust."

The proximity of contemporary fiction to the wasteland of social media is revealed in many ways, including the rise of a subspecies of thriller we might call internet gothic, with ominous titles like *Follow Me* (2015), *Friend Request* (2017), *Shame on You* (2017), and *Troll* (2017). It leverages the creepy convergence of intimacy and anonymity online, figuring the villain either as a psychopath empowered to stalk his victims in new

Internet Gothic Internet gothic follows a long if minor tradition of connecting communication media to horror. The genre stands adjacent to works one might describe either as works of internet realism or Social Media Sci-Fi, including M. T. Anderson's early entrant *Feed* (2002). See also Joshua Mohr, *All This Life* (2015), Robert Charles Wilson, *The Affinities* (2015), Rob Reid, *After On: A Novel of Silicon Valley* (2017), Sean Gandert, *Lost in Arcadia* (2017), Tim Maughan, *Infinite Detail* (2019), the Analog novels of Eliot Peper beginning with *Bandwidth* (2018), Lauren Oyler's *Fake Accounts* (2021), and Patricia Lockwood's *No One Is Talking about This* (2021).

ways, or as the "system" itself in the form of an artificial intelligence gone mad (see figure on p. 245). D. B. Thorne's *Troll* is a particularly effective example, telling the story of a neglectful father searching for clues to the whereabouts of a daughter who was being harassed online before she disappeared.[23] So maddeningly adept is the harasser at displaying his all-knowing, anonymous ubiquity to the panicky protagonist, at first it seems like it must somehow be the internet itself who is the troll, as though the Writey Novel experiment had come to evil-genius fruition instead of petering out into nonsense. So much so that it is a slight letdown when he turns out instead to be the father's *other* child, a lost son he never even acknowledged let alone neglected. Reducing the crime to an oedipal drama, this leaves the medium of harassment off the hook.

The convergence of contemporary fiction and social media is also visible in some works of the small-press avant-garde. As what David Wells aptly calls "a fiction of the Internet—a representation of an infinitely extending and seemingly available world," Megan Boyle's *Liveblog: A Novel* (2018) presents a less pulpy but no less symptomatic instance.[24] In the tradition of Andy Warhol's *a: a Novel* (1968) and Goldsmith's *Soliloquy* (2001), Boyle's project began as an experiment in exhaustive self-surveillance, this time conceived as auto-therapy. Keeping more or less continuous track of her actions by blogging about them in real time on her own Tumblr site, Boyle would correct a chronic "failure to follow through with tasks I said I'd do," taking ownership of her life and prospects for happiness. Warding off misunderstanding in assertive all caps, she warns her readers at the outset that

THIS IS NOT GOING TO BE INTERESTING **I AM NOT GOING TO TRY TO MAKE THIS SOUND INTERESTING OR TRY TO MAKE YOU LIKE ME OR THINK ABOUT IF YOU ARE READING THIS OR ENJOYING READING THIS, IT'S JUST GOING TO BE WHAT IT IS: A FUNCTIONAL THING THAT WILL HOPEFULLY HELP ME FEEL MORE LIKE IMPROVING MYSELF.**[25]

It was self-publication as self-discipline as self-improvement, and on one level it sits squarely within the conception of fiction-as-therapy we have been tracking throughout this book. But in this case it is a therapy of writing—the original modality of "narrative therapy" in fact—not reading.[26] The irony was her assumption—as she later concluded was a mistake—that drug use (or abuse) was crucial to sustaining that writing. The flaw in this thinking is visible even in her disavowal, as shared above, of her desire to be interesting, where the writing is not an act of self-improvement in itself but something she does in hopes of feeling like working toward that end in the future. It makes sense, then, when 640-some closely printed pages later, we find the author recording how she has been "hearing voice of [omitted] in my head saying, 'is the liveblog getting in the way of other ways you could be being productive?'"[27] Here, then, is the specter of writing as wasting time, as expense rather than virtuous production.

What's interesting about this particular waste of time is how it registers, as on a photographic negative, the "real job" this writer does not have. Entries in the blog are rigorously time-stamped and littered with to-do lists and super-egoic expectations for productivity such as we might hear them from any young professional knocking out some emails before heading to the gym. Productivity, for Boyle, is difficult to manage in ways more ordinary to her demographic cohort—she does a lot of hanging around, surfing the internet, doing drugs, driving her car to the mini-mart, drinking smoothies and diet Red Bull, and does not even do much reading—but its shadow is visible in the form of a prodigious accumulation of words, in the work of art or proto-art that is her blog. Far from a litany of pleasures taken, as the more defiantly countercultural version of the project might have been, the novel's catalog of casual acts of transgression and wasteful slackerdom are tinged with a kind of pre-professional masochism. My favorite instance comes near the beginning, when, finding herself listening to a very bad song, Boyle decides that "I kind of like how awful listening to it feels."[28]

The question is: am I really wasting time if I am writing in real time about the time I am wasting? *Liveblog* makes the question intriguingly difficult to answer, layering function and dysfunction one upon the other in a palimpsest. And how about someone reading about someone wasting time? Is that expense of time in any sense productive? Boyle declares her independence from the reader's needs at the outset, but something obviously changes when, three years later, a long series of blog posts are gathered up and published with the subtitle "a novel" by the small press Tyrant Books. That form of publication would appear to be an affirmation of the novel's potential interest to readers even absent anything in it we could confidently call a plot or other completed narrative form. Rather, it is the serial presentation of the thoughts and actions of a depressed person, a young woman, an individual. Sometimes it is crazily witty and charming, though often enough (and by design!) it is dead on the page, a despair-inducing slog. It is not a "good novel." It isn't trying to be. The principle of its unity as an artwork is not internal but external, not organic but conceptual. One could similarly pronounce that the entire internet, in all its infinite ongoing blab, shall henceforth be considered her artwork.

And yet, despite its all but utter lack of properly "political" content beyond the sexual politics latent everywhere in it, Boyle's waste of time manages to articulate, or at least to perform, and maybe even to monumentalize, a desire for fundamental change. The state of being it calls forth would not be the life of yuppie efficiency its author never does achieve, but a breakthrough to some new, wholly other state of being on the far side of a bonfire of our vanities.

The Abjection of the Novel

According to a famous report from the National Endowment for the Arts, *Reading at Risk* (2004), mentioned in chapter 5, only 45 percent of Americans read even one work of fiction, poetry, or drama in any given year. The report was meant to sound a klaxon of alarm, of course, but in regard to this percentage, one might make a counterpoint that in absolute terms, even limited to the US, it amounts to an *enormous number* of people who at least occasionally spend time reading works of literature, some 150 million. What's interesting is how that many-ness, when it becomes an object of novelistic representation in its own right, can only produce zombie novels. Which is great for zombie novels, but leaves us wondering whether the novel as such, the literary novel, can convincingly master or even keep up with the world it now inhabits. Granted that the novel still "works" for a great many readers, are the affordances of the "bourgeois novel" simply too limited, too monochromatic, to convert the massified, multi-mediated, post-bourgeois world into transcendentally successful narrative art as we once found it in *Middlemarch* (1872) or *War and Peace* (1869)? Do we need to lower our expectations for the genre based on its changed cultural circumstances?

While I share her aversion to moralizing about social media usage, there is finally something unconvincing about Virginia Heffernan's insightful effort to recuperate the internet as, in itself, a "massive and collaborative work of realist art."[29] True, in contrast to the natural world, and very much like the world built in a novel, the world of the World Wide Web is a comprehensively signifying one. To interface with it is to enter a virtual space saturated with human intention. And yet, crucially, left to its own devices, this space cannot achieve the successful novel's essential effect of aesthetic coherence in the presentation of a fictional world. Instead, like time itself, it goes on and on endlessly, generating what Niklas Luhmann, continuing our theme, has described as a crisis of "surplus meaning" akin to that produced by the invention of writing and, later, the printing press.

In those cases, in his account, after long periods of upheaval social order was successfully reasserted in the rise of recognized monopolies on expertise, first in the form of the literate clergy, then by the establishment of credentialed disciplines and professions. We still await an equivalently functional social mechanism for the reduction of surplus meaning birthed by the internet, assuming we want one. The contemporary crisis of authority is of course easiest to see in the political sphere, where traditional gatekeepers of information are regularly bypassed for one or another purveyor of fever dream, but it is everywhere, including in the sphere of literary and cultural criticism. Where is the cultural authority of the novel as an art form to be found amid this surplus?

The irony and even poignancy of the current situation of the novel will be particularly evident to readers of one of the genre's greatest theorists, Mikhail Bakhtin. For him, it was the essence of the novel form to enter into the "zone of maximal contact" with the historical present, exposing itself to discourses high and low, near or far-flung, in open-ended profusion.[30] Surplus was its specialty.[31] As the most profound literary expression of what he took to be the essential human truth of *dialogism*—the inherent ongoing-ness and sociality of all communication—the novel in Bakhtin's account was a "carnivalesque" rebuke to the monological authoritarianism of the literary forms that preceded it. Chief among them was the national epic, born of ritualistic orality, where events take place in the sealed chamber of a completed past. Coming into its own in an increasingly literate world, the novel was by contrast like a "creature from an alien species" (4) descended into the system of literature, infiltrating it and orienting it toward an unknown, open, cosmopolitan future. It was a genre of "indestructible" modernity still in development even in the early to mid twentieth century when Bakhtin was writing, and uniquely able to take plenitude as a theme. And yet, even for him, it was crucial to any given novel's success that it achieve what he described as the "intently active unity of a consummated whole."[32]

To read Bakhtin with an eye to the present is to be struck by how his vision of liberating *novelization* has been at once realized and utterly negated. Realized, in that the monological authority of the ancient epic world is in full retreat under the reign of postmodern pluralism, where everything is purported to be a matter of choice or point of view. Negated, in that the regime of consumer choice and its associated neoliberal labor practices is an overwhelmingly coercive and indeed monological one holding sway more or less worldwide. Once upon a time the central organizing image, or "chronotope," as Bakhtin called it, of the novel's eager advance into the unknown was the road. Now, in the form of the "information superhighway," that road leads to the chaotic sameness, or personified entropy, of the zombie horde.

The rise within the general multiplicity of the internet of a handful of platform monopolies makes the logic clear: infinitely various messages but only one true "platform," and thus one true meta-message: the necessity of corporate capitalism and consumerist way of life. In this and many other ways the internet is the Bakhtinian novel turned inside out, the long historical development of its narrative strategies for absorbing and composing the brouhaha of modernity giving way to the free-floating, multi-purposed, billion-fold iteration of a network communications protocol and its associated micro-genres, the post, the tweet, the take, the thread. Perhaps, then, it is the *bad novel* that best expresses our historical moment.

Consider the case of the author Al K. Line, who is said to live in rural England with his wife, son, and dogs. That's the only public information available on the internet about a writer who, since 2014, has self-published no fewer than forty-two novels in the horror genre via Amazon's Kindle Direct Publishing service, beginning with the four volumes of the *Zombie Botnet* series that appeared in sequence that year (see figure on p. 252).[33]

Like all postapocalyptic fiction, it fantasizes a radical simplification of the world. This is managed on the one hand by the world's depopulation and, on the other hand, by its de-mediation as the power grid goes out. Together they clear the field for a return to visceral existential confrontations. Like so many fictions of its kind, the *Zombie Botnet* novels follow a small group of still-human survivors across the wasted landscape, in this case the landscape of Wales. They are forever on the move, pausing only for hopeless defense of some flimsy and invariably inadequate shelter. If the world has been simultaneously depopulated

The Zombie Botnet Series Line's zombie series is most notable for its explicit linking of the zombie plague with internet use.

and de-mediated in postapocalyptic narrative, it has also been unsettled, the drama staged, in the manner of picaresque, as a series of random encounters on the road.

Line's conceit is that the zombie plague has spread in the form of a viral packet of internet images that, viewed even for a second, convert viewers instantly into the compulsively hateful flesh-eaters they already were in a metaphorical sense, simply as internet users. The first order of business for the survivors Line puts at the center of the series is to unplug, lest they become infected, too. The second is to hit the road, their story becoming a kind of pilgrimage toward nothing in particular when they decide that, settlement being too dangerous, they will simply keep moving forever. But in a sense this program of bodily movement cycles them right back into the media system they have escaped. Their movement along the roads of rural Wales embodies the logic of open-ended seriality driving the production of the novels that contain it; the series does not so much conclude as peter out in ellipses, overtaken, in the career of Al K. Line at least, by a new series, a series of series, in theory ad infinitum.

This—the timely serial provision of new narrative product for one's audience—is as we've seen how the game of self-publishing is played. It is reminiscent of an earlier moment in the print culture of the novel when serialization was the norm and was regularly taken as a challenge to the integrity of the novel as a work of art. Nowadays, as a popular novelist, you are not so much crafting a perfect object as, somewhat like a blogger or regular poster, constructing a narrative *feed*.

Your reader, meanwhile, is not so much reading a novel as taking a hit of a narrative drug of a kind that works for them but will soon wear off. If the individual units sold in this way by Al K. Line are somewhat ragged affairs, replete with misspellings ("dieing" for dying is the least forgivable, one would think, for a would-be professional horror novelist)[34] and other forms of shoddiness, they are held together in the transcendental form of the genre—in this case, *zombie novel*—as such. Trading on its familiarity, the zombie novel needs only to mobilize the necessary tropes in some fashion for the whole thing to sort of work for some readers, if only it can find them. This is the lower-brow version of the (merely) conceptual unity Megan Boyle produces when she points at her blog and declares it "a novel." Neither has much to do with the frankly harder-won coherence of the aforementioned *Middlemarch* or *War and Peace*, to which we might add works like Henry James's *The Golden Bowl* (1904) or Ralph Ellison's *Invisible Man* (1952), which, even in their significant bulk, manage to convince us that every one of the many sentences compiled under their covers is necessary to some larger, complex aesthetic articulation.

Not that any work of genre fiction is or could ever be a pure repetition of a generic form. In the march of time and entropy, innovations are bound to arise as they did in Howey's injection of a self-loathing ghost into the zombie killing machine, and they do here simply in the literalism and transparency of *Zombie Botnet*'s relation to the commercial media environment in which it came into being. If this does not redeem the series aesthetically, it arguably does so intellectually as an incidental laying bare of the device.

Early in the second volume of the series, appropriately entitled *Zombie 2.0*, Kyle and Mike enter a library in search of some information they need to survive. Kyle, the younger of the two, is confused:

"I didn't even know that people still went to the library," said Kyle. "Why would you bother? Didn't people just look shit up Online, or buy from Amazon for their Kindles?"

"Fucking hell, Kyle, you kids are on another planet. Look, not everyone has a bloody Kindle or Kobo or fucking i-whatever you twat, and there is such a thing as leading a more sociable life. You know, where you actually have to talk to other people ..."

"So what's the deal with libraries then? They have every book there is, or what?" ...

"Look Kyle, of course they don't have every fucking book there is you dick-head. There are over a hundred and seventy million books in print, and who the fuck knows how many more in digital form now that any idiot can write and publish a book— even if it's shit."[35]

I'm not sure about Mike's numbers, but his anxieties are widely felt. They are also, in his case, perfectly self-reflexive, his author having contributed more than his share of works to the horde of zombie books roaming the wastelands of the literary field. The mistake, though, would be to think that this over-population of the literary field through the affordances of the internet has no bearing on the works that rise to the top, impressive in many ways, and perhaps even ennobling of their readers, though they remain. No reader who would describe themselves as "a serious reader" reads only one book seriously. They may be invested in transformative encounters with the unity of the work of narrative art, but all will soon be looking toward the next occasion for literary pleasure, the next book in the queue.

If, historically, it was the glory of the novel to embrace the open-endedness of the modern world, containing and composing it, the shame of the novel in the Age of Amazon is to have been turned inside out to that world and exposed, word by word, to the endlessly cacophonous unfolding of commercialized sociality in real time. Its fate—if only in the dark mirror of my depiction of contemporary literary history as apocalypse— is to be one text among too many just like it, unable to justify its reason for being. In this, the abjection of contemporary self-published zombie fiction is perhaps only the exaggerated case of the abjection of the contemporary novel as such. If that is true then the coherence we seek, the comprehensively meaningful world we want to inhabit, is elsewhere than in the novel as we know it.

Coda: The Commoditization of Culture

It was Jeff Bezos who intuited the potential link between the internet and books and sought to conjoin them, first as a mechanism enabling the distribution of printed paper volumes that had themselves, historically, been the product of a revolutionary new copying technology, the printing press; then, after the advent of the Kindle, as a distributor of downloadable digital simulacra of books; and finally, upon the introduction of the Kindle Direct Publishing platform, as a force for the populist disintermediation of the relation between writer and reader. As the more aggressive user of the internet, and as a company initially more concerned to capture market share than profits, Amazon has presented traditional publishing companies and their authors with the specter not of the commodification of literature, a long-standing fact, but of its *commoditization*: the reduction of intellectual property to a less and less profitable—because increasingly interchangeable and widely available—class of generic goods.[36]

Commoditization is one way to describe what is by any measure the extraordinary proliferation of works of fiction in our time, but even more so of their easy availability and relatively low cost. How do readers find their way to these books? Mostly they don't. Even if there were the inclination, there is not enough time. When they do, what was once a relatively deliberate process of selection based on the reputation of famous authors has been complicated—or simplified, depending on your perspective—by recommendation algorithms and book marketing initiatives that ensure the reader's next purchase is just a click away. That next purchase may be a work from the same author, or it may simply be one with an eye-catching title or cover and $2.99 price tag, puffed up perhaps by a bunch of fake reviews purchased from one of the many outfits providing that service for a fee, or gently coerced from readers given a copy of the work for free.

To say that, through the combined agency of Amazon and the internet, the specter of commoditization hangs over contemporary literature is of course to admit that, as specter, it is not quite yet manifest, and might never be given the profound commitment of the publishing industry to the singularity of book titles and author names as brands. There is no modern literary field to speak of except as it has evolved over the centuries with legal claims to copyright typically vested in an individual. There is no contemporary book market as we know it except as it is organized by the assignment of an ISBN or at least ASIN (Amazon's in-house tracking system) number to each and every commercially published book; no book marketing except as it is geared to producing distinctions between works you should buy and those you can ignore.[37]

To the extent that they still succeed in producing these distinctions, fears of market oversaturation are overblown, at least from the reader's point of view. What concern of hers are millions of data files sitting in a server somewhere? From the average author's point of view, however, it is cause for legitimate worry, as readers learn to price literary experience at rates too low to sustain even a highly accomplished midlist author in their livelihood without other sources of financial support. The fear of commoditization is the fear that, like so many sacks of flour or boxes of nails, literary works might be laid bare as marginally distinct and meagerly profitable instances of a generic cultural staple.

What fiction would lose on that account, it seems to me—a certain glamor—would be partially recompensed in the revelation of its basic necessity. We need novels like we need food to eat and clothing and shelter—at least some of us do, numbering in the hundreds of millions. For Amazon, as we have seen throughout this book, all books are in this sense "used" books, objects of utility whether or not they are new. Until now, the question has been what *kinds* of use they are imagined as having, whether it is as a bearer of virtual quality time (chapter 1) or corporate self-representation (chapter 2) or existential supplement (chapter 3) or structured fantasy (chapter 4) or existential scaling device (chapter 5). The assumption throughout these discussions has been that Amazon succeeds in providing readers with novels they want.

But what about when novels, becoming lost in a sea of content, have no use to readers at all? What does it mean to think of them as inert lines of code? What status should the "great unread," as Margaret Cohen has called the copious leavings of literary history, the books we never talk about, have in our understanding of contemporary literature?[38] What should we make of the underlist?

In the practice of literary criticism in its historically oriented mode, the number of works of the past understood to be relevant to scholars and their students is drastically reduced by the formation of canons. One need only read the tiniest fraction of the thousands of novels published in nineteenth-century France to be considered exceptionally well-read in that field. Something similar occurs when scholars of contemporary literature converge on a relative handful of recently published texts as representative of the present. Almost always they gravitate toward works of high artistic esteem as indicated by prizes and other quality signals. To a much lesser extent, they might also—as this book has done—look to examples interesting for reasons of their extraordinary popularity, like *Fifty Shades of Grey*, whose outsize (even if ultimately relatively fleeting) presence at the center of culture makes them seem representative in a different way. The great unread in this context is made up not so much of works once read yet now forgotten, but of works that have *never been read by anyone* except (but even here there is room for doubt) their author and perhaps a few friends. We can only hope that, for their authors, the effort was worth it, if only as a healthy exercise of their creative powers.

The average reader needn't worry about them. For the scholar of the contemporary novel, however, they represent a troubling surplus, a challenge to our ability to know the literary field, since who's to say that the deepest truth of the matter doesn't reside on the outskirts of that field, in the wasteland?

One conceivable approach to this dilemma would be to use computational methods on this vast literary data set, assuming it could be gathered and queried in a satisfying way. For now, a frankly less diligent, purely speculative, possibly crazy framing of the matter will have to suffice. This one transvalues the monumental waste of internet-enabled literary history as a collective demand for transformation. It sees it as representing the possibility of a world organized fundamentally otherwise than this one is. Strange and almost traitorous as it sounds, it posits literary waste as clearing conceptual space for a world that *doesn't need so much fiction*, at least not as we know it, having progressed beyond a desire for the forms of therapy it currently offers.

After all, doesn't the very uselessness of the great unread of contemporary fiction bring it into ironic alignment with the work of genius in the great tradition of aesthetic theory? The latter's power has always been understood to be a function of its transcendence of mere utility. The values it embodies are supposed to be higher ones than the satisfaction of everyday needs. That's why the Amazonian view of literature, putting popular utility foremost, is so offensive to that tradition.

The works of the underlist transcend utility, too, if from the opposite direction, going low where literary art goes high. What is achieved by the magisterial individual artist in the great tradition is achieved in the wastelands of Amazonia by the unread authorial masses in toto. Their anonymous collective achievement of transcendent uselessness is maintained in its perfection by never being examined, only contemplated from afar.

Afterword

Boxed In

Coziness is not a quality much sought after by literary scholars in the texts they study and teach, but it is the selling point of an entire genre of contemporary fiction, a thriving subcategory of the crime novel called cozy mystery (in the UK, "cosy" mystery). A fixture in the publishing industry for some time now, the cozy mystery can seem as though designed for the contempt of persons for whom literature, to be valuable, should offer a *challenge* of some sort to readers, whether to easy comprehension or unexamined beliefs or ignorance of historical circumstances other than their own. What is also sometimes called the village mystery blocks every path to critical esteem, opting for soothing provincialism, cultural homogeneity, and quirky gentility over more demanding confrontations with the truth of modern crime. Often enough it is supplied with add-ons such as a food theme, as in Joanne Fluke's best-selling *Chocolate Chip Cookie Murder* (2000) and its twenty-four sequels, each tied to a different baked good and including recipes, or other gimmicks like the recruiting of a house cat to the investigative team.[1]

Whatever their differences, they are written to strict generic specifications: the cozy mystery should feature an amateur female sleuth solving crime in a small town. There should be no explicit sex or profanity in the novel, and all the killing should occur offstage, preferably by relatively civilized means such as poison or, as we have it in Debbie Young's *Best Murder in Show* (2017), a craftily arranged bee sting.[2] Although very much a phenomenon of the present, the cozy mystery looks to the midcentury example of Agatha Christie—with her estimated 2 billion books sold—for inspiration, drawing from it a parade of newly configured Miss Marples, frequently a younger version thereof. No wonder, then, that the cozy mystery has garnered precious little attention from critics, almost none in fact, barely an article or two in a twenty-five-year period otherwise characterized by an increasing recognition of the potential excellence and interest of works written within popular generic conventions.

Without exactly disputing the implicit verdict of literary scholars on the value of the cozy mystery, which in fact has no ambitions of the sort one might offend by not taking it seriously as high art, one can make a case for its interest as one of the literary forms by which the overwhelming tendency of the Age of Amazon toward the provision of *more* meets its dialectical response in the symbolic provision of *less*. That dialectic has been one of the central concerns of the preceding pages, which have attempted to trace the links of the contemporary novel to the consumer economy, examining the consequences of their convergence in the gigantic operations of Amazon. The argument has been that contemporary fiction makes its way by either aligning itself with or resisting the flood of muchness by which the modern sensorium is assailed, or by executing some more complex combination of the two. Doing the first, the literary work tends toward the maximalism of the epic, toward geographical and historical sprawl, while the second tends toward the minimalism of romance, assuring its readers that the deepest truths are to be discovered in the small world of the romantic couple if not in the author-protagonist's intimate relation to herself. Throughout, the project has been to define the literary field from as low a vantage point as possible in the status hierarchy, seeing it as structured for the reliable satisfaction of what Northrop Frye called the "imaginative needs of the community" rather than as a series of pinnacles of aesthetic achievement.[3]

Seen in this perspective, the cozy mystery is a kind of romance, and in fact both its continuities and discontinuities with the romance novel are highly significant. Like the romance, it is a genre strongly associated with female authors, female protagonists, and female readers. Unlike the romance, it displaces the love story, concentrating instead on the quirks of village life as they are revealed in the heroine's investigation of a crime. It is common enough to find cozy mystery plots set in motion by the protagonist's departure alike from city life and from a relationship with a man. Doing so, she rethinks her life goals, trading obsession with the would-be alpha billionaire for membership in a small, richly embodied community.

This is what we see in *Best Murder in Show*, self-published via the Kindle Direct Publishing service, where twenty-something heroine Sophie Sayers takes flight from a good-for-nothing boyfriend for residence in the Cotswold cottage she has just inherited from her great aunt. Exhibiting the self-reflexivity evident everywhere in the KDP world once one begins to look for it, that great aunt was a writer—a travel writer, not a mystery writer, although the allusion to Agatha Christie's slightly less prolific contemporary, Dorothy Sayers, is hard to miss. While lacking her aunt's wanderlust, in fact negating it, Sophie Sayers wants to be a writer, too. As she gets to know her new neighbors and learns their ways, taking a job at the local bookshop and joining the village writers' group, one gets the uncanny sense that something very much like Debbie Young's *Best Murder in Show* is the work she is destined to write.

And in fact, Debbie Young, resident of a Cotswold village like the one depicted in her novels, is nothing if not a self-consciously "indie" writer, having mixed her work on the now six *Sophie Sayers Village Mystery* novels and other projects with a strong commitment to a group called the Alliance of Independent Authors (ALLi). Based in the UK, it offers various kinds of support to those who, like herself, have decided to launch a literary career without the benefit (or bane) of a traditional publishing contract. In this, the longing for coherent community so evident in her fiction finds parallel expression in the formation of a community of underdog writers, albeit one far-flung enough that it is mostly held together by the internet. It is not the first time in this book we have witnessed an impulse toward mutual aid that is surely one of the most appealing features of the KDP world, tied together as it is by the medium of listservs and other social media.

Indeed, one of the strangest things about *Best Murder in Show*, and to a certain extent about contemporary cozy mystery in general, is its vexed relation to the medium that facilitated its coming into being. Not that the internet is absent from Young's fictional village of Wendlebury Barrow—passing reference is made to Facebook and Google and eBay and email, and Sophie has a smartphone like any woman of her station would. But it is as though willfully suppressed in its possible significance to a village culture whose raison d'être, symbolically at least, is its disconnection from all that. It has its own sources of stimulation, including the eponymous yearly Village Show, which finds Sophie on a float winding through town dressed up as Virginia Woolf, although she hasn't gotten around to reading that author yet: "The sense of community that bound us was almost palpable. There was so much to observe and take in. Like any aspiring writer, I'm a natural people watcher, but I quickly reached sensory overload."[4]

The most glaring absence in Young's depiction of the village is Amazon, a common presence in the contemporary UK, even in the Cotswolds, to which deliveries are made as reliably as anywhere else. This might not be so noticeable if it weren't for the significance of a bookshop to the novel's plot: it is run by a man who becomes Sophie's low-intensity love interest, and is where she proves her value to him as an employee by concocting marketing strategies and product diversification schemes that will finally make it profitable. Echoing one of the feel-good stories of recent publishing history—the persistence and even thriving of a number of independent bookstores once thought to be at the point of extinction—this shop offers its local customers the personal touch, and tea and biscuits, they still crave. The problem of Amazon never arises there; it's as if revealing the corporate wizard behind the curtain of self-publishing would contradict the novel's desire to ground itself in provincial authenticity.

Even stranger, however, almost too obvious to notice, is that a genre explicitly intended to sooth the nerves of the stressed-out modern reader is centered on a *murder* to begin with. It has become a self-conscious joke in the genre—the way, book after book in a series, murder follows these citizen sleuths around in a fashion that would surely drive real gentleladies to death-haunted madness. Murder is not particularly cozy, is it, even if it is murder by bee sting?

It is a contradiction that the genre has sustained since Christie, and it sends one searching for explanations. One idea—it suits *Best Murder in Show* to a T—would be to say that the murderer embodies the outside world as it has come to infiltrate the village. Expelling him from the social body secures that village in its continuance as a safe, small world, even as the investigation secures Sophie's status as an insider there, someone who has finally, as the last line of the book has it, "come home."[5] The solution of the crime is thus also the solution to the modern problem of belonging—at least until the next book in the series, when the ritual will need to be repeated. In the enormously popular adjacent subgenre of mystery called the murder thriller, the precise opposite is often the case: what is exposed in the solution to the crime are the sins of the community elders whose bad blood spills down through the generations. The quaintness of the community, such as it may have seemed, was only a façade. And yet the latter, noir version of crime makes sense in a genre that is trying to shock and thrill and disturb its readers. In the cozy mystery it is an anomaly.

But who among us is completely coherent? It occurred to me at some point as I was writing this book that, for all its grasping after a certain interpretive totality, the account of literary history it was giving bears some relation to a cozy mystery. As much as, come to think of it, it might also be analogized to science fiction or epic fantasy or horror, take your pick. Such is the kinship of generic form to the larger patterns by which we try to make narrative sense of things—think, here, of Hayden

White's insight that to even begin to think and write about history is to avail oneself of one genre or another—that any of that pursuit's generic objects of study could easily be seen as a mirror of its own interpretive designs.[6] In this case, the cozy mystery occurs on the scene of literary life, also known to scholars as the *literary field*, which is nothing if not a village green of sorts when compared to the grizzlier battlefields of modernity. The would-be victim is the novel, poor thing. It is being stalked by an uncouth interloper, a corporate person named Amazon. Is that the corpse of the novel over there? It was Amazon in the library with a candlestick.

The difference of course is that the solution to the crime of the corporatization of literary life was announced here at the outset, before the investigation had even really begun. Also, the ancillary benefits to most of us of this "crime" make a great many millions of us complicit in it, somewhat like the passengers on the Orient Express. Not least of those benefits are those gained by the countless readers and writers who, in and around Amazon, are finding their literary needs met in ways I do not want to discount or hold myself above.

I still remember the experience of reading Ellen Willis's brief 1970 essay "Women and the Myth of Consumerism" a few years ago as part of a study of the classic theorizations of the consumer economy in preparation for writing this book. Having found many of these readings highly convincing, it was a shock to read an essay that began: "If white radicals are serious about revolution, they are going to have to discard a lot of bullshit ideology created by and for educated white middle-class males. A good example of what has to go is the popular theory of consumerism." What follows in Willis's essay is a brisk but highly creditable summary of exactly the texts I had recently been revisiting and mentally applauding, showing how they rely on a grossly simplified figure of the woman as shopper and as dupe. Then comes the punchline: "There is nothing inherently wrong with consumption. Shopping and consuming are enjoyable human activities and the marketplace has been a center of social life for thousands of years."

This was bracing enough—and instructive because true. The marketplace and capitalism are not the same, and there are reasons to believe some version of the former would persist in any new mode of production with any degree of division of labor and significant geographical spread. The diversity of human wants and needs is neither a new nor an entirely "consumer capitalist" thing, and neither is trade. Keeping faith with the traditional emphases of Marxism, Willis's second point is to insist that the problems we should be most concerned about are located in the sphere of production—in the neutralization of the laborer's agency in the matter of not only how but what things are made. In the meantime,

> the profusion of commodities is a genuine and powerful compensation for oppression. It is a bribe, but like all bribes it offers concrete benefits … Under present conditions, people are preoccupied with consumer goods not because they are brainwashed but because buying is the one pleasurable activity not only permitted but actively encouraged by our rulers.[7]

Hardly a celebration of consumer culture as we know it, this nonetheless seemed to me to suggest a crucial nuance in any viable critical attitude we might adopt toward it. It would be less contemptuous of those who indulge (almost everyone) in surplus consumption while also more realistic about the power of the therapeutic pleasures it offers in the absence of a better system. I resolved that my analysis would try to keep faith both with the merciful empathy of Willis's perspective and with the severity of her critique of the economic system that does not in fact meet our deepest needs. Maintaining that balance has admittedly not been easy.

The limits to Willis's analysis, conducted in 1970, year of the first Earth Day, come into view when we consider the links between mass commodity consumption and environmental degradation and climate change.

It is a point easiest to see, ironically, in postapocalyptic fictions like Edan Lepucki's *California* (2014), where most of those commodities are gone. Lepucki's self-consciously literary take on the postapocalyptic genre briefly came to fame in the context of Amazon's notorious dispute with the publishing conglomerate Hachette over e-book pricing, when it refused to make Hachette books available for pre-ordering in retaliation for the publisher's refusal to allow all e-book prices to be reduced to a $9.99 maximum. When Lepucki's novel was offered as an example of a young writer falling victim to Amazon's thuggery on the late-night TV show *The Colbert Report*—Colbert himself having been a Hachette author—its sales surged. Appropriately enough, in the ruined Southern California of the novel, all commodities are very expensive indeed, and some—for the novel's protagonist, Frida, unaccountably, the most important is a turkey baster—achieve talismanic power as tokens of a vanished plenitude: "In a world so disconnected from the past, her connection to these objects had been her only strategy for remaining sane. It still was."[8]

That said, by the end of the novel, fearing for her unborn child, Frida has moved with her husband, Cal, into one of the restricted Communities dotting the wasteland where life retains a militant semblance of middle-class normalcy. Hers is called the Pines, but there is apparently also one up north started by Amazon, another by Walmart. The attachment to random domestic commodities she felt amid the scarcities of the wild was in retrospect only the first step in a return to consumerism on the old exploitative, destructive, Amazonian model, justified now by the needs of the children: "Frida knew she was thinking of her own family, that she had begun to see them as special: separate from the rest of the world with all its attendant suffering and corruption. Maybe it was wrong, but it was the choice she had made."[9] While it does not celebrate this choice, the novel does not seriously challenge it, as though wanting, as literary fiction so often does, to remain realistic even when it envisions a radically altered world: *Can a mother in her situation have been expected to do otherwise than, in effect, sign up for Prime? Dream on.*

This realism points to the limits of the novel's—and of our—political imagination. Defining the wasted worlds of the postapocalyptic novel no less than the fleece-lined cocoons of cozy mystery, these limits are surely the most consequential example of the *less* at the core of Amazon's *everything*.

Notes

Preface

1 MacKenzie Bezos, *The Testing of Luther Albright* (New York: Harper Perennial, 2005); *Traps* (New York: Vintage, 2013).
2 See the separately paginated back matter of *Luther Albright*, p. 10.
3 *Traps*, p. 46; Roland Barthes, "The Reality Effect" (1968), in *The Rustle of Language*, trans. Richard Howard (Berkeley: University of California, 1989).
4 Scott Galloway, *The Four: The Hidden DNA of Amazon, Apple, Facebook, and Google* (New York: Portfolio/Penguin, 2017), p. 33.

Introduction

1 James A. Dewar, *The Information Age and the Printing Press: Looking Backward to See Ahead* (Santa Monica, CA: RAND Corporation, 1998); Tom Wheeler, *From Gutenberg to Google: The History of Our Future* (Washington D.C., Brookings Institution Press, 2019).
2 Simone Murray, *The Digital Literary Sphere: Reading, Writing, and Selling Books in the Internet Era* (Baltimore: Johns Hopkins University Press, 2018).
3 See Eric Hayot's forthcoming work on the implications of the decline of significant innovation in all the arts.
4 Ted Striphas, *The Late Age of Print: Everyday Book Culture from Consumerism to Control* (New York: Columbia University Press, 2009).
5 Michael Kozlowski, "Project Fiona—The Tale of the Very First Kindle e-Reader," Good e-Reader, December 4, 2018.

6 That said, as Sarah Brouillette has rightly insisted, it is a crucial fact of contemporary literary life that the traditional "literary disposition"—a taste for higher things, for literature as serious art as well as escapist entertainment—is in significant retreat in the world at large as the conditions for its continuance have decayed; and, one might add, in retreat even among the well-off fractions of the middle class that have historically sustained it as a seat of cultural authority. This being the case, Amazon was bound to want to facilitate a different, more populist—a corporate populist—relation to literature, one that accommodates the literary fiction crowd without taking as gospel their account of how and why literature matters, although matter it surely does. See Sarah Brouillette, "Neoliberalism and the Decline of the Literary," in *Neoliberalism and Contemporary Literary Culture*, ed. Mitchum Huehls and Rachel Greenwald Smith (Baltimore: Johns Hopkins University Press, 2017), pp. 277–90. I borrow the term "corporate populism" from Jerome Christensen, "Spike Lee: Corporate Populist," *Critical Inquiry* 17, no. 3 (Spring 1991), pp. 582–95. On the connection between contemporary populism and digital technology, see Jay David Bolter, *The Digital Plenitude: The Decline of Elite Culture and the Rise of New Media* (Cambridge, MA: MIT Press, 2019).

7 Dan N. Sinykin, "The Conglomerate Era: Publishing, Authorship, and Literary Form, 1965–2007," *Contemporary Literature* 59, no. 4 (Winter 2017), pp. 462–91.

8 Laura McGrath, "Literary Agency," *American Literary History* 33, no. 2 (Summer 2021), pp. 350–70.

9 Herbert Marcuse, *One-Dimensional Man: Studies in the Ideology of Advanced Industrial Societies* (1964; repr., London: Routledge, 2002). See also Raymond Williams, "Advertising: The Magic System," in *Culture and Materialism* (London: Verso, 2005).

10 Todd McGowan, *Capitalism and Desire: The Psychic Cost of Free Markets* (New York: Columbia University Press, 2016).

11 See Peter Brooks, *Reading for the Plot: Design and Intention in Narrative* (Cambridge, MA: Harvard University Press, 1984).

12 Kate Soper, *Post-Growth Living: For an Alternative Hedonism* (London: Verso, 2020).

13 Lina M. Khan, "Amazon's Antitrust Paradox," *Yale Law Journal* 126, no. 3 (2017), pp. 710–805; Timothy Wu, *The Curse of Bigness: Antitrust in the New Gilded Age* (New York: Columbia Global Reports, 2018); Steve Wasserman, "The Amazon Effect," in *Literary Publishing in the Twenty-First Century*, ed, Travis Kurowski et al. (Canada: Milkweed, 2016), pp. 32–57. Amazon's

strategy for resisting claims that it is a monopoly is to define the competitive domain as *all of retail*, not just online retail.

14 And sure enough—a stunning statistic!—there are roughly half as many companies being traded on US stock exchanges now as at the time of Amazon's founding in the mid-1990s. See Michael Wursthorn and Gregory Zuckerman, "Fewer Listed Companies: Is That Good or Bad for Stock Markets?," *Wall Street Journal*, January 4, 2018.

15 An efficient anatomy and critique of this influence is available in James Kwak, *Economism: Bad Economics and the Rise of Inequality* (New York: Pantheon, 2017).

16 See Adam Winkler, *We the Corporations: How American Businesses Won Their Civil Rights* (New York: Liveright, 2018).

17 "Amazon's dominance hides a cold reality about its service: it is getting worse." So writes David Dayen in *Monopolized: Life in the Age of Corporate Power* (New York: The New Press, 2020), p. 210.

18 Mark McGurl, *The Program Era: Postwar Fiction and the Rise of Creative Writing* (Cambridge, MA: Harvard University Press, 2009).

19 The long history of "sacral" as opposed to "everyday" economies as they pertain to the novel is discussed in Günter Leypoldt, "Degrees of Public Relevance: Walter Scott and Toni Morrison," *Modern Language Quarterly* 77, no. 3 (September 2016), pp. 369–93. It is worth noting that the former, insofar as it persists in our time, is largely underwritten by the institution of the school, which continues to present novels to students as embodiments of values not directly subject to market valuation.

20 The correspondingly less explicit, more shameful midcentury phase of the novel's nonetheless intense relation to the market is analyzed in Evan Brier, *A Novel Marketplace: Mass Culture, the Book Trade, and Postwar American Fiction* (Philadelphia: University of Pennsylvania Press, 2010). An important study of the cultural politics of late twentieth-century bookselling, in particular on the conflict between bookstore chains and independent booksellers, is available in Laura J. Miller, *Reluctant Capitalists: Bookselling and the Culture of Consumption* (Chicago: University of Chicago Press, 2006).

21 Timothy Laquintano, *Mass Authorship and the Rise of Self-Publishing* (Iowa City: University of Iowa Press, 2016), p. 97. See also Laura J. Miller, "Whither the Professional Bookseller in an Era of Distribution on Demand?," in *The International Encyclopedia of Media Studies*, vol. 2, ed. Angharad N. Valdivia and Vicki Mayer (Chichester, UK: Wiley-Blackwell, 2013), p. 173.

22 This framing is partly inspired by Timothy Aubry, *Reading as Therapy: What Contemporary Fiction Does for Middle-Class Americans* (Iowa City: University of Iowa Press, 2011). I only differ from Aubry, who focuses his account on middlebrow fiction, in thinking that the therapeutic paradigm can be extended from the middlebrow into frankly "merely entertaining" genre fiction, on one side, and toward works of more pointedly elevated literary status on the other. In other words, the modalities of literary therapy or self-care are many and not confined to middlebrow forms, although one readily concedes that the middlebrow makes its therapeutic aspirations more explicit (as virtuous "self-improvement") than in other domains. See also Leah Price, *What We Talk About When We Talk About Books: The History and Future of Reading* (New York: Basic, 2019), especially chap. 4, "Prescribed Reading."

23 Philip Rieff, *The Triumph of the Therapeutic: Uses of Faith after Freud* (Wilmington, DE: ISI Books, 2006), pp. 15, 10; originally published: New York, Harper and Row, 1966. See also Northrop Frye, "Literature as Therapy," in *The Eternal Act of Creation: Essays, 1979–1990* (Bloomington: Indiana University Press, 1993), pp. 21–34. In Merve Emre's compelling analysis of postwar US reading practices and institutions, she recounts how readers came to be sorted into "good readers" (influenced by New Critical teaching practices), who read works for their aesthetic qualities alone, and "bad readers," for whom literature was increasingly conscripted to various utilitarian ends, most importantly nationalist ones. See Merve Emre, *Paraliterary: The Making of Bad Readers in Postwar America* (Chicago: University of Chicago Press, 2018).

24 Rieff, *The Triumph of the Therapeutic*, pp. 12, 54, 208.

25 In this I follow the example of Sianne Ngai, who has rejuvenated contemporary aesthetic theory by refusing the assumption that popular categories of judgment—for example, when we call something "cute"—are not worth deeper consideration of their philosophical import and politically diagnostic power. That said, this book differs from Ngai's in moving from the question of aesthetic judgment to the matter of the *uses* and *functions* of contemporary fiction specifically—that is, to matters more proper to literary-economic sociology than to aesthetic theory per se. Sianne Ngai, *Our Aesthetic Categories* (Cambridge, MA: Harvard University Press, 2012).

26 See Mavis Reimer et al., eds., *Seriality and Texts for Young People: The Compulsion to Repeat* (London: Palgrave, 2014).

27 V. Propp, *The Morphology of the Folktale*, trans. Laurence Scott (Austin: University of Texas Press, 1968).

28 One exception would be John Cawelti, a pioneer in the scholarly study of popular fiction, who noted that "while standardization is not highly valued in modern aesthetic ideologies, it is, in important ways, the essence of all literature." John Cawelti, *Adventure, Mystery and Romance: Formula Stories as Art and Popular Culture* (Chicago: University of Chicago Press, 1977), p. 9. In J. Hillis Miller's *Fiction and Repetition*, by contrast, repetition is what produces undecidability in interpretation—a rather ingenious but, in our context, unhelpful deconstruction of a structure of desire for more of the same. J. Hillis Miller, *Fiction and Repetition: Seven English Novels* (Cambridge, MA: Harvard University Press, 1985).

29 Thomas J. Roberts points out that "a work of junk fiction is as form-intensive as a sonnet or villanelle and ... is read in part for the formal pleasure it provides." Thomas J. Roberts, *An Aesthetics of Junk Fiction* (Athens: University of Georgia Press, 1990), p. 9.

30 Leah Price reports that, according to a Nielson study, 80 percent of YA novels in 2014 were sold to readers older than seventeen. Price, *What We Talk About*, p. 10.

31 Norman N. Holland, *The Dynamics of Literary Response* (1968; repr., New York: Norton, 1975).

32 Nick Levey, "Post-Press Literature: Self-Published Authors in the Literary Field," *Post45*, February 3, 2016.

33 Lucien Karpik, *Valuing the Unique: The Economics of Singularities*, trans. Nora Scott (Princeton: Princeton University Press, 2010).

34 On the unprecedented speed with which literary works are now "metabolized" in contemporary culture, see Julia Straub, "Literary Reviewing and the Velocity of Book Histories in Times of Digitization," *Anglia* 139:1 (2021), pp. 224, no. 41.

35 Michael Clune, *Writing against Time* (Stanford, CA: Stanford University Press, 2013).

36 This skepticism is absent in perhaps the most direct recent treatment of the question, Josie Billington's *Is Literature Healthy?* (Oxford: Oxford University Press, 2016). Her answer is yes.

37 Lauren Berlant, *Cruel Optimism* (Durham, NC: Duke University Press, 2011).

38 I take inspiration here from Dave Beech, *Art and Value: Art's Economic Exceptionalism in Classical, Neoclassical and Marxist Economics* (Chicago: Haymarket, 2016). While Beech is

preoccupied mostly with the situation of visual art, his sensible resistance to the idea that it really has been "subsumed" by the industrial labor process is galvanizing.

39 A notable exception to the relative independence of novelistic labor would be something like James Frey's company Full Fathom Five, now apparently defunct, where the controversial memoirist sought to revivify the "industrial" mode of fiction production by hiring a great many low-paid writers to produce Young Adult fantasy and science fiction series under a pen name.

40 I take seriously Gabriel Zaid's suggestion, in his subversively upbeat *So Many Books*, that the relative cheapness of book publishing—as compared, say, to moviemaking, and this was before the advent of KDP's reduction of the cost to near zero—is its strength, allowing for a pluralistic pursuit of small-scale preoccupations and eccentricities. The only problem with this supply-side celebration of abundance is its disregard for the institutional contexts in which books, once they exist, will circulate and be read, or not. By the same token, the facilitation of "diversity" in publishing, which is one of KDP's undeniable achievements, does not touch the difficult question of access to new works in a deeper sense: all the things over and above the mere existence of books that have to come together to make a person into a reader or, for that matter, writer. See Gabriel Zaid, *So Many Books: Reading and Publishing in an Age of Abundance*, trans. Natasha Wimmer (Philadelphia: Paul Dry, 2003).

41 Brad Stone, *The Everything Store: Jeff Bezos and the Age of Amazon* (New York: Little Brown, 2013).

42 See, for instance, John B. Thompson, *Merchants of Culture: The Publishing Business in the Twenty-First Century*, 2nd ed. (New York: Plume, 2012) and *Book Wars: The Digital Revolution in Publishing* (Cambridge: Polity Press, 2021).

43 The key texts here are Georg Lukács, *The Theory of the Novel: A Historico-philosophical Essay on the Forms of Great Epic Literature*, trans. Anna Bostock (Cambridge, MA: MIT Press, 1971); M. M. Bakhtin, *The Dialogic Imagination: Four Essays*, trans. Caryl Emerson and Michael Holquist (Austin: University of Texas Press, 1981); Ian Watt, *The Rise of the Novel: Studies in Defoe, Richardson and Fielding* (Berkeley: University of California Press, 1971).

44 David Cunningham, "Capitalist Epics: Abstraction, Totality and the Theory of the Novel," *Radical Philosophy* 163 (September/October 2010).

45 See, for instance, Nantina Vgontzas, "Amazon after Bessemer," *Boston Review*, April 21, 2021.

46 Jeff Bezos, "2020 Letter to Shareholders," aboutamazon.com, April 15, 2021.

47 For instance, Bezos recently announced a sizable Climate Pledge Fund designed to support "green" technologies, businesses and causes its directors (privately) deem worthy of investment.

1 Fiction as a Service

1 George Packer, "Cheap Words," *New Yorker*, February 17, 2014.

2 See, for instance, Alec MacGillis, *Fulfillment: Winning and Losing in One-Click America* (New York: Farrar, Straus and Giroux, 2021).

3 John B. Thompson, *Merchants of Culture: The Publishing Business in the Twenty-First Century*, 2nd ed. (New York: Plume, 2012), p. 322. Thompson speaks, however, of the "hidden revolution" in publishing, dating back to the 1980s, consisting in a *"revolution in the process"* of text production, which by the 2000s yielded the digital file "ready to be delivered in whatever form the market demanded" (326). See also Adam Hammond, *Literature in the Digital Age: An Introduction* (Cambridge: Cambridge University Press, 2016).

4 The sheer difficulty of knowing how many novels and other books have been published is ably discussed by Erik Fredner, "How Many Novels Have Been Published in English (An Attempt)," Stanford Literary Lab blog, March 14, 2017.

5 The 70 percent royalty is paid on texts priced by their authors in the Amazon-stipulated range of $2.99 to $9.99, but otherwise falls to 35 percent. Needless to say, this strongly qualifies the author's entrepreneurial "freedom" as a self-publisher via KDP.

6 Bill Gates, "Friction-Free Capitalism," in *The Road Ahead* (New York: Viking, 1995), pp. 180–207.

7 Kashmir Hill, "I Tried to Block Amazon from My Life. It Was Impossible," *Gizmodo*, January 22, 2019.

8 Nick Srnicek, *Platform Capitalism* (Malden, MA: Polity, 2017). See also Jaron Lanier, *Who Owns the Future?* (New York: Simon and Schuster, 2014).

9 One important exception to this rule is Jasper Bernes's study of the poetry of the service economy, *The Work of Art in the Age of Deindustrialization* (Stanford, CA: Stanford University Press, 2019).

10 Arlie Russell Hochschild, *The Managed Heart: The Commercialization of Human Feeling* (Berkeley: University of California Press, 1983). The coincidence of the rise of the service economy

with rising inequality is documented in Saskia Sassen, "Service Employment Regimes and the New Inequality," in *Globalization and Its Discontents: Essays on the New Mobility of People and Money* (New York: Norton, 1998), pp. 137–51.

11 This parallels the notorious redefinition of the college student as customer, which in turn may have something to do with the extraordinary success of the discipline of creative writing, which, responsive to intense (customer) demand, is the only growth sector within literary studies more broadly.

12 John Rossman, *The Amazon Way: 14 Leadership Principles behind the World's Most Disruptive Company* (CreateSpace, 2014).

13 Robert Spector, *Amazon.com: Get Big Fast* (New York: Harper-Business, 2002), p. 48.

14 Rossman, *The Amazon Way*, p. 7.

15 Interestingly, after enduring a great deal of negative publicity, Amazon settled its dispute with Hachette and other publishers more or less on the latter's terms. See David Streitfeld, "Amazon and Hachette Resolve Dispute," *New York Times*, November 13, 2014.

16 Rossman, *The Amazon Way*, p. 8. In this respect, Amazon parallels a broader process that Markus Krajewski describes as the early twenty-first-century "transferal of the classic service functions to technical media." See Krajewski, "Ask Jeeves: Servants as Search Engines," trans. Charles Macrum III, *Grey Room*, no. 38 (Winter 2010), p. 13.

17 Brad Stone, The Everything Store: Jeff Bezos and the Age of Amazon (New York: Little Brown, 2013), p. 27.

18 Stone, *The Everything Store*, p. 10.

19 Kindle Direct Publishing, "Guide to Kindle Content Quality," kdp.amazon.com.

20 Hugh Howey, "My Advice to Aspiring Authors," hughhowey.com, March 14, 2013.

21 "Hugh Howey Goes from Bookstore Clerk to Self-Publishing Superstar," *Geek's Guide to the Galaxy*, podcast, episode 83, April 4, 2013.

22 See Timothy Laquintano, *Mass Authorship and the Rise of Self-Publishing* (Iowa City: University of Iowa Press, 2016).

23 John Locke, *How I Sold 1 Million eBooks in Five Months!* (Telemachus, 2011), p. 15.

24 Hugh Howey, "Wool, Part One" (Amazon Digital Services: Broad Reach Publishing, 2011).

25 Hugh Howey, *Wool* (CreateSpace, 2013); *Dust* (CreateSpace, 2013); *Shift* (CreateSpace, 2013).

26 Ed Pilkington, "Amanda Hocking, the Writer Who Made Millions by Publishing Online," *Guardian*, January 12, 2012.

27 Jasinda Wilder, *Alpha* (Amazon Digital Services: Jasinda Wilder, 2014).

28 Locke, *How I Sold One Million eBooks*, p. 38.

29 Monica Brooks, *Loving the White Billionaire: A Sexy BWWM Romance* (Amazon Digital Services, 2015).

30 M. S. Parker and Cassie Wild, *Serving Him: An Alpha Billionaire Romance* (Amazon Digital Services: Belmonte Publishing, 2015).

31 A fine start on comprehending the Tingle phenomenon is made in Andrew Ferguson, "The President Is a Shrieking Pile of Void Crabs; or, the Cosmically Horrific Satire of Dr. Chuck Tingle," an unpublished manuscript posted on academia.edu.

32 Kevin Killian, *Selected Amazon Reviews* (Hooke, 2006); Nick Thurston, *Of the Subcontract: Or Principles of Poetic Right* (York, UK: Information as Material, 2013).

33 Hugh Howey, *The Shell Collector* (CreateSpace, 2014), p. 162.

34 See, for instance, J. D. Porter, "Popularity/Prestige" *Pamphlets of the Stanford Literary Lab* 17, 2018; James English et al., "Mining Goodreads: Literary Reception Studies at Scale," Price Lab for Digital Humanities, 2018; Melanie Walsh and Maria Antoniak, "The Goodreads 'Classics': A Computational Study of Readers, Amazon, and Crowdsourced Amateur Criticism," *Post45*, April 21, 2021. General theorizations of the significance of Goodreads for literary history include Lisa Nakamura, "'Words with Friends'; Socially Networked Reading on Goodreads," *PMLA* 128, no.1 (January 1, 2013), pp. 238–43; Simone Murray, "Secret Agents: Algorithmic Culture, Goodreads and the Datification of the Contemporary Book World," *European Journal of Cultural Studies*, Dec. 5, 2019.

35 A longer and differently focused version of this discussion of time concepts—but still including several of the formulations and phrasings I use here—is Mark McGurl, "Real/Quality," in *Time: A Vocabulary of the Present*, ed. Joel Burges and Amy Elias (New York: NYU Press, 2016).

36 Quoted in Richard L. Brandt, *One Click: Jeff Bezos and the Rise of Amazon.com* (London: Penguin 2012), p. 4.

37 *Michigan Technic* 72, no. 4 (1954). No page numbers.

38 Regis McKenna, *Real Time: Preparing for the Age of the Never Satisfied Customer* (Cambridge, MA: Harvard Business School Press, 1997), p. 3.

39 Jasper Bernes, "Logistics, Counterlogistics, and the Communist Prospect," *Endnotes*, no. 3 (September 2013).

40 Alison K. Clarke-Stewart, *Interactions between Mothers and Their Young Children: Characteristics and Consequences* (Chicago: Society for Research in Child Development, 1973).

41 Kazuo Ishiguro, *The Remains of the Day* (New York: Vintage, 1990), p. 71.

42 This is a point made differently by Mathias Nilges in "Neoliberalism and the Time of the Novel," *Textual Practice* 29, no. 2 (2015), pp. 357–77.

43 Nicholson Baker, *Vox* (New York: Vintage, 1993); *The Fermata* (New York: Vintage, 1995).

44 Baker, *Vox*, pp. 11, 126.

45 Baker, *The Fermata*, pp. 271, 303.

46 Jonathan Crary, *24/7: Late Capitalism and the Ends of Sleep* (London: Verso, 2013), p. 20.

47 Ishiguro, *The Remains of the Day*, p. 23.

48 Chester Himes, *If He Hollers Let Him Go* (1945; repr., New York: Thunder's Mouth, 2002), p. 203.

49 Frantz Fanon, *Black Skin, White Masks*, trans. Richard Philcox (New York: Grove, 2008), p. 118.

50 Deborah Brandt, *The Rise of Writing: Redefining Mass Literacy* (Cambridge: Cambridge University Press, 2015).

51 Brandt, *The Rise of Writing*, p. 20.

52 Brandt, *The Rise of Writing*, p. 22.

53 Kinohi Nishikawa, *Street Players: Black Pulp Fiction and the Making of a Literary Underground* (Chicago: University of Chicago Press, 2018).

54 Vickie M. Stringer, *Let That Be the Reason* (New York: Upstream, 2001), p. 121.

55 Vickie M. Stringer, with Mia McPherson, *How to Succeed in the Publishing Game* (Columbus, OH: Triple Crown, 2005). On the overwhelming whiteness of mainstream publishing, see Richard Jean So, *Redlining Culture: A Data History of Racial Inequality and Postwar Fiction* (New York: Columbia University Press, 2021).

56 Colson Whitehead, *John Henry Days* (New York: Anchor, 2001).

57 Linda Hutcheon, *A Poetics of Postmodernism: History, Theory, Fiction* (London: Routledge, 1988).

58 It is a quality of the novel that, if Alexander Manshel is correct, is somewhat belated here given the wholesale shift in the literary field toward a less epistemologically troubled historicism beginning in the late 1990s. See Alexander Manshel, "Colson Whitehead's History of the United States," *MELUS: Multi-Ethnic Literature of the United States*, 2020.

59 Whitehead, *John Henry Days*, pp. 19–21.

60 Does the small nonprofit press—e.g., Greywolf or Coffeehouse—offer a possible exit from this dilemma? The beginnings of an answer are offered in Dan Sinykin and Edwin Roland, "Against Conglomeration: Nonprofit Publishing and American Literature after 1980," *Post45*, Issue 7, April 21, 2012.

61 Jarret Kobek, *I Hate the Internet: A Useful Novel against Men, Money, and the Filth of Instagram* (Los Angeles: We Heard You Like Books, 2016).

62 Nicholas Thoburn, *Anti-Book: On the Art and Politics of Radical Publishing* (Minneapolis: University of Minnesota Press, 2016).

63 Kobek, *I Hate the Internet*, pp. 11, 3.

64 Kobek, *I Hate the Internet*, p. 11.

65 Kobek, *I Hate the Internet*, p. 25.

66 Bruce Robbins, "The Sweatshop Sublime," *PMLA* 117, no. 1 (2002).

67 Quoted in George Anders, "Amazon's Web Services Delight: 16.9% Margins, More Joy Ahead," *Forbes*, April 23, 2015.

68 Louis Bedigian, "Amazon's Quarter Was a 'Full-On Crusher,'" *Benzinga*, July 23, 2015.

69 McKenna, *Real Time*, p. 12.

70 Quoted in "Amazon's Jeff Bezos Looks to the Future," *Charlie Rose*, transcript of interview broadcast on December 1, 2013.

71 Stewart Brand, *The Clock of the Long Now: Time and Responsibility* (New York: Basic, 1999).

72 Neal Stephenson, *Seveneves* (New York: William Morrow, 2016).

73 Thompson, *Merchants of Culture*, p. 332.

2 What Is Multinational Literature?

1 Ernest Cline, *Ready Player One* (New York: Broadway, 2011).

2 Jesper Juul, *Half-Real: Video Games between Real Rules and Fictional Worlds* (Cambridge, MA: MIT, 2005).

3 Thomas Pavel, *Fictional Worlds* (Cambridge, MA: Harvard University Press, 1986).

4 The inertial appeal of the dual-structure tradition is strong enough to have already spawned a variant of LitRPG, called GameLit, in all ways like its parent except that the stats readouts have been removed in favor of the qualitative and integral measures of success we find in normal fantasy novels. In this it is indistinguishable from a long-running subspecies of game-novels based on Dungeons & Dragons, which typically "forget" their origins in the RPG.

5 Vasily Mahanenko, *Survival Quest: Way of the Shaman, Book 1* (Magic Dome, 2017).

6 D. Rus, *AlterWorld: Play to Live Book 1*, trans. Irene Woodhead and Neal Mayhew (Amazon Digital Services, 2014).

7 The Russian-ness of it all—one notes the early-mover status of several Russian writers in the LitRPG space—is interesting, suggesting a potentially significant geopolitical backdrop to this cultural phenomenon. As Rus's *Play to Live* saga unfolds over later volumes, its Russian nationalism becomes more and more strident, culminating in an epic battle for the soul of the game fought against dark virtual hordes from the East.

8 Nick Yee, *The Proteus Paradox: How Online Games and Virtual Worlds Change Us—and How They Don't* (New Haven, CT: Yale University Press, 2014); Jane McGonigal, *Reality Is Broken: Why Games Make Us Better and How They Can Change the World* (New York: Penguin, 2011). See also Nick Dyer-Witheford and Greig de Peuter, "Immaterial Labor: A Worker's History of Videogaming," *Games of Empire: Global Capitalism and Video Games* (Minneapolis: University of Minnesota Press, 2009), pp. 3–33.

9 McGonigal, *Reality Is Broken*, p. 53.

10 Rus, *AlterWorld*, loc. 2479 of 4782.

11 Andrew Karevik, *CivCEO: The Accidental Champion, Book 1* (Amazon Digital Services, 2019), loc. 240 of 3538.

12 It is closely akin to the *official world* described in the recent work of Mark Seltzer, but distinct from it. The official world in Seltzer's account is the scene of what in sociological theory is called "reflexive modernity": "a type of world that consists both of itself and an unremitting commentary on itself." Which is to say, it is our hypermediated world, a thing in the making for some 500 years but vastly reinforced by the rise of successive waves of mass media culminating in the internet. "Gamelike, violent, yet extremely formal," Seltzer's official world is suffused by a sense of reality in suspense, in which map and territory, model and actuality refuse to be resolved into easily separable things. So, too, is the corporate world larger than the corporate workplace, both itself and the ideas it has about itself. The corporate world, however, is a more pointedly *capitalist* construction than Seltzer's, which appears in his account as much a product of the Enlightenment as of private enterprise, although it certainly includes the cultural pathologies particular to the latter. It is also a more *partial* structure than the official world, which is the "modern world" in its entirety. It is a place where individual corporations compete with each other, and where the

corporate form as such still competes with nominally nonprofit entities like states. The otherworldly elegance of Seltzer's formulations is such that one can easily be hypnotized into believing, as the official world believes of itself, that the fervor of its reflections on its own situation has in fact de-realized that situation, made it (merely) game-like. As against the eerie sense of interchangeability and formality of Seltzer's brilliant vision of the official world, the thematics of the corporate world center on the fundamental social and other *inequalities* and *hierarchies* and *struggles* that characterize it. No less a product of reflexive modernity, they are the engine of its historicity, one thing among others that make a given point in the 500-year continuum of global modernization seem starkly different from another. Mark Seltzer, *The Official World* (Durham, NC: Duke University Press, 2016), p. 4.

13 See, for example, Pheng Cheah, *What Is a World? On Postcolonial Literature as World Literature* (Durham, NC: Duke University Press, 2016).

14 Mark J. P. Wolf, *Building Imaginary Worlds: The Theory and History of Subcreation* (New York: Routledge, 2012).

15 Steven Savage, *Way with Worlds: Crafting Great Fictional Settings*, vol. 1 (CreateSpace, 2016).

16 David Grann, *The Lost City of Z: A Tale of Deadly Obsession in the Amazon* (New York: Vintage, 2010). The film version developed by Amazon Studios (dir. James Gray) was released to Amazon Prime Video customers in 2016. Jerome Christensen pierces through some of the larger methodological considerations of reading for the corporate allegory in film in *America's Corporate Art: The Studio Authorship of Hollywood Motion Pictures* (Stanford, CA: Stanford University Press, 2012). See also J. D. Connor, *The Studios after the Studios: Neoclassical Hollywood, 1970–2010* (Stanford, CA: Stanford University Press, 2015), and Michael Szalay, "'The Real Home of Capitalism': The AOL Time Warner Merger and Capital Flight," in *The Routledge Companion to Literature and Economics*, ed. Michelle Chihara and Matthew Seybold (New York: Routledge, 2019).

17 Lydia DePillis, "Its Amazon's World. We Just Live in It," CNN Business, October 4, 2018.

18 Leigh Claire La Berge, *Scandals and Abstraction: Financial Fiction of the Long 1980s* (Oxford: Oxford University Press, 2014); Arne De Boever, *Finance Fictions: Realism and Psychosis in a Time of Economic Crisis* (New York: Fordham University Press, 2018); Alison Shonkwiler, *The Financial Imaginary: Economic Mystification and the Limits of Realist Fiction* (Minneapolis: University

of Minnesota Press, 2017); Paul Crosthwaite, *The Market Logics of Contemporary Fiction* (Cambridge: Cambridge University Press, 2019).

19 Peter Drucker, *Concept of the Corporation* (1946; repr., New Brunswick: Transaction, 1993); Alfred D. Chandler Jr., *Scale and Scope: The Dynamics of Industrial Capitalism* (Cambridge, MA: Harvard University Press, 1990).

20 Laura J. Miller, *Reluctant Capitalists: Bookselling and the Culture of Consumption* (Chicago: University of Chicago Press, 2007). Ralph Clare, *Fictions Inc.: The Corporation in Postmodern Fiction, Film, and Popular Culture* (New Brunswick, NJ: Rutgers University Press, 2014); Dan Sinykin, "The Conglomerate Era: Publishing, Authorship and Literary Form, 1965–2007," *Contemporary Literature* 85, no. 4 (2017).

21 Laura McGrath, "Literary Agency," *American Literary History* (April 19, 2021).

22 Jasper Bernes, *The Work of Art in the Age of Deindustrialization* (Stanford, CA: Stanford University Press, 2017), pp. 1; 19.

23 Here I am echoing the title of Amy Hungerford's *Making Literature Now* (Stanford, CA: Stanford University Press, 2016), which explores several other sites of gatekeeping and marketing in the contemporary literary field.

24 Thomas J. Peters and Robert H. Waterman Jr., *In Search of Excellence: Lessons from America's Best-Run Companies* (New York: Harper and Row, 1982); Terrence E. Deal and Allan A. Kennedy, *Corporate Cultures: The Rites and Rituals of Corporate Life* (Reading, MA: Addison-Wesley, 1982).

25 Robert Brenner, *The Economics of Global Turbulence: The Advanced Capitalist Economies from Long Boom to Long Downturn, 1945–2005* (London: Verso, 2006).

26 Peters and Waterman, *In Search of Excellence*, p. xx.

27 Peters and Waterman, *In Search of Excellence*, pp. 56, 61, 75.

28 Deal and Kennedy, *Corporate Cultures*, p. 16.

29 A phenomenon analyzed by James Manyika et al. in "A New Look at the Declining Labor Share of Income in the United States," McKinsey Global Institute, May 2019.

30 Robert E. Weir, *Beyond Labor's Veil: The Culture of the Knights of Labor* (University Park, PA: Penn State Press, 1996).

31 The death throes of union power and influence in the US 1970s are compellingly detailed in Jefferson Cowie, *Stayin' Alive: The 1970s and the Last Days of the Working Class* (New York: The New Press, 2010).

32 This is the context in which to read not just LitRPG but a spate of novels, from Douglas Coupland's *Microserfs* (1995) to Max

Barry's *The Company* (2006), Joshua Ferris's *Then We Came to the End* (2007), Ed Park's *Personal Days* (2008), and Halle Butler's *The New Me* (2019)—not to mention hit TV shows like *The Office* (2005–13)—where the white-collar cubicle farm comes into focus as the scene of a kind of soul-killing serfdom. Pitched relentlessly in the mode of light satire, these works suggest that its remedy is, alas, not militant solidarity of the laboring multitude but psychic self-remove through irony. For an analysis of this genre, see Ralph Clare, "Conclusion: Corporate Hegemony, Cubed," in *Fictions Inc.*, pp. 180–206.

33 Gantt's novel is included in Mary C. Grimes, ed., *The Knights in Fiction: Two Labor Novels of the 1880s* (Urbana: University of Illinois Press, 1986); Halle Butler, *The New Me* (New York: Penguin, 2019). See also Natasha Stagg, *Surveys* (South Pasadena, CA: Semiotext(e), 2018) and Hilary Leichter, *Temporary: A Novel* (Minneapolis: Coffee House, 2020).

34 Terrence E. Deal and Allan A. Kennedy, *The New Corporate Cultures: Revitalizing the Workplace after Downsizing, Mergers, and Reengineering* (Reading, MA: Perseus, 1999).

35 Both events are detailed in Brad Stone, *The Everything Store: Jeff Bezos and the Age of Amazon* (New York: Little Brown, 2013).

36 Andrew S. Grove, *Only the Paranoid Survive: How to Exploit the Crisis Points That Challenge Every Company* (New York: Crown Business, 1999).

37 Karl Marx and Friedrich Engels, *The Communist Manifesto*, in *The Marx-Engels Reader*, 2nd ed., ed. Robert L. Tucker (New York: Norton, 1978), p. 476.

38 An observation inspired by Martin Puchner, *Poetry of the Revolution: Marx, Manifestos, and the Avant-Gardes* (Princeton: Princeton University Press, 2005).

39 Marx and Engels, *The Communist Manifesto*, p. 477.

40 See, for instance, Pheng Cheah, *What Is a World?*, pp. 60–91.

41 Heike Geissler, *Seasonal Associate*, trans. Katy Derbyshire (South Pasadena, CA: Semiotext(e), 2018), p. 38. The German original was published in 2014. A US-centric version the story of low-wage employment, including at an Amazon fulfillment center, is told as nonfiction in Emily Guendelsberger, *On the Clock: What Low-Wage Work Did to Me and How It Drives America Insane* (New York: Little, Brown and Co., 2019).

42 Geissler, *Seasonal Associate*, pp. 39, 13, 96.

43 As reported in "Translation Database: Amazon Crossing Is the Story," Three Percent, rochester.edu, 2015.

44 "World Lite: What Is Global Literature?" (unsigned editorial), *n+1* 17 (Fall 2013).

45 Tierno Monénembo, *The King of Kahel*, trans. Nicholas Elliott (Las Vegas, NV: Amazon Crossing, 2010).

46 Monénembo, *The King of Kahel*, p. 5.

47 Rebecca Gable, *The Settlers of Catan*, trans. Lee Chadeayne (Las Vegas, NV: Amazon Crossing, 2011; Petra Durst-Benning, *The Glassblower*, trans. Samuel Willcocks (Amazon Crossing, 2014); *The American Lady* (Amazon Crossing, 2015); *Paradise of Glass* (Amazon Crossing, 2015).

48 Laura Gallego, *Omnia*, trans. Jordi Castells (Seattle: Amazon Crossing, 2016).

49 Gallego, *Omnia*, pp. 70, 149.

50 Jesse Tevelow, *Authorpreneur: Build the Brand, Business, and Lifestyle You Deserve* (Amazon Digital Services, 2018).

51 See, for instance, Andrew H. Plaks, "The Novel in Premodern China," in *The Novel*, ed. Franco Moretti, vol. 1, *History, Geography, Culture* (Princeton: Princeton University Press, 2006), pp. 181–213.

52 Jia Pingwa, *Happy Dreams*, trans. Nicky Harman (Seattle: Amazon Crossing, 2017), pp. 132, 462.

3 Generic Love, or, The Realism of Romance

1 E. L. James, *Fifty Shades of Grey* (New York: Vintage, 2012), p. 12.

2 James, *Fifty Shades of Grey*, pp. 3, 11, 12.

3 Quoted in Max Weber, *The Protestant Ethic and the "Spirit" of Capitalism and Other Writings*, trans. Peter Baehr and Gordon C. Wells (New York: Penguin, 2002), p. 9.

4 The insufficiency of the Weberian account of capitalism to explain the modern consumer economy is perhaps most forcefully elaborated in Daniel Bell, *The Cultural Contradictions of Capitalism* (New York: Basic Books, 1975).

5 James, *Fifty Shades of Grey*, pp. 4, 269.

6 James, *Fifty Shades of Grey*, p. 54.

7 See National Endowment for the Arts, *Reading at Risk: A Survey of Literary Reading in America*, Research Division Report #46 (Washington, DC: National Endowment for the Arts, 2004). Women make up approximately 60 percent of those who read fiction at all, and the typical female reader reads more than her novel-reading male counterpart.

8 Bezos eventually relented on this matter, allowing publishers to set the prices of their e-books.

9   E. L. James, *Fifty Shades Darker* (New York: Vintage 2012), p. 40.

10 Jane Austen, *Pride and Prejudice* (1813; repr., New York: Bantam, 1981), p. 27.

11 Niklas Luhmann, *Love as Passion: The Codification of Intimacy*, trans. Jeremy Gaines and Doris L. Jones (Stanford, CA: Stanford University Press, 1998), pp. 45, 46; emphasis in original.

12 To switch theoretical idioms, modern love is a product of what René Girard called "mimetic desire," the desire for what someone else already desires, in this case as embodied in a literary romantic ideal of true love. René Girard, *Deceit, Desire and the Novel*, trans. Yvonne Freccero (Baltimore: Johns Hopkins University Press, 1965).

13 This is one of the major themes of Stephanie Coontz's *Marriage, A History*: that what might seem like the trivialization of marriage in our time in fact stems from our making new and in many ways greater demands upon this institution than ever before. Stephanie Coontz, *Marriage, A History: How Love Conquered Marriage* (New York: Penguin, 2005).

14 Daniel Harris, *Cute, Quaint, Hungry and Romantic: The Aesthetics of Consumerism* (Boston: Da Capo, 2000), pp. 84–5, 101, 99.

15 Nancy Armstrong, *Desire and Domestic Fiction: A Political History of the Novel* (New York: Oxford University Press, 1987).

16 Janice A. Radway, *Reading the Romance: Women, Patriarchy, and Popular Literature* (1984; repr., Chapel Hill: University of North Carolina Press, 1991), p. 15.

17 Cora Kaplan, "*The Thorn Birds*: Fiction, Fantasy, Femininity," in *Formations of Fantasy*, ed. Victor Burgin et al. (New York: Methuen, 1986), pp. 142–66.

18 James, *Fifty Shades of Grey*, pp. 75, 336.

19 James, *Fifty Shades of Grey*, p. 11.

20 Erich Fromm, *Escape from Freedom* (New York: Henry Holt, 1941). Interestingly, for our purposes here, Fromm's follow-up *The Art of Loving* (1956) objects to conceptions of love as something one "falls" into, and criticizes its capture by the logic of consumerism: "Love is an activity, not a passive affect; it is a 'standing in' not a 'falling for.' In the most general way, the active character of love can be described by saying love is primarily *giving*, not receiving." See *The Art of Loving* (New York: Harper, 2006), 21.

21 James, *Fifty Shades of Grey*, p. 224.

22 For obvious reasons of its proximity and salience to the democratic rise and popular success of fascism, the problem of choice

figures in this critical literature as a question mainly of political psychology. And there is no doubt a strong link, although not necessarily a causal one, between the success of the literary alpha billionaire in the marketplace and the rise of his surly and self-pitying plutocratic avatars to excessive prominence in the political world. They come together on the common ground of market spectacle, one a search for high book sales, the other for high cable news ratings, in surreal culmination of a process first noticed in Joe McGinnis's classic account of the 1968 election, *The Selling of the President, 1968* (New York: Trident, 1969).

23 James, *Fifty Shades of Grey*, p. 23.

24 Fredric Jameson, *The Antinomies of Realism* (London: Verso, 2013).

25 An insight confirmed—albeit in different terms—by Andrew Piper, whose computational exploration of the *differentia specifica* of fictional texts, as opposed to non-fictional ones, is the former's " 'phenomenological investment.' Seen quantitatively, the particular nature of fictional discourse since the nineteenth century has been its profound investment not simply with the world around us, but with our perceptual encounter with that world, the way 'making sense' is explicitly related with the physical senses." See Andrew Piper, *Enumerations: Data and Literary Study* (Chicago: University of Chicago Press, 2018), p. 99.

26 Affect would also—here Jameson amplifies Brian Massumi, Teresa Brennan, and other affect theorists—appear to be the more politically promising of the two, pointing to the unpredictable potentialities of embodied life rather than to done deals. Who knows even now what future we might collectively, dialectically, feel our way toward?

27 Jameson, *Antinomies of Realism*, p. 45.

28 Linda Williams, "Film Bodies: Gender, Genre, and Excess," *Film Quarterly* 44, no. 4 (1991), pp. 2–13.

29 Jennifer Fleissner, *Women, Compulsion, Modernity: The Moment of American Naturalism* (Chicago: University of Chicago Press, 2004).

30 Goran Blix, "Story, Affect, Style," *nonsite.org*, March 14, 2014.

31 A pioneering exception to the rule of literary critical disavowal of the importance of neoclassical economics is Regenia Gagnier, *The Insatiability of Human Wants: Economics and Aesthetics in Market Society* (Chicago: University of Chicago Press, 2000).

32 Needless to say, it is not sufficient to explain Amazon as a reflection of this tendency in economic theory. Even staying within the realm of economic theory, one would for instance want to

add the kind of thinking about transaction costs associated most famously with Ronald Coase's seminal "The Nature of the Firm" (1937). For Coase, the existence of the firm is explained by the relative efficiency it affords in not having to constantly negotiate new contracts with laborers. This is as true at Amazon as any other firm, with the added appeal to the customer that the Amazon interface reduces transaction costs (including the expense of time looking around for what you need) of shopping in various places. Ronald Coase, "The Nature of the Firm," *Economica* 4, no. 16 (1937), pp. 386–405.

33 Ronald Schleifer, *Modernism and Time: The Logic of Abundance in Literature, Science, and Culture, 1880–1930* (Cambridge: Cambridge University Press, 2000).

34 Nicholas Xenos, *Scarcity and Modernity* (London and New York: Routledge, 1989), p. 1.

35 In practice, opportunity cost is calculated by factoring in the forgone utility of the *single next best alternative* to the action taken, as though there aren't at each moment a practical infinity of consequential actions we can take.

36 Staffan Linder, *The Harried Leisure Class* (New York: Columbia University Press, 1970).

37 James, *Fifty Shades of Grey*, p. 3.

38 The concept of opportunity cost first found expression in formal economic theory in 1848, in Frédéric Bastiat's essay "What Is Seen and What Is Not Seen," where, against the idea that the unfortunate occurrence of a broken window is at least good for society in providing work to the glazier, Bastiat notes that the money we happily see spent on the new window will invisibly *not* be spent on something else which might have been more valuable still. See Frédéric Bastiat, "What Is Seen and What Is Not Seen," in *Selected Essays on Political Economy*, trans. Seymour Cain (Irvington-on-Hudson, NY: Foundation for Economics Education, 1995).

39 Martin Heidegger, *Being and Time*, rev. ed., trans. Joan Stambaugh (New York: SUNY Press, 2010); Martin Hägglund, *Dying for Time: Proust, Woolf, Nabokov* (Cambridge, MA: Harvard University Press, 2012).

40 Alfred Gell, *The Anthropology of Time: Cultural Constructions of Temporal Maps and Images* (Oxford: Berg, 1992).

41 Gell, *The Anthropology of Time*, p. 217.

42 Catherine Gallagher, "The Rise of Fictionality," in *The Novel*, ed. Franco Moretti, vol. 1, *History, Geography, Culture*, (Princeton: Princeton University Press, 2007).

43 Ian Watt, *The Rise of the Novel: Studies in Defoe, Richardson and Fielding* (Berkeley: University of California Press, 1957).

44 Eva Illouz, *Hard-Core Romance: Fifty Shades of Grey, Best-Sellers, and Society* (Chicago: University of Chicago Press, 2014).

45 Two works particularly useful in thinking through the chromatic crypto-identity politics of *Fifty Shades of Grey* are David Batchelor's *The Luminous and the Grey* (London: Reaktion Books, 2014) and *Chromophobia* (London: Reaktion Books, 2000).

46 Lauren Berlant, *The Female Complaint: The Unfinished Business of Sentimentality in American Culture* (Durham, NC: Duke University Press, 2008).

47 Fredric Jameson, *Archaeologies of the Future: The Desire Called Utopia and Other Fictions* (London: Verso, 2007).

48 Henry James, *The Portrait of a Lady*, ed. Robert Bamberg (New York: Norton, 1975).

49 The vast and various territory of female homosociality lying to the side of the male/female marriage plot in the Victorian period is explored in Sharon Marcus, *Between Women: Friendship, Desire, and Marriage in Victorian England* (Princeton: Princeton University Press, 2007).

50 James, *Portrait of a Lady*, p. 263.

51 James, *Portrait of a Lady*, p. 14.

52 James, *Portrait of a Lady*, pp. 363, 7, 356.

53 Virginia Woolf, *Mrs. Dalloway* (New York: Harcourt, 1925).

54 Woolf, *Mrs. Dalloway*, pp. 10, 39–40.

55 Woolf, *Mrs. Dalloway*, pp. 70–1.

56 Gell, *The Anthropology of Time*, p. 86.

57 Tommy Andres and Ariana Tobin, interview with Packard, "How 'Choose Your Own Adventure' Was Born," *Marketplace*, April 11, 2014.

58 Edward Packard, *The Cave of Time: Choose Your Own Adventure #1* (New York: Bantam, 1979).

59 Packard, *The Cave of Time*, p. 21.

60 Packard, *The Cave of Time*, p. 57.

61 Kristy Flowers, *Jane Murray: My Open Marriage—Live the Sexual Dream!* (Kristy Flowers Books, 2015), loc. 2196, 2388, 2177.

62 Flowers, *Jane Murray*, loc. 2522.

4 Unspeakable Conventionality

1   Mommy Claire, *Mommy Claire Chronicles—Volume II: Erotic Tales of Female Domination, Adult Baby Diaper Love and Age Play* (AQT Enterprises, 2017), loc. 338 of 3217.

2   Mommy Claire, *Mommy Claire Chronicles*, loc. 402 of 3217.

3   Mommy Claire, *Mommy Claire Chronicles*, loc. 360 of 3217; loc 3134 of 3217.

4   Mommy Claire, *Mommy Claire Chronicles*, loc. 3134 or 3217.

5   The story of the Kindle device's development is recounted by Zehr in his contribution to the Computer History Museum Oral History Project, Catalog no. 102739919, May 14, 2014, computerhistory.org.

6   Matthew Kirschenbaum, *Track Changes: A Literary History of Word Processing* (Cambridge, MA: Harvard University Press, 2016).

7   Neal Stephenson, *The Diamond Age: Or, A Young Lady's Illustrated Primer* (New York: Bantam Spectra, 2008). On Lab126's interest in this novel, see Michael Kozlowski, "Project Fiona: The Tale of the Very First Kindle E-Reader," goodereader.com, December 4, 2018, and Brad Stone, "Fiona," in *The Everything Store: Jeff Bezos and the Age of Amazon* (New York: Little Brown, 2013), chap. 8, "Fiona," pp. 236–7.

8   Ibid., p. 64.

9   See for instance, Tithi Bhattacharya, ed., *Social Reproduction Theory: Remapping Class, Recentering Oppression* (London: Pluto, 2017).

10   Jane Tompkins, *Sensational Designs: The Cultural Work of American Fiction, 1790–1860* (Oxford: Oxford University Press, 1986), p. 200.

11   Rita Felski, *Uses of Literature* (Malden, MA: Blackwell, 2008).

12   Timothy Aubry, *Reading as Therapy: What Contemporary Fiction Does for Middle-Class Americans* (Iowa City: University of Iowa Press, 2011).

13   Anis S. Bawarshi and Mary Jo Reiff, *Genre: An Introduction to History, Theory, Research, and Pedagogy* (West Lafayette, IN: Parlor Press, 2010), p. 4.

14   Carolyn R. Miller, "Genre as Social Action," *Quarterly Journal of Speech* 70, no. 2 (1984).

15   Although not credited there, Miller's conception of genre in action is helpfully retooled for literary studies in Group Phi, "Doing Genre," in *New Formalisms and Literary Theory*, ed. Verena Theile and Linda Tredennick (New York: Palgrave, 2013).

16 Adena Rosmarin, *The Power of Genre* (Minneapolis: University of Minnesota Press, 1985).

17 John Rieder, *Science Fiction and the Mass Cultural Genre System* (Middletown, CT: Wesleyan University Press, 2017).

18 For Walter Benn Michaels, *Fifty Shades* is an expression of contemporary neoliberalism, showing us a world in which labor (Ana's labor of love for Christian) is increasingly performed at will and without a contract. See Walter Benn Michaels, "Fifty Shades of Libertarian Love," *Los Angeles Review of Books*, May 22, 2015. For Eva Illouz, the astounding popularity of the book stems from its "resonance" with the lived contradictions of women's lives after feminism. See Eva Illouz, *Hard-Core Romance: Fifty Shades of Grey, Best-Sellers, and Society* (Chicago: University of Chicago Press, 2014).

19 See, for instance, the introduction to Diana Caine and Colin Wright, eds., *Perversion Now!* (Palgrave, 2017), p. 2: "What is the fate of transgression in such an apparently permissive age?"

20 Andrew Hoberek, "Literary Genre Fiction," in *American Literature in Transition, 2000–2010*, ed. Rachel Greenwald Smith (Cambridge: Cambridge University Press, 2017), pp. 61–75, 66. See also Tim Lanzendörfer, "Introduction: The Generic Turn? Toward a Poetics of Genre in the Contemporary Novel," in *The Poetics of Genre in the Contemporary Novel*, ed. Lanzendörfer (Lanham, MD: Lexington Books, 2016), pp. 1–16.

21 Jeremy Rosen, "Literary Fiction and the Genres of Genre Fiction," *Post45*, August 7, 2018. See also Günther Leypoldt, "Social Dimensions of the Turn to Genre: Junot Díaz's *Oscar Wao* and Kazuo Ishiguro's *The Buried Giant*," *Post45*, March 31, 2018.

22 Northrop Frye, *The Secular Scripture: A Study of the Structure of Romance* (Cambridge, MA: Harvard University Press, 1976), pp. 15, 6.

23 Sandra M. Gilbert and Susan Gubar, *No Man's Land: The Place of the Woman Writer in the Twentieth Century* (New Haven, CT: Yale University Press, 1989).

24 In addition to Radway and Illouz, see for instance Carol Thurston, *The Romance Revolution: Erotic Novels for Women and the Quest for a New Sexual Identity* (Urbana: University of Illinois Press, 1987; Tania Modleski, *Loving with a Vengeance: Mass Produced Fantasies for Women* (New York: Methuen, 1984); Stephanie Harzewski, *Chick Lit and Postfeminism* (Charlottesville: University of Virginia Press, 2011).

25 Sarah Brouillette, "Romance Work," *Theory and Event* 22, no. 2 (April 2019), pp. 451–64.

26 Terry Lovell, *Consuming Fiction* (London: Verso, 1987).

27 Norman N. Holland, *The Dynamics of Literary Response* (1968; repr., New York: Norton, 1975).

28 Helen Gurley Brown, *Having It All: Love, Success, Sex, Money Even if You're Starting with Nothing* (New York: Simon & Schuster: 1982).

29 Eva Illouz, *Consuming the Romantic Utopia: Love and the Cultural Contradictions of Capitalism* (Berkeley: University of California Press, 1997).

30 Roland Barthes, *The Pleasure of the Text*, trans. Richard Miller (New York: Hill and Wang, 1975), p. 14.

31 Barbara Deloto and Thomas Newgen, *The House of Enchanted Feminization* (independently published, 2019).

32 Anne Jamison, *Fic: Why Fan Fiction Is Taking Over the World* (Dallas: SmartPop, 2013). See also Francesca Coppa, "A Brief History of Media Fandom," in *Fan Fiction and Fan Communities in the Age of the Internet*, ed. Karen Hellekson and Kristina Bussel (Jefferson, NC: McFarland, 2006), pp. 41–59.

33 Aarthi Vadde, "Amateur Creativity: Contemporary Literature and the Digital Publishing Scene," *New Literary History* 48, no. 1 (2017), p. 27.

34 B. F. Dealeo, *Fifty Shades of Brains* (Seattle: Ambauminable, 2013).

35 Illouz, *Hard-Core Romance*, p. 13.

36 See Anne Jamison, a leading scholarly authority on fan fiction: "Fifty Shades, then, grew not out of one source—Stephenie Meyer's Twilight Saga—but out of a system of mutually derivative and transformative texts ... The 'Office' genre. 'Mogul' Edward. The BDSM fic. The more assertive Bella." Jamison, "When Fifty Was Fic," in *Fifty Writers on Fifty Shades of Grey*, ed. Lori Perkins (Dallas, TX: Perseus, 2012).

37 Franco Moretti, "The Dialectic of Fear," *New Left Review* 136 (1982), pp. 67–85.

38 Sarah Jeong, "Bad Romance," *The Verge*, July 16, 2018. On self-publishing and the larger questions of intellectual property, see Timothy Laquintano, *Mass Authorship and the Rise of Self-Publishing* (Iowa City: University of Iowa Press, 2016), chap. 5.

39 Jeffrey Eugenides, *The Marriage Plot: A Novel* (New York: Farrar, Straus and Giroux, 2011), pp. 22–3.

40 See Marshall Boswell, "The Rival Lover: David Foster Wallace and the Anxiety of Influence in Jeffrey Eugenides's *The Marriage Plot*," *MFS: Modern Fiction Studies* 62, no. 3 (Fall 2016), pp. 499–518.

41 Adelle Waldman, *The Love Affairs of Nathaniel P.* (New York: Picador, 2013), p. 3.

42 Eugenides, *The Marriage Plot*, p. 58.
43 Keith Gessen, *All the Sad Young Literary Men* (New York: Penguin, 2008), p. 97.

5 World-Scaling

1 Niklas Luhmann, *The Reality of the Mass Media*, trans. Kathleen Cross (Stanford, CA: Stanford University Press, 2000), p. 1.
2 Orrin E. Klapp, *Opening and Closing: Strategies of Information Adaptation in Society* (Cambridge: Cambridge University Press, 1978); *Overload and Boredom: Essays on the Quality of Life in the Information Society* (Praeger, 1986).
3 N. Katherine Hayles, *Chaos Bound: Orderly Disorder in Contemporary Literature and Science* (Ithaca, NY: Cornell University Press, 1994).
4 Debjani Ganguly, *This Thing Called the World: The Contemporary Novel as a Global Form* (Durham, NC: Duke University Press, 2016), p. 1.
5 Claudio Celis Bueno, *The Attention Economy: Labour, Time and Power in Cognitive Capitalism* (London: Rowman and Littlefield, 2017).
6 Simone Murray, *The Digital Literary Sphere: Reading, Writing, and Selling Books in the Internet Era* (Baltimore: Johns Hopkins University Press, 2018). See also R. Lyle Skains, *Digital Authorship: Publishing in the Attention Economy* (Cambridge: Cambridge University Press, 2019).
7 Alice Bennett, *Contemporary Fictions of Attention: Reading and Distraction in the Twenty-First Century* (London: Bloomsbury, 2018).
8 See, for instance, Victor Nell, *Lost in a Book: The Psychology of Reading for Pleasure* (New Haven, CT: Yale University Press, 1988); Richard J. Gerrig, *Experiencing Narrative Worlds: On the Psychological Activities of Reading* (New Haven, CT: Westview, 1993); Patrick Colm Hogan, *The Mind and Its Stories: Narrative Universals and Human Emotion* (Cambridge: Cambridge University Press, 2003); Keith Oatley, *Such Stuff as Dreams: The Psychology of Fiction* (Malden, MA: Wiley-Blackwell, 2011); Norman N. Holland, *Literature and the Brain* (Gainesville, FL: PsyArt Foundation, 2009); Blakey Vermeule, *Why Do We Care about Literary Characters?* (Baltimore: Johns Hopkins University Press, 2011); Lisa Zunshine, *Why We Read Fiction: Theory of Mind and the Novel* (Columbus: Ohio State University Press, 2012).

9   National Endowment for the Arts, *Reading at Risk: A Survey of Literary Reading in America*, Research Division Report #46 (Washington, DC: National Endowment for the Arts, 2004).

10 Ganguly, *This Thing Called the World*, p. 21.

11 Mikhail Bakhtin, *The Dialogic Imagination: Four Essays*, trans. Michael Holquist and Caryl Emerson (University of Texas Press, 1983).

12 Ernest Hemingway, "Big Two-Hearted River, Part One," in *The Nick Adams Stories* (New York: Scribner, 1981), p. 184.

13 William Faulkner, *Go Down, Moses* (New York: Vintage, 1990), pp. 243–5.

14 In this view, a model might be useful precisely in its *failure* to account for a given text or for some feature of the literary field as a whole. In that case, if that exception seems crucial, one redesigns or abandons the model, and so on. Doing so, one has secured a powerful criterion for the evidentiary interest of a given text within a given research frame as either strongly exemplary of a given position in the genre system, or as a fascinating violation of its norms.

15 If, according to Franco Moretti, works like Goethe's *Faust*, Whitman's *Leaves of Grass*, and Joyce's *Ulysses* should be described as instances of "modern epic," our ongoing relation to them as readers conspicuously dependent on "scholastic institutions," then works of epic fantasy from Tolkien through George R. R. Martin to N. K. Jemisin, bearing no such dependency, would have to be called "postmodern epic." See Franco Moretti, *Modern Epic: The World System from Goethe to Garcia Márquez*, trans. Quentin Hoare (London: Verso, 1996), p. 5.

16 See, for instance, Günter Leypoldt, "Social Dimensions of the Turn to Genre: Junot Diaz's *Oscar Wao* and Kazuo Ishiguro's *Buried Giant*," *Post45*, March 31, 2018; Jeremy Rosen, "Literary Fiction and the Genres of Genre Fiction," *Post45*, August 7, 2018.

17 I discuss this opposition at greater length in Mark McGurl, "The Novel's Forking Path," *Public Books*, April 1, 2015.

18 I owe this observation—the relative critical neglect of the realism in magical realism—to Ramón Saldívar.

19 Alexander Beecroft, *An Ecology of World Literature: From Antiquity to the Present Day* (New York: Verso, 2015).

20 Don DeLillo, *Underworld* (New York: Scribner, 1997).

21 Patrick Jagoda, *Network Aesthetics* (Chicago, University of Chicago Press, 2016). See also Scott Selisker, "Social Networks," in *American Literature in Transition, 2000–2010*, ed. Rachel Greenwald Smith (Cambridge: Cambridge University Press, 2017) pp. 211–23.

22 Caroline Levine, *Forms: Whole, Rhythm, Hierarchy, Network* (New York: Oxford University Press, 2015). See also Anna Gibson, "*Our Mutual Friend* and Network Form," *Novel: A Forum on Fiction* 48, no. 1 (2015), pp. 63–84.

23 DeLillo, *Underworld*, p. 16. Not that, I hasten to add, paranoia has gone out of style. Rather, it lives on in a thriving popular subgenre we could call "internet gothic," discussed briefly in chapter 6.

24 Graley Herren, "'The Martiniad': Nick Shay as Embedded Author within Don DeLillo's *Underworld*," *Critique: Studies in Contemporary Fiction* 56, no. 4 (2015), pp. 449–65.

25 DeLillo, *Underworld*, p. 89; emphasis added.

26 Amitav Ghosh, *Sea of Poppies* (New York: Farrar, Straus and Giroux, 2008); *River of Smoke* (New York: Farrar, Straus and Giroux, 2011); *Flood of Fire* (New York: Farrar, Straus and Giroux, 2015).

27 Binayak Roy, "Reading Affective Communities in a Transnational Space in Amitav Ghosh's *Sea of Poppies*," *Nordic Journal of English Studies* 15, no. 1 (2016), pp. 47–70.

28 Ghosh, *Sea of Poppies*, pp. 8–10.

29 Ghosh, *Sea of Poppies*, p. 46.

30 Ghosh, *Sea of Poppies*, p. 503.

31 Elleke Boehmer and Anshuman A. Mondal, "Networks and Traces: An Interview with Amitav Ghosh," *Wasafiri* 27, no. 2 (2012).

32 Bae Suah, *Nowhere to Be Found*, trans. Sora Kim-Russell (Seattle: Amazon Crossing, 2015).

33 Anna Moschovakis, *Eleanor, or, The Rejection of the Progress of Love* (Los Angeles: Semiotext(e), 2018), pp. 10, 11, 21.

34 Olivia Laing, *Crudo* (New York: Norton, 2018), p. 1.

35 Thanks to Nika Mavrodi for pointing this out to me.

36 Tao Lin, *Shoplifting from American Apparel* (New York: Melville House, 2009), pp. 13, 57.

37 Where are the "literary" novels of our time testifying to the triumph of romantic love? There are a few, no doubt, including Chimamanda Ngozi Adichie's *Americanah* (New York: Anchor Books, 2013).

38 The suggestion here is that "alienation" can be considered an achievement rather than simple malady. The question of connection and disconnection in contemporary global literature, including Lin's *Taipei*, is explored in Jason Gladstone, "Network Unavailable: Informal Populations and Literary Form," *American Literary History* 31, no. 1 (2019).

39 Tao Lin, *Taipei* (New York: Vintage, 2013).

40 Lin, *Taipei*, p. 16.

41 Lin, *Taipei*, p. 8.

42 Lin, *Taipei*, p. 16.

6 Surplus Fiction

1 The Writey Novel site is archived on the Internet Archive Wayback Machine: https://web.archive.org/web/20161208165921/https://writeynovel.com.

2 Charles Pulliam Moore, "Now's Your Chance to Write a Book with the Help of the Entire Internet," *Splinter News*, February 2, 2016.

3 There's also a phrase near the beginning, the metacommentary "[l]ooks like this is vulnerable to botting. [y]ou should fix that!" followed immediately by the rejoinder "fuck your mom."

4 Strange enough, in its barely credible naivety, that one begins to wonder if the experiment wasn't designed for failure all along.

5 Sarah Jeong's *Internet of Garbage* (New York: Forbes Signature Series e-books, 2015) was an early critical look at the phenomenon. See also P. W. Singer and Emerson T. Brooking, *Like War: The Weaponization of Social Media* (Boston: Houghton Mifflin, 2018).

6 Louis Althusser, "Ideology and Ideological State Apparatuses," in *Lenin and Philosophy and Other Essays*, trans. Ben Brewster (New York: Monthly Review, 1971), pp. 127–88.

7 See Mark Seltzer's theorization of the "pathological public sphere" in his *Serial Killers: Death and Life in America's Wound Culture* (New York: Routledge, 1998).

8 "Self-Publishing Grew 40 Percent in 2018, New Report Reveals," October 15, 2019, proquest.com.

9 An inquiry begun in Daniel Punday, *Writing at the Limit: The Novel in the New Media Ecology* (Lincoln: University of Nebraska Press, 2012).

10 Ava Kofman, Francis Tseng, and Moira Weigel, "The Hate Store: Amazon's Self-Publishing Arm Is a Haven for White Supremacists," ProPublica, April 7, 2020.

11 A. American, *Going Home* (New York: Plume, 2013), pp. 7–8.

12 Hugh Howey, *The Plagiarist* (CreateSpace, 2011).

13 John B. Thompson, *Book Wars: The Digital Revolution in Publishing* (Cambridge: Polity, 2021), p. 185.

14 See, for instance, Gerry Canavan, "'We *Are* the Walking Dead': Race, Time and Survival in the Zombie Narrative," in *Zombie Theory: A Reader*, ed. Sarah Juliet Lauro (Minneapolis: University of Minnesota Press, 2017), pp. 413–32. I have more to say about the ironically rude health of the contemporary zombie in Mark McGurl, "The Zombie Renaissance," *n+1*, Issue 9, April 27, 2010.

15 Jessica Hurley, "History Is What Bites: Race, Zombies, and the Limits of Biopower in Colson Whitehead's *Zone One*," *Extrapolation* 56, no. 3 (2015).

16 Hugh Howey, *I, Zombie*, hughhowey.com, 2012.

17 Ling Ma, *Severance* (New York: Farrar, Straus and Giroux, 2018).

18 Zygmunt Bauman, *Wasted Lives: Modernity and Its Outcasts* (Cambridge: Polity, 2004), p. 97.

19 Georges Bataille, *The Accursed Share: An Essay on General Economy*, vol. 1, *Consumption*, trans. Robert Hurley (New York: Zone, 1991).

20 Jean-Joseph Goux, "General Economics and Postmodern Capitalism," trans. Kathryn Ascheim and Rhonda Garelick, *Yale French Studies*, no. 78 (1990), pp. 206–24.

21 Kenneth Goldsmith, *Wasting Time on the Internet* (New York: Harper Perennial, 2016).

22 Tiziana Terranova, *Network Culture: Politics for the Information Age* (London: Pluto, 2004); Jodi Dean, *Blog Theory: Feedback and Capture in the Circuits of Drive* (Malden, MA: Polity, 2010).

23 D.B. Thorne, *Troll* (London: Corvus, 2017).

24 David Wells, "'Liveblog' and the Limits of Autofiction," *New Yorker*, November 29, 2018.

25 Megan Boyle, *Liveblog: A Novel* (New York: Tyrant, 2018), p. 5.

26 See, for instance, Michael White, *Maps of Narrative Practice* (New York: Norton, 2007).

27 Boyle, *Liveblog*, p. 642.

28 Boyle, *Liveblog*, p. 36.

29 Virginia Heffernan, *Magic and Loss: The Internet as Art* (New York: Simon and Schuster, 2016), p. 8. She would be on stronger ground to claim that a given website or page, or better yet application, could so be considered, inasmuch as these units have boundaries associated with coherent intentions.

30 Niklas Luhmann, *Social Systems*, trans. John Bednarz Jr. (Stanford, CA: Stanford University Press, 1996), p. 11.

31 For a further elaboration of this theme in the context of Victorian fiction, see Emily Steinlight, *Populating the Novel: Literary Form and the Politics of Surplus Life* (Ithaca: Cornell University Press, 2018). Steinlight helpfully points out how, compared to nonfictional genres, fiction might be understood as a "surplus" to documentary referentiality.

32 Bakhtin, *The Dialogic Imagination: Four Essays*, trans. Michael Holquist and Caryl Emerson (University of Texas Press,1983), pp. 4, 31; Bakhtin, "Author and Hero in Aesthetic Activity," in *Art and Answerability: Early Philosophical Essays*, trans. Viadim Lupanov (Austin: University of Texas Press, 1990), p. 12.

33 Al K. Line, *Zombie Botnet*, vols. 1–4: *#zombie, Zombie 2.0, Alpha Zombie, Zombie Slaver* (Amazon Digital Services, 2014).

34 Al K. Line, *#zombie: Zombie Botnet*, 1, p. 66.

35 Al K. Line, *Zombie 2.0: Zombie Botnet*, 2, p. 66.

36 See John B. Thompson, *Merchants of Culture: The Publishing Business in the Twenty-First Century*, 2nd ed. (New York: Plume, 2012), p. 376: "'One of the greatest threats facing the creative industries today is,' as one perceptive retailer put it, 'the increasing commoditization of content by non-content players, which is driving down the value of intellectual property.'"

37 James English, Amy Hungerford, and Günter Leypoldt are three critics who have ably explored the evolution and elaboration of the "judgment devices" of contemporary literature, the various ways we elevate some works over others, including by announcing their status as best sellers. See James English, "Quality Signals in an Age of Abundance," *Western Humanities Review* 70, no. 3 (Fall 2016); Amy Hungerford, *Making Literature Now* (Stanford, CA: Stanford University Press, 2016); Günter Leypoldt, "Degrees of Public Relevance: Walter Scott and Toni Morrison," *Modern Language* 77, no. 3, (September 2016), pp. 369–93.

38 Margaret Cohen, "Narratology in the Archive of Literature," *Representations* 108, no. 1 (Fall 2009), p. 59.

Afterword

1 Joanne Fluke, *Chocolate Chip Cookie Murder* (Amazon, 2013); Leighann Dobbs, *Ghostly Paws* (Amazon Digital Services, 2014).

2 Debbie Young, *Best Murder in Show* (Amazon Digital Services, 2017).

3 Northrop Frye, *The Secular Scripture: A Study of the Structure of Romance* (Cambridge, MA: Harvard University Press, 1976), p. 6.

4 Young, *Best Murder in Show*, p. 135.

5 Young, *Best Murder in Show*, p. 205.

6 Hayden White, *Metahistory: The Historical Imagination in Nineteenth Century Europe* (Baltimore: Johns Hopkins University Press, 2014).

7 Ellen Willis, "Women and the Myth of Consumerism," in *The Essential Ellen Willis*, ed. Nona Willis Aronowitz (Minneapolis: University of Minnesota Press, 2014), pp. 40–2.

8 Edan Lepucki, *California* (New York: Back Bay, 2014).

9 Lepucki, *California*, p. 388.

Index

Index

Index

Index